Managing Work-life Balance

A guide for HR in achieving organisational and individual change

David Clutterbuck has published widely on management, with over 40 books to his name. Having first explored the topic of work-life balance well over 30 years ago, he brings a keen analytical eye to the issue of creating a culture supportive of work-life balance. He is senior partner of Clutterbuck Associates, Chairman of the Item Group and Visiting Professor at Sheffield Hallam University.

The Chartered Institute of Personnel and Development is the leading publisher of books and reports for personnel and training professionals, students, and for all those concerned with the effective management and development of people at work. For details of all our titles, please contact the Publishing Department:

tel: 020–8263 3387
fax: 020–8263 3850
e-mail: publish@cipd.co.uk
The catalogue of all CIPD titles can be viewed on the CIPD website:
www.cipd.co.uk/bookstore

Managing Work-life Balance

A guide for HR in achieving organisational and individual change

David Clutterbuck

Chartered Institute of Personnel and Development

Published by the Chartered Institute of Personnel and Development, CIPD House, Camp Road, London, SW19 4UX

First published 2003

Design by Beacon GDT, Mitcheldean, Gloucestershire
Typeset by Fakenham Photosetting Ltd, Fakenham, Norfolk
Printed in Great Britain by The Cromwell Press, Trowbridge, Wiltshire

British Library Cataloguing in Publication Data
A catalogue of this manual is available from the British Library

ISBN 0 85292 969 2

The views expressed in this manual are the author's own and may not necessarily reflect those of the CIPD.

The CIPD has made every effort to trace and acknowledge copyright holders. If any source has been overlooked, CIPD Enterprises would be pleased to redress this for future editions.

Chartered Institute of Personnel and Development, CIPD House,
Camp Road, London SW19 4UX
Tel: 020 8971 9000   Fax: 020 8263 3333
E-mail: cipd@cipd.co.uk Website: www.cipd.co.uk
Incorporated by Royal Charter. Registered Charity No. 1079797.

Contents

Acknowledgements

I am indebted to a number of people in making this book a reality: my wife, Polly, who immediately saw the irony in the project ('Physician, heal thyself!'); Pam Walton and Pauline Henderson at the Work-Life Balance unit at the DTI; my academic tutor at King's, David Guest, who pointed me in the direction of alternative theoretical models of work-life balance. Also of great help have been Alison Carter of the Institute for Employment Studies; Tom Hastings, my research assistant, who handled much of the final detail work; and two members of the Clutterbuck Associates' team, Tanya Yazdanpanahi and Nicki Foster, who critiqued the evolving concepts. Finally, great thanks are due to Mike Huss of employment law specialists, Peninsula, who has contributed to the chapter on the legal complexities of work-life balance.

David Clutterbuck

Foreword

This book owes its origins to a wedding cake. The cake was made in the middle 1970s, when as a young management journalist I was writing about the conflict between work and family life (then known as 'corporate bigamy' – being married to the job as well as one's spouse). It appeared on the front cover of *International Management* and depicted the groom at the altar, interrupting the ceremony to take a telephone call and dictate a memo to his secretary. The bride sat weeping over the cake and the vicar looked on helplessly.

Who ate the cake I can't remember. But the image has stuck with me for nearly 30 years, during which time the conflict between work and non-work lives has become increasingly more patent and, to many people, increasingly less soluble. The problem is not just one of work intruding more and more into home life – although that is evident – it is also one of having so much more to do in our lives. People want to see the world, to enjoy a variety of sports, to subscribe to multitudes of television channels. Suddenly, one life is not enough to achieve even a fraction of what is available to us, let alone what our imagination could open up for us. We are, it is true, a little longer-lived and more likely to remain active into our Third Age, but until we can clone ourselves, there will never be enough time and energy to meet all our aspirations and obligations. There just aren't enough slices in the cake!

The thinking behind this book has emerged from a variety of sources: extensive reading of both practitioner and academic literature; interviews with line managers and human resources professionals; and discussions with groups of students and participants on in-company training programmes. The initial realisation was how complex the issue is and how unhelpful so much of the literature (both popular and academic) is in helping people work out appropriate responses to the issues. As a result, a number of models have been developed to try to explain more clearly the interactions between different forces that affect the work-life balance equation. In particular, the *Quality Model for Work-Life Balance* attempts to provide a structure against which organisations can benchmark their efforts to create a culture supportive to work-life balance.

The book also includes details from a survey of 74 employers, ranging in size from under 20 employees to 10,000-plus. The aim of the survey was to gain some insights into what policies organisations have towards work-life balance, how those policies are put into practice, and how/ whether their impact is measured.

The intent in the book is to provide the HR professional with a practical guide through the hype and into pragmatic implementation of approaches that will deliver sustainable change. This is quite a challenge, because *in spite of a great deal of investment in work-life balance policies, very few, if any companies have made a significant difference to the lives of most of their employees*. Our initial research question was therefore: 'Why can't companies make work-life balance work?'

The answer, it seems, is that those which fail to see significant results across the business almost all have tackled the issues in a piecemeal manner, rather than seeking integrated, holistic solutions that blend the three legs of the work-life balance stool – policy, support for the individual employee and culture change. The latter involves in particular changing the attitudes and behaviours of line managers at all levels.

Much of the information and guidance in this book has high relevance for top managers, both in their own lives and as the guardians of culture in their organisations. However, it is aimed squarely at the HR professional, who has the challenging tasks of making the business case for work-life balance and of being the architect of the culture changes necessary for building a culture that supports and sustains good practice in managing work-life balance. This is *not* a nuts-and-bolts book on flexible working, and the reader should not expect either detailed technical content or detailed explanation of the increasingly complex legal framework around work-life issues. What you will find in the following pages is a comprehensive approach to bringing work-life issues onto the boardroom agenda, and to developing a clear and practical strategy for harnessing work-life balance as a source of sustainable competitive advantage. These are combined in the Quality Model for Work-Life Balance, examined in Chapter 7. (Activist readers may wish to read that concluding chapter first!)

If you have already achieved significant success in implementing work-life balance in your organisation, this book should provide some more structure around which to explore and improve. If you are still in the early stages, it should provide insights into where and how to achieve rapid and sustainable results. Either way, this is an issue the HR function ignores at its peril!

David Clutterbuck
April 2003

Readers of this book who have online facility may also download a self-diagnostic which helps them assess their satisfaction with their own work-life balance. To access the diagnostic, go to www.worklifequality.co.uk.

List of Figures

List of Tables

Introduction:

A contract with the devil?

When I joined this firm, I thought I was just selling my time and mental energy for eight hours, five days a week. I soon found that there were invisible clauses in the contract. What I'd really signed away was body and soul, any right to a home life or keeping fit, and the right to switch off from work and give full attention to other aspects of my life. Bit by bit, the job has stolen all my spare capacity for giving. What makes it worse is that I've become addicted to it. I can't really imagine any other way of life. Sometimes I feel guilty, but mostly I haven't time for that. If I really thought about it, I'd be angry. Maybe I'm just pathetic . . .

The speaker is a manager in his early thirties, married, with two young children. His sense of being trapped, of being afraid to examine his situation too closely in case he has to admit to being a failure in other important parts of his life, is very common. In the 1970s, when conflict between work and other aspects of life first became an issue, it was referred to as corporate bigamy – being married to the job and the spouse. The *New Yorker* carried one of the most poignant of its cartoons. As two executives cross the road in Manhattan, one says, 'What I don't understand is why you have to trade quality of life for standard of living.'

For so many people at work today, even that trade is not available. Working long hours does not necessarily lead to income levels that provide a comfortable standard of living. While they may not exist on a subsistence diet in terms of food, they often have to make do with subsistence levels of mental regeneration in terms of leisure and enjoyment of their families.

Recent studies of learning and childhood have revealed the critical importance of play in the generation of mental energy. The proverb *All work and no play makes Jack a dull boy* is quite accurate. As adults, the pressure to focus on work and to see play as a frivolous diversion has become widely institutionalised and is perhaps one of the primary reasons why so many companies complain of lack of creativity and an inability to maintain high levels of customer-friendliness.

For the CEO or HR director, work-life balance is an issue that is claiming increasing attention. An inability to manage employees' needs for a more holistic, fulfilling life contributes to most of the problems that sap competitive advantage and reduce profitability – amongst them:

- employee absenteeism through stress
- failure to retain talent

- insufficient initiative and creativity
- low levels of customer service
- unethical behaviour
- low commitment and motivation.

These are all issues we address in Chapter 1 of this exploration of how companies can best respond to what is fast becoming the key social issue of the decade.

But how did we get to the state where work-life balance has become such a problem?

A hundred years or so ago, our Victorian ancestors routinely worked six days a week, ten hours a day. As the twentieth century gathered pace, the twin pressures of social reform and technological change combined to drive down working hours and increase the quantity of holidays. Then a strange thing happened – those same pressures began to exert precisely the opposite effect, with the result that many people today are working very similar hours to their forebears, but more intensively.

The social pressure for quantity of leisure has to a considerable extent been replaced – particularly among the ever-increasing professional classes – with pressure for quality of leisure. We travel farther to take our holidays and spend more on them. We inhabit better-quality housing, eat out far more, and discretionary spending is a much higher proportion of our income. In order to achieve this, we work longer hours, or perhaps have more than one job. The cost of a higher standard of living *is* often a lower quality of life.

Economists looking into the technological future 100 years ago imagined that automation would gradually free us from the tyranny of work. Even in the 1970s and 1980s, erudite authors were discussing whether we would have to ration work, so that as many people as possible had a fair share. Their mistake was to view technological advance in terms of manufacturing. While it is true that automation demands less and less human intervention in the process of making things, our economy has shifted inexorably into one where most people produce intangibles. We spend our money on car and health insurance, entertainment, advice on just about any element of our lives, and often vain attempts to save time.

Instead of freeing us, the technologies of the past two decades have increasingly enchained us. The tyranny of time has twinned with the tyranny of work. Whereas it didn't matter 100 years ago whether a document arrived in another country a day or a week later, today almost everything is required instantaneously. The more accurately we can measure and manage time, the more important it becomes to us. (According to a recent article in *Scientific American,* 'a time error of a millionth of a second from an individual satellite could send a signal to a GPS receiver that would be inaccurate by as much as a fifth of a mile' – more than enough to ground an oil tanker in a sea channel.[1])

Digital technology has also made us instantly available, wherever and whenever we are. A study two years ago by UMIST[2] found that 83 per cent of managers are contacted by their employers out of working hours, many of them regularly. More than 75 per cent regularly work beyond their contracted hours. One of the most common complaints I hear from professionals working for multinational organisations is that they are expected to be available for calls in the timeframe of the dominant nationality of the organisation – whether that is 11 o'clock in the evening or 4 o'clock in the morning their time. Fewer and fewer places on the Earth's surface are now out of reach of mobile telephone transmission. We are literally on call most of the waking day, and sometimes beyond.

The world 'will never seem to sleep' – customers and global operations demand 24-hours-a-day service. This has three impacts:

- Technology makes working from any location, at any time possible.

- The HR function is expected to help employees adjust to remote working.

- Geographical borders are becoming obsolete as multimedia technologies allow people to interact instantaneously, wherever they are. The talk is of 'electronic immigration', using labour wherever it is.[5]

The ability to separate our work and our non-work lives is being steadily eroded, but the flow has been largely one-way – from work into home. Trying to create a clear divide between the two worlds simply doesn't work for most people – the tidal forces against are too strong. Creating an ebb-tide – where home and non-work are allowed to intrude into work space and work time – is resisted by employers and employees alike. Moreover, we lack the practical tools to do so without disrupting the workplace in much the same way as work intruding into home disrupts home life.

True, technology and social pressure may flip again and provide the solutions to some of these problems. Survey evidence suggests that 86 per cent of people use the Internet at work (most claiming to do so outside their normal working hours or in a brief lunchtime) to sort out domestic issues.[3] Artificial Intelligence may one day allow us to leave much of the decision-making to computers which have become familiar with the way we think. The obsession of the developed world with consuming things is already beginning to give way to an appreciation of the value of consuming ideas. Achieving greater work-life balance is a higher priority for Generation Z than for its predecessors. One study of graduating students from 11 countries found that 57 per cent considered balancing work and personal life was their primary career goal.[4] However, a significant proportion of people in employment still view themselves as having more commitment to work than to other parts of their lives (in the UK, 14 per cent over-all and 20 per cent in the private sector). (A quarter put non-work first, and the remainder said work and non-work were equal in terms of their commitment.)

Technology won't come to the rescue for some time yet, however. In the meantime, it is more likely to increase the pressures that allow work to dominate our lives. Society changes relatively slowly. So where can we look for help?

GOOD INTENTIONS THWARTED

In the UK, the Government has been promoting the concept of work-life balance for some time and many of the largest employers have signed up to the principles. In practice, not a great deal has been achieved. For most professional employees, work-life balance is something that occurs only when you retire or are made redundant. Occupational stress is on the increase, as are real working hours. Since Tony Blair launched his work-life balance campaign in March 2000, the proportion of workers putting in more than 60 hours a week has risen from 12 to 16 per cent. The proportion of women working more than 60 hours has risen from 6 to 13. Good intentions clearly aren't enough.

So why haven't the good intentions of employers been translated into practice for more than a tiny proportion of employees? From our current research into the issue, it appears that the main reason lies in the failure to view the issue holistically. Tackling part of the problem is not enough; to make a difference, employers need to attack it simultaneously at three levels. Specifically, these are:

- *policy* – setting the environment: establishing and communicating family-friendly policies, such as parental leave, support for carers, unpaid sabbaticals, crèche provision, flexible working hours or jobsharing

- *capability* – equipping people with the skills to create their own work-life balance. (People often get trapped into a dysfunctional lifestyle because they do not know clearly what they want and/or because they are afraid to pursue it.) Capability is also about enabling managers to organise work more effectively, and to help employees make use of opportunities available

- *culture* – here the focus is on attitudes and support systems. Even where there are very positive policies towards work-life balance and where people have a strong desire to achieve personal change in this respect, they may be inhibited by fear or organisational inertia. Will I be seen as making less of a contribution? Will my job or my promotion be more at risk? Will my colleagues resent what I am doing? How supportive will my manager and my colleagues be? These are all key questions that define whether people take the opportunities offered to them.

MAKING A DIFFERENCE: THE ROLE OF HR

Although in our research we did encounter a handful of senior people in HR who claimed to have established what was for them a healthy balance between their work and non-work lives, they formed a very small minority. But HR's role in creating a culture supportive of work-life balance is vital and substantial. Only HR can make a convincing case for the business impact of investing time and money in promoting good work-life balance (WLB) practice; only HR can craft and sell in to top management viable strategies for taking advantage of the competitive potential that a proactive approach to WLB brings; only HR can design and integrate the wide portfolio of policies needed; and only HR can develop and implement the processes for measuring progress against WLB goals.

As we shall see in Chapter 1, in which we consider the business case, WLB is just one more of those vital activities which HR can only achieve with the active co-operation and commitment of top management. Educating top managers about their responsibilities and supporting them in making changes in their own lives is not always easy. People at the top often don't *want* to break old habits. Yet it is remarkable how often HR professionals report that they are pushing at an open door. On the executive programmes at the leading business schools, for example, one of the most popular elective subjects is work-life balance. And what executives recognise is good for them can be relatively easy to sell as good for all employees.

HR's key role is to have the courage to conduct the WLB debate at all levels in the organisation, pushing it on the agenda wherever and whenever possible, with the aim always in mind of developing a truly strategic approach to these issues. If and when HR succeeds in bringing the majority of top managers on board too, it will have the wherewithal to bring about genuinely radical change.

MAKING A DIFFERENCE: THE ROLE OF TOP MANAGEMENT

One of the positive stories about former US president Jimmy Carter was his stand against unnecessary long hours at the White House. Carter would reportedly walk round the building from time to time after normal working hours and remind people that the world wasn't going to end if they left what they were doing till tomorrow. By contrast, consider this account from a middle manager in a multinational company:

> My official working hours were nine to five, but my director was always in the office by 7.30 am. I soon learnt from his disapproving expression and the behaviour of my colleagues that arriving any later than 8.15 was not acceptable. The same was true in the evening. He would always be there till seven and would ring in till that time if he was out of the office. You just didn't dare go before half past six, even if you'd finished everything you had to do. I found myself taking on more and more work simply to justify the extra hours I was putting in.

Less than one in ten of the directors I have interviewed in our current research sees himself or herself as a good role model for work-life balance. 'Do as I say, not as I do' is not a very powerful message to the organisation.

In addition to examining what kind of example they provide personally, top management can support the drive towards work-life balance by demonstrating an interest in and concern for employees' experiences in this context, by publicly recognising the contribution of people who work alternative hours, and by working to integrate policies so that they are consistently supportive of work-life balance. One company, for example, had a set of policies aimed at stimulating work-life balance and another set to manage succession planning. One of the criteria within the succession planning process was 'commitment' – a term that was generally interpreted to exclude part-time employees and those whose family responsibilities prevented them from working all hours when projects demanded it. Even when top management attempted to spell out that this was not their intention, they were not believed until several high-level appointments of part-timers and carers demonstrated that they were serious.

Some companies, such as BP, have set up websites which have specific information about work-life balance policies and provide advice on how to take advantage of them. Again, however, it is the reality of what people see happening in the workplace that determines whether policies will be taken seriously by either the employee beneficiaries or those managers who administer the policies on a daily basis.

MAKING A DIFFERENCE: CREATIVE THINKING SPACE

It's a true but sad reflection on the way we organise work that very few people come to work to think. In seminar after seminar, around the developed and increasingly in the developing world too, I find that people do their real thinking out of office hours, in the car, on the train, or in the period between going to bed and going to sleep. Working time and, to a large extent, non-work time is primarily about doing. Top management often reinforces this view by expecting people to be seen to work. Putting one's feet on the desk and relaxing is not perceived as a constructive activity.

Chilling evidence of the shrinking of reflective time comes from a recent survey by Yell.com, which finds that the nominal one-hour lunch break – an important opportunity to recuperate mental energies in the middle of the working day – is fast vanishing, having now shrunk on average to just 35 minutes. A growing minority of employees (7 per cent) don't have time to take a lunch break at all.[6]

Yet all the evidence we have is that reflective space – time to think deeply and in a focused way – is critical to effective working. Instead of back-to-back meetings, companies can encourage people to build buffer periods in which they can reflect on what they have just done and on what they want to achieve from the next meeting. Practical experience shows that people who manage their time in this way accomplish far more, more quickly. Decisions taken in meetings, where the participants have thought about what they want to say, hear and achieve, are clearer and achieved in much shorter time.

It is up to top management to develop a culture that is more aware of the value of using time as an intelligent resource, rather than allowing people to become the victims of time. Once again, it helps to be a good role model.

MAKING A DIFFERENCE:
GIVE EMPLOYEES THE TOOLS TO CREATE THEIR OWN WORK-LIFE BALANCE

A number of employers, such as the Nationwide Building Society, have offered employees briefings or training in how to set about creating a better balance of work and non-work for their own lives. There are a number of issues which people may need help to tackle, including:

- what they actually *want* from each aspect of their lives – how important each aspect is to them now and how important they expect it to be in the future
- how they sort out conflicting demands on their time, physical energy and emotional energy – as important within the workplace and within the home as between work and home
- how they achieve the self-discipline required to set boundaries and to say no when demands from others threaten to breach those boundaries
- how to recognise and manage the stress that comes from conflicting or excessive demands upon them.

Simply having an opportunity to think these issues through can help greatly. Where training is not available, some organisations have found that employees are increasingly bringing issues of work-life conflict to internally or externally resourced counselling facilities. The topic is also one of the top three issues discussed by executives using external coaches or mentors.

MAKING A DIFFERENCE:
THE LINE MANAGER AS THE KEY TO CULTURE CHANGE

Like top managers, ordinary line managers can influence the environment for work-life balance in several ways. Firstly, they too will be role models for the members of their teams. The more seriously they take work-life balance issues, the greater the encouragement for others to do the same. Secondly, they can learn how to be more comfortable with *achievement-focused* management (where what matters is what people accomplish, no matter where or how long they work) and how to let go of the traditional *input-focused* style of management that expects managers to monitor people's activity. Achievement-focused management requires them to trust and empower people to do what they have agreed. It also requires the manager to spend less time in checking up and more in ensuring the quality and quantity of interaction between team members.

The line manager also needs to be skilled in helping people manage conflicting demands upon them. He or she must work with the team to identify what work is both urgent and important (and therefore may take precedence over other demands), what can be left till tomorrow, and what should not be done at all. He or she must also assist people in finding accommodations that ensure that a better work-life balance for one or two people does not mean an unacceptable burden for others. Keeping such issues on the agenda and encouraging dialogue about them is a good starting point. Empowering the members of the team to negotiate their own solutions is a natural evolution of this approach.

There seems to be a strong connection between flexibility (of working time, place and practice) and people feeling in control of their working lives. Equally strong appears to be the connection between feeling in control of factors at home, such as spending more quality time with one's family, lower stress levels and better sleeping patterns; and factors at work such as productivity and retention.

THE PAYBACK

The evidence from numerous studies is that corporate investment in work-life balance pays major dividends. For example, a 2001 study of women working in telecommunications companies found that investment in work-life balance was closely correlated with higher retention and workforce diversity.[7] Other surveys and case studies have linked a positive approach to work-life balance to productivity, creativity, positive attitudes towards work, and employee commitment (willingness to 'go the extra mile' on behalf of the customer or the company). Commitment has in turn been linked to financial performance, one international study finding that companies with committed employees provide an average return to shareholders of 112 per cent over three years, compared to 90 per cent for companies with average commitment.

The real payback, however, is the creation of a working environment that rebalances the psychological contract between employer and employee. Companies perceived as being among the best employers to work for outperform the stock market average on most key indicators. It is now becoming more and more difficult to be an employer of choice if employees have to make what they perceive as too great a sacrifice of their non-work lives. The issue of work-life balance has forced itself onto the management agenda in recent years. Now it is time for it to infiltrate and change radically the business culture.

WHAT DO WE MEAN BY 'WORK-LIFE BALANCE'?

All three of the words in this much-used phrase have a high ambiguity of meaning. When we talk about work, do we just mean paid-for employment, or do we also include voluntary work, housework, and/or physical recreation, such as digging the garden? The distinction between work and non-work is often blurred by the extent to which we enjoy the task we are doing. Work may be synonymous with 'chore'; equally, it may be synonymous with 'effort', as in 'having a good work-out'. In terms of the work-life balance debate, however, there seems to be a reasonable consensus that work relates to *the time and energy people contract to expend to a third party in return for a defined reward*. This may encompass voluntary work, where the payback lies in psychosocial or generative rewards.

The word 'life' evokes a range of meanings, from simple existence to a life sentence. In the context of work-life balance, however, it is typically taken to be the antithesis of work – ie not-work or non-work. This seems to me to be a rather narrow and largely unhelpful definition. Life in reality involves an accumulation of experiences, the opportunity to experiment and learn, being able to establish and grow meaningful, fulfilling relationships and, paradoxically, the opportunity to engage in meaningful, fulfilling activities (ie to enjoy one's work). For the purposes of this book, we define 'life' as *the opportunity to achieve in a diverse range of contexts*.

'Balance' generally implies some sense of equity or reasonableness. Workaholics are presumed to be unbalanced because they do not conform to expected norms about where and how they invest their time and energy, in the same way that a person with obsessive compulsive disorder is observed to be dysfunctional. However, reasonableness is very much in the eye of the beholder – a workaholic may be more fulfilled than a more laid-back counterpart who has no passionate interests. And equity, it can be argued, is not an essential component of balance. People who feel they lead a relatively balanced life may still spend longer at work than at play. The fact that there is conflict between work and non-work doesn't mean that there is a feeling of imbalance. There must be a real or perceived negative impact for imbalance to be an issue. What matters is the individual's ability to accommodate and resolve such conflicts.

A working definition of 'balance' in the context of work-life balance is: *a state where an individual manages real or potential conflict between different demands on his or her time and energy in a way that satisfies his or her needs for well-being and self-fulfilment*. Some observers would also add reference to the impact on other key stakeholders, such as close family members.

Achieving work-life balance can arguably be boiled down to:

- being aware of different demands on your time and energy

- having the ability to make choices in the allocation of time and energy
- knowing what values you wish to apply to choices
- making (conscious) choices.

If, as appears to be the case, balance is more complicated than simply comparing work and non-work, then there has to be a practical framework for thinking about how we allocate our resources of time and energy. In Chapter 2 we discuss six critical lifestreams, two of them related to 'work' and four to 'life'. A simpler version of the same concept is expressed in Figure 1 *The allocation of space and time*. In theory, at least, people who wish to be fulfilled need to allocate time and consideration to:

- themselves ('me-time') – recharging their batteries, taking care of their own physical and emotional needs
- close others – family, close friends and other people with whom they have strong emotional ties
- paid employment – as the means to finance the fulfilment of various needs
- distant others – for example, involvement in voluntary activities for the larger community.

Figure 1 The allocation of space and time

Innermost circle: space/time for me

First circle out: space/time for close others

Second circle out: space/time for paid employment

Outermost circle: space/time for distant others (eg community)

A factor common to all four of these categories is that each contributes to creating meaning in the individual's life. The emphasis one person places on a category will obviously differ considerably from the emphasis placed on it by another. And his or her perception of whether a good balance is the result will not necessarily match the perception of other stakeholders in terms of time and energy. A spouse or child, for example, might feel that he or she should have a greater share of attention. Giving up 'me-time' to accommodate such expectations is a common response amongst parents of young children, and it is for this reason that they are particularly likely to feel dissatisfied with their work-life balance.

FIVE STATES OF BALANCE/IMBALANCE

Another practical way of looking at work-life balance is as a spectrum. At one extreme is *subsistence*, where people work long hours out of necessity, with little resource left over for investment in other aspects of their lives. Next comes *conflict,* where the individual recognises conflicting demands and struggles to resolve them. Squarely in the middle is *integration*, where the person has more or less achieved a satisfactory level of fulfilment in multiple aspects of his or her life. *Idleness* describes the situation of those who are either unable to work (through disability or unemployment, for example) or unwilling to engage in productive activity. At the far extreme is *hedonism*, where the individual has no need to work and devotes his or her energies to play and/or non-work activities.

Alongside this notion of balance there is more to be said on the subject of conflict. Conflict occurs when one part of a person's life intrudes dysfunctionally or excessively into another. The normal assumption is that the intrusion is primarily from work into non-work, but in reality there are many situations where the flow can be the other way round. For example, marital problems or illness may be reflected in irritable behaviour at work; or urgent needs in the role of dependent carer can require employees to leave at short notice when providing alternative cover is not feasible. (One company with a strong work-life balance ethic found it difficult to cope with a requirement by several staff to watch their children in the same school nativity play – service coverage was cut to the bone for a few hours.)

Parasuraman and Greenhaus summarise the problem thus:

> *The most prevalent type of work-family conflict occurs when the time demands of one role make it difficult or impossible to . . . participate fully in the other; when the symptoms of psychological strain in one role . . . spill over into the other; when behaviours used in one role are used inappropriately in the other.*

It is interesting to note here that people's judgements about their job and their employer often ignore the impact of one upon the other. The *Sunday Times* 100 Best Companies to Work For survey[8] reveals that being exhausted after work is not a predictor of feeling that the company demands too much of you. The company which in the 2003 survey had the highest score against the statement 'Most days I feel exhausted when I come home from work' was Majestic Wine Stores, where 75 per cent of employees agreed with the statement, yet it was one of the top 40 per cent of employers. Working hard, and even working long hours, does not necessarily correlate with a perception of poor work-life balance.

People's sense of work-life balance is, to a considerable extent, the product of the climate or environment in which they conduct their lives. There is evidence that having a friendly and supportive environment at work promotes satisfaction with work-life balance,[9] and that having a supportive family environment contributes similarly.[10]

However, work family programmes will not solve stress problems. They simply help people manage the conflicts better.

THE STRUCTURE OF THIS BOOK

In Chapter 1 we examine the business case for employers to invest in work-life balance and for the Human Resources function to promote the benefits of a culture that supports work-life balance. Making the business case is not as straightforward as many enthusiasts would have us believe. While each aspect of flexible working – for example, from telecommuting to annualised hours – can be shown to provide an ample return to employers in individual cases, this does not mean that the same will be true in all cases, nor that the aggregate effect will exceed the sum

Figure 2 Our route map

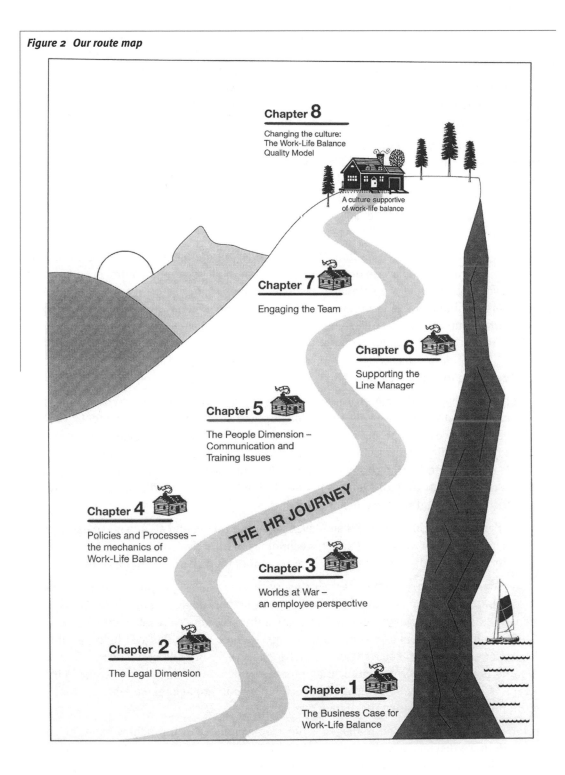

of the parts. It can and does happen that flexibility for some employees results in less favourable circumstances, and hence lower motivation, for others. Moreover, the chain from introducing a policy to support work-life balance to increased business profit has several intervening links. Break any of these and the effect of work-life balance will be muted. What does seem to be universally the case, however, is that a work-life culture delivers more benefits to all stakeholders than simply having *ad hoc* policies and practices.

Chapter 2, written by Mike Huss, senior employment law specialist at Peninsula, provides a broad overview of the legislative framework, both UK and European. It is clear that new legislation in this area will continue to be passed and that obligations on employers will increase. Many of the HR professionals we interviewed for this book emphasised the value of being proactive and ahead of the legislation over constantly striving to catch up. Not only does a proactive approach appear to be cheaper in the long run, but it is less demanding on HR time.

In Chapter 3 we look at the issues from the point of view of the individual and the support HR can give to people in being aware of work-life choices and taking greater control over their work and non-work lives. While the company has a responsibility not to put pressure on them to work excessive hours over long periods and to try to accommodate people's need for flexible working arrangements (as long as these can be achieved without damage to the business), the ultimate responsibility and accountability for maintaining work-life balance rests with the employee. The company may educate them and encourage them, but employees have to decide how they want to manage their time and make their own choices.

In Chapter 4 we get to the meat of policy and process – the specifics of work-life balance provision. At this stage we deal with the various options for flexibility one by one. Later in the book (Chapter 8) we examine how to integrate them into a broad, customised package that supports the work-life balance culture. Policies, as we have already observed, are only of value if they are implemented by the company in the form of practical processes. Policies seem to fall into three main categories: those related to time flexibility, those related to place flexibility, and the various benefits that reinforce flexible working.

Processes, in turn, are only of value if employees are both willing and able to make use of them. Critical factors here are work organisation, technology and HR systems, each of which have to be adjusted to ensure that they support rather than undermine work-life balance objectives.

Chapter 5 delves into some of the mechanisms for reaching out to people and overcoming the individual barriers that prevent them from making use of the work-life balance options available to them. In particular it focuses on how the organisation communicates with employees about work-life balance issues and provides appropriate training where this will help people both make better, more courageous choices and be supportive of colleagues' work-life balance needs. HR itself can aid the communication process by demonstrating good practice in its own ranks – it is noticeable that organisations which struggle to implement work-life balance often have HR functions that present a negative role model.

Chapter 6 focuses on the line manager – the pivotal person in the achievement of culture change. Here we discuss how HR can help the line manager gain the confidence, competence and commitment to make work-life balance a valued means of achieving team goals, rather than another problem to manage. We also examine what it means for the line manager to be a personal role model for work-life balance.

Chapter 7 focuses on the team itself and how it can help the manager and individual team members address the practicalities of achieving both superior task performance and a fulfilling life inside and outside of work. Accommodations between team members and creativity in designing solutions that meet the needs of the business and those of the individual are best achieved through team dialogue.

Finally, in Chapter 8 we pull all the strands together into an integrated model, which we call the *Work-life balance quality management model*. This provides a clear route map for implementing and measuring progress in work-life balance. In particular, it links policy, process and people activities clearly with outcomes for the three key stakeholders: employees, the organisation and the community. The quality model provides a practical means of benchmarking good practice and assessing improvement in work-life balance over time.

In pulling together the ideas and approaches in this book, we have concentrated heavily on the practical. The experienced HR professional should, at the very least, find in these pages a ready blueprint for moving his or her organisation more rapidly along the path to a work-life balance positive culture. Every HR professional we have spoken to, who has committed to helping top management build such a culture, has found it to be a challenge, but one with great payoffs in terms of personal satisfaction. And they have individually found that they, too, have had to re-evaluate their own lives and choices – and that they are the better for it!

REFERENCES AND READING

1 STIX G. (2002) 'Real time'. *Scientific American*. September. pp20–23.
2 WORRALL L. *and* COOPER C. L. (1999) *The Quality of Working Life: 1999 survey of managers' changing experiences*. London, Institute of Management.
3 NOP survey on work/life balance for Yell.com. October 2002.
4 PRICEWATERHOUSECOOPERS (1999) *International Student Survey*. London, PriceWaterhouse Coopers. Available at: http://www.pwcglobal.com [Accessed 10 July 2003].
5 www.pearnkandola.com
6 GALINSKY E., JOHNSON A. A., *and* FRIEDMAN D. E. (1993) *The Work-Life Business Case: An outline of a Work in Progress*. New York, Families and Work Institute.
7 WOMEN IN CABLE AND TELECOMMUNICATIONS FOUNDATION (2001) *Diversity Through Investment*. Chantilly, VA, Women in Cable and Telecommunications. Available at: http://www.wict.org/foundation/bestpractices/bpwhitepaper.pdf [Accessed 10 July 2003].
8 MCCALL A. (ed.) (2003) '100 best companies to work for'. *Sunday Times Supplement*. 2 March.
9 GUEST D. *and* CONWAY N. (1998) *Fairness at Work and the Psychological Contract*. London, Institute of Personnel and Development.
10 GUEST D. *and* CONWAY N. (2000) *The Psychological Contract in the Public Sector:* the results of the 2000 CIPD survey of the Employment Relationship. London, Chartered Institute of Personnel and Development.

1

The business case for work-life balance

This chapter explores why organisations need to attach greater priority to work-life balance than they have done traditionally, and provides the HR professional with the wherewithal to make and present the business case. It also places work-life balance in the context of the psychological contract between employees and the organisation.

Like anti-wrinkle cream, the virtues of work-life balance have been oversold. Many enthusiasts talk as if there were a direct and obvious link between investment in work-life balance and a direct bottom-line payback. The reality is that such evidence is very hard to glean. Nonetheless, the body of evidence supporting the implementation of work-life balance policies is substantial – it is just almost entirely indirect in its impact. What we are looking at is not a straight cause-and-effect interaction, but a chain of events most, if not all, of which do seem to be convincingly linked.

Figure 3 is an attempt to capture that chain of events.

The first observation is that investment in work-life balance is a long way down the chain to profit improvement. For example, studies show no direct association between family-friendly

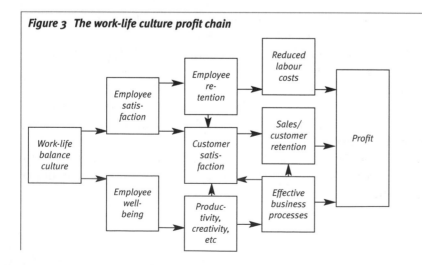

Figure 3 The work-life culture profit chain

policies (an important element of work-life balance approaches) and people's satisfaction with their level of work-life balance. Professor David Guest, of King's College, London, suggests that this is either because these policies are not implemented effectively, or because they 'lessened but not diminished the problem'.[1] A second observation is that the links between the elements described here are relatively complex – so much so that it would be remarkable if a direct link could be made. A third is that it is hard to argue convincingly *against* any of the links in the chain. In the rest of this chapter, we will try to explore some of those links, along with some of the broader correlations between facets of work-life balance and business performance.

WARNING:

THIS CHAPTER CONTAINS COPIOUS QUANTITIES OF STATISTICS.

Readers allergic to statistical data may find it easier to skim-read the first half of the section. Readers who have to substantiate the business case with hard data should find more than enough for their needs!

The reasons organisations have chosen to invest time, resources and energy in promoting work-life balance vary widely. It is easy to think of the work-life balance movement as another recent US import, but that is far from the case. Indeed, it is possible to find the real roots of corporate interest in work-life balance in a multitude of mainly European threads, from the desire of Quaker businesses in the nineteenth century to enable their employees to become 'whole persons', through the Scandinavian-driven experiments in semi-autonomous working in the 1970s, to the early Dutch attempts to distribute work in the 1980s.

The USA v Europe

The USA is awash with literature and studies on work-life balance (WLB) and these have inevitably formed a significant part of the research for this book. However, there have traditionally been two very different philosophies behind the WLB movements on the two continents, and it is useful to be aware of these before embarking on any great programme of cultural change. 'While US companies generally offer work-life programs as a competitive advantage, the EU mandates them as a function of social responsibility,' concludes an investigation and comparison by Georgia State University.[2] It continues:

The effects of the work-life programs demonstrate that competitive advantage and social responsibility are not opposite goals but intertwined: companies gain a competitive advantage from recruiting, retention, productivity increases and better customer service while also helping the society in which they operate.

Organisations in the UK have the opportunity to get the best of both worlds – to be seen to be applying legislation proactively (and perhaps exceeding its provisions, where this will enhance corporate reputation and support specific corporate goals) and to establish clear strategies for using flexibility in the workplace as a means of achieving competitive advantage.

The legislative framework within the EU and the UK tends to push social compliance to the fore in the case that companies build for WLB and the priorities they attach to WLB solutions. After all, it doesn't help the case much for a company to have a positive attitude but be in breach of legislation! Part of the challenge for HR in the UK is to give the competitive advantage case equal or greater prominence – and to be believed by what is often a somewhat cynical workforce.

IMPACT ON EMPLOYEES

Very few companies, if any, deliberately set out to create workplaces that are unattractive. But many still operate on the tacit assumption that what employees want first and foremost is money. Even where surveys contradict this view, they struggle to accept that, above a threshold that varies from individual to individual, sustainable non-monetary rewards are far more important for retention, motivation and commitment.

Companies, which aim to motivate people primarily by money, are finding increasing resistance. As a senior HR manager in the London office of a multinational finance company explains:

> *A few years ago, the psychological contract was simple. You worked hard, for long hours, and you expected to make sacrifices in your non-work life. There'd be a lot of challenge in your work and a great deal of travel. In return, you stood to make a lot of money, through bonuses, and you expected to be able to retire before your mid-forties and enjoy all those pleasures you'd denied yourself till then. The problem is, we can't fulfil that promise now. Without the expectation of becoming independently wealthy relatively young, why should people make sacrifices in other parts of their lives?*

According to a recent survey by the Department of Trade and Industry, one in three employees would prefer flexible working hours to a £1,000 pay rise. The right to work flexibly is valued by employees more highly than any other 'perk', including a company car.

A Jobtrak.com survey of more than 3,000 US college students at Brigham Young University shows that their number one recruiting incentive is WLB. In a similar vein, recent graduates from 11 countries, surveyed by PricewaterhouseCoopers in 2000, placed work-life balance at the top of their wish-list in selecting a job and career. This is an increase from 45 per cent to 57 per cent over the same survey in 1998. Significantly, the graduates do not see any substantial conflict between work-life balance and achieving long-term career goals. However, this idealism seems to be gradually worn away as they become acculturated to the working norms of the organisation. No matter how determined they are not to be sucked into the long hours habit, they find that they are slowly but surely trapped into being so. As they see their work-life balance ebb away, they rationalise it to themselves as something that is only temporary – but it rarely is.[3]

Surveys by pollster Harris also reveal that working men under 40 value spending time with their family more than having challenging work or a high salary. Some 70 per cent claimed they would be willing to exchange some of their salary for more family time.

Gemini Consulting, in a study across the USA, Europe, Russia and Japan, found that balancing the needs of work and family was the first priority of workers in all countries, bar Russia, where it came second to pay (probably not surprisingly, given the problems many Russians seem to have getting paid!).

Figures from a survey in the Republic of Ireland illustrate how big the change in people's priorities has been. In 1962, 83 per cent of Irish workers thought that work demands should take preference over personal and family needs; now only 37 per cent have the same view.[4] Another recent survey finds that 50 per cent of MBA students want to be offered the flexibility to work from home.[5] Yet another survey finds that 83 per cent of working mothers and 72 per cent of working fathers experience conflict between the desire to do a good job at work and the desire to see more of their families.[6]

Even attitudes to what is expected of managers are changing rapidly. The proportion of people who think 'senior positions require more commitment than merely 9-to-5' fell from 82 per cent to 58 per cent between 1999 and 2002. Only a third of people agree that senior managers who have children under 15 should be expected to work late and at weekends whenever necessary. Greater responsibility and longer hours are no longer automatically linked in public perception.

It's easy to underestimate the gap between what employees want and what they perceive they are getting. Employers who point to high scores in staff attitude surveys for job satisfaction may be missing the point. A study by the University of Connecticut found that while, in a sample of 1,000 employees, 88 per cent said they had high job satisfaction, 95 per cent also said they were worried that work took them away too much from their families, and 87 per cent said they lost sleep worrying over work responsibilities.

Moreover, discussion of what employees want is often overly simplistic. Employees vary greatly in their circumstances, personalities and ambitions. What they want in terms of their work and non-work lives also changes significantly as they evolve through various life stages, acquiring and shedding responsibilities. Perhaps the only common factor in what employees want is the desire for an employer to be sufficiently flexible to fit their individual circumstances. A substantial proportion also want their employer to view them not simply as a hired pair of hands or bundle of neurons, but as a whole person, who is defined not just by the job they do, but by the rich web of activities, interests and relationships in which they engage, both within and outside work.

The comment a few lines above about the change in the psychological contract is not an isolated observation. The reality is that the psychological contract between employer and employee is changing constantly. In the developed countries at least, those in work have typically progressed well beyond the basic levels of the hierarchy of needs. The emphasis of the psychological contract has therefore moved inexorably further and further towards an exchange that emphasises a broader sense of self-fulfilment – how do my work and the company that employs me enable me to become the person I want to be? Whereas that person might once have been defined primarily in terms of career and work role, changing social attitudes and the increasing participation of women in the workforce, particularly at more senior levels, have made the definition much more holistic. The person someone aspires to be may now be a combination of many life facets – lawyer or accountant, fantastic parent, an accomplished cook, a good friend, a contributor to good causes, and so on. The dilemma for employers, and hence for HR, is:

- *to what extent does the psychological contract between this company and its employees enable them to become the persons they want to be?*

Alternatively,

- *to what extent does it interfere with their aspirations to become that person?*

The increasing perception by women that the psychological contract does not meet their current needs is demonstrated by the very high proportion of married women (over 50 per cent) who say they would prefer either not to work at all or to work only part-time, once they have children.[7]

The social change that is occurring among fathers is captured in an article in *Harvard Business Review*, which comments:

> *A new organisational man has emerged – one who wants to be an involved father with no loss of income, prestige and corporate support – and no diminished sense of manhood. . . . Corporations may lose their best and brightest men if they don't address the needs of the 1990s man.*[8]

According to the US Center for Ethics and Corporate Responsibility the number one ethical issue for corporations is 'a difficulty in performing at a high level at work, while maintaining a strong commitment to one's family at the same time'.[9] A recent survey of 500 male managers by *Management Today* found that a third would trade career progression for more time with their families. The survey also found that many felt guilty about neglecting family responsibilities – one in five had missed his or her child's Christmas play in 2002.[10] Three quarters of respondents said they paid more attention to work-life issues than their fathers; 84 per cent of those with children under five said the same.

The effects of these conflicts between the image, which many men (and women) feel obliged to put forward to suggest that they are confident and in control, and the reality of their guilt about not managing to invest sufficiently in their family was revealed in a study by sociologist Robert Weiss.[11] He interviewed 80 executives defined by their organisation as functioning well. What he actually found was that all wanted to be seen not just as successful in business, but as

> *good fathers, good providers, good men. . . . However, each of them reported stress and irritability; half had trouble sleeping; most had few close friends, choosing instead to compartmentalise their lives to get through the day.*[12]

It's not just a family matter

It's easy from much of what has been written about work-life balance to equate it to family-friendly policies. But this sells the whole concept short and may in some circumstances stimulate a backlash from those without families. Companies which have focused their work-life balance policies on parents report that this has marginalised the issue amongst managers and employees. Even where the flexible working options are available to parents of both genders, men tend to avoid them because they are seen to be addressing the issues of working mothers. Career-minded women also avoid them, on the grounds that they don't want to give yet another advantage to men.

Family-friendly policies also do not necessarily provide for the growing army of employees who care for disabled and/or elderly relatives. Nor do they allow for the special needs of people with a hidden disability, such as diabetes or ME, who may need to manage their lives around a health regime; or people, who are studying in their spare time and need to attend classes and workshops; or people, who manage a smallholding in addition to their main job, or who perhaps are building their own home; or people who are helping their spouse establish a business . . . The list goes on. Drawing an arbitrary line that suggests flexible working is all right for one group and not for another is neither logical nor useful. It is difficult to advance a tenable argument why policies on working flexibility should not apply to all employees. Why, in principle, should it be more acceptable for an employee with young children to be able to adjust his or her hours, than for someone who wishes to compete at an amateur level in his or her chosen sport? While in general there is little evidence of a widespread resentment among employees without dependents for benefits given to those who do have dependents, the issue surfaces regularly in research among employee groups.

Another issue which is beginning to surface more frequently is the fact that these arbitrary lines already exist, not just in the formal criteria many companies apply in identifying who is eligible to work flexibly, but in the informal cultures that define what is and what is not permissible. For example, the likelihood of working from choice some days at home each month increases substantially with seniority – it is not only accepted but expected in many organisations that middle and senior managers will spend some time at home doing the tasks that require concentrated thinking. Where this privilege does not extend to all employees, those who are denied the opportunity to work in this way can only conclude that they are in some way less worthy or less trusted.

Any sense of unfairness or inequity can seriously undermine the psychological contract between the organisation and its employees – especially when the contract is under increased pressure as a result of downsizing or 'lean management'. In both these circumstances, the net result is that more work is expected from fewer employees. Where the organisation fails to automate and 'work smarter', the employees simply have to cope with greater volume of work, which obliges them to work longer hours. Where an organisation does automate, work often becomes more concentrated and continuous, meaning that employees are more drained at the end of the day. (A high proportion even of employees working for Top 100 Best Employer companies report that they are exhausted by their work.) It is interesting that many US companies have responded to the post-2001 recession by increasing the attention they pay to work-life balance issues and by investment in policies and activities that support work-life balance.[13] The reason does not appear to be altruism so much as recognition that employee motivation is a fragile flower that needs nurturing. It seems at odds with a business culture that is often accused of short-termism, but it is hard to get even short-term results out of a disaffected workforce.

The impact of downsizing and lean management is often made worse by the perception on the part of many men that they are defined by their role as breadwinner and by the job that they do. Comments *Harvard Business Review* author Michael Kimmer:

> *In an expanding economy, hitching one's manhood to a career may make some sense. In a recession, it's a recipe for feelings of failure.*[14]

According to researcher Monique Connor and her colleagues,[15] the big six international accountancy firms (now the big four) have recognised that they should respond to employee's different needs by giving them:

- the opportunity to advance through their careers at different paces while contributing to the success of the firm

- the opportunity to assume different workloads – for short or long periods

- more flexibility to balance work and family life.

They also aim to convey the message that the firm is willing to explore ways to meet individual needs *and* the needs of clients by embracing policies and practices that ultimately support higher retention. Many of these companies have found that, having institutionalised these expectations and practices during the good times, it is much easier to find accommodations between the employers' need for more flexibility and the employees' desire for alternative working. When the principles are accepted at the corporate level and processes are familiar to implement flexibility at the local level, appropriate dialogue is much less difficult and there is less suspicion between the two sides.

IMPACT ON THE ORGANISATION

As we saw earlier in the chapter, a proactive approach to work-life balance will not normally affect productivity, competitiveness, the bottom line or the return on equity in a direct manner. Rather, it creates the environment where intervening variables can line up behind the delivery of these basic measures of business performance. Nonetheless, there is a great deal of support from credible observers for the notion that work-life balance and business performance are inextricably linked.

For example, the link with competitiveness is championed by Denise Kingsmill, deputy chair of the Competition Commission, who asserts 'We still have a very old-fashioned stance to the number of hours people work and a culture of presenteeism', and suggests that this is at least part of the reason the UK lags behind in terms of productivity by comparison with much of the rest of the developed world.

In similar vein, while he admits that the evidence for greater productivity through investment in work-life balance is largely anecdotal, Richard Donkin of the *Financial Times* points out that there are also broader benchmarks which are harder to explain away:

> *French manufacturers are way ahead of the British in securing annualised hours agreements, which is one reason why they can maintain higher productivity with a 35-hour week. They focus on organising the necessary work. In the UK we still tend to concentrate on time spent at work, so much of which, we must acknowledge, is wasted.*[16]

Certainly, employees' perception of their own productivity is that it increases with flexible working or teleworking.[17] A study of employees in companies employing over 500 staff, by BT Cellnet, found that four out of five employees working flexibly think their productivity has improved; 70 per cent of them think the increase is at least 10 per cent. The main reasons given for feeling that they are more productive are:

- having fewer interruptions

- being able to use commuting time for more useful activities

- less stress
- greater control over where and when they do their work.

Managers at some of the USA's largest companies who have direct reports working flexibly through flexitime or telecommuting some of their working week, generally have a positive experience.[18] Seven out of ten claimed there was an improvement in flexibility.

Some statistical support is also available from studies such as that by the Resource Connection and the Industrial Society, which found that 70 per cent of flexible workers were seen to produce a higher output than their full-time desk-bound colleagues, and performed better than when working under non-flexible arrangements. Flexible workers also demonstrated higher resilience, leadership and commitment than those working standard full-time hours, as rated by their managers. The study further showed that seven out of ten senior managers who jobshared were seen to have a 30 per cent higher output than one person doing the same job.[19]

Other studies have found that both managers and employees perceive an increase in productivity from providing employees with greater flexibility in working times and locations.

Various studies suggest a strong correlation between good people management processes in general and the bottom-line performance of companies. For example, Watson Wyatt's regular Human Capital Index finds that North American and European companies rated as having very good HR practices deliver three times as much value to shareholders as those at the other end of the spectrum. There is also a small but significant market value difference in market value (3.5 per cent) between those with flexible working arrangements, such as telecommuting, flexitime and jobsharing, and those without.

Another US study, by Sibson and Co., a firm of consultants in New Jersey, looked at the impact of high labour turnover on earnings and stock prices. It concluded that for call centres, high-technology companies, speciality retailers and fast-food vendors (all sectors where labour turnover is above 50 per cent a year), earnings and stock value were depressed by 38 per cent from this factor alone. Among the factors that cost money is expensive mistakes, which often exceeds new employees' wages for the first few weeks.

Recruitment and retention

For many organisations, people costs are the highest costs. It is not surprising, then, that a study by Towers Perrin in 2001 found a sharp difference between high- and low-performing businesses in the way they regard their people. It used to be that companies would routinely put phrases such as 'People are our greatest asset' in annual reports – then promptly demonstrate through layoffs or other actions that they didn't really believe it at all. Now high-performing companies are making the sentiment a practical reality. They are identifying which employees have the knowledge, skills and commitment to help create and sustain competitive advantage; they are making them aware of their importance and how they can contribute; and they are making sure that they keep these people, through motivating and rewarding them. They are also doing all they can to attract more people of the same kind.

Because it is difficult to target benefits solely at these key employees (who could range from a shop assistant to a senior manager), these companies by and large make policies apply equally to all. This sense of egalitarianism also seems popular with most of the talented employees they want to keep. The days of perks for managers and favourites are gone in most high-performing organisations.[20]

The arguments for an intensive focus on retaining people of ability are well made in the book *The War for Talent*,[21] whose authors say:

> *In 1900, only 17 per cent of all jobs required knowledge workers; now 60 per cent do. More knowledge workers means it's more important to get great talent, since the differential value created by the most talented knowledge workers is enormous.*

Their study concentrated, it is true, on middle and senior managers (some 13,000 of them), but the same principles seem to apply – companies are becoming more and more reliant on having talented people, switching them on and keeping them. At the same time, employees are more mobile than ever before.

Other studies on both sides of the Atlantic provide similar data. They indicate that at any one time, just over a third of employees are minded to move on to another employer. (One even suggests that two thirds would leave if a good opportunity for advancement arose.) They may not be actively looking, but they are sufficiently dissatisfied to be minded to quit. A Reed International study of 800 employees found that 31 per cent were passively job-seeking by keeping their eyes on the job market, while another 14 per cent were actively on the lookout.[22] Whether they did leave depended on opportunity (and the more valuable they were, the more likely they were to find an opportunity) and how negatively they felt about the psychological contract with the organisation and the relationships with their boss and working colleagues.

An impromptu and limited study I initiated in a major UK employer attempted to establish what proportion of people who were minded to leave would look actively for other opportunities in the organisation. Only one person in six would do so. The main reasons for this reluctance to search inside the organisation were concerns about the response of their boss and/or colleagues if it became known they were looking to move on. Those employees who were looking internally all felt they had a supportive boss and colleagues. Significantly, a Gallup survey of 2 million employees in 700 companies in 2000 found that most valued having a caring boss more highly than pay or fringe benefits.

The Saratoga Institute assesses the average cost of losing an employee at 150 per cent of his or her annual salary, taking into account costs of recruiting a replacement, training them, downtime before they arrive, time for them to come up to speed, and costs in quality while they learn the job. Some key employees – say a top salesperson – may cost the company many times more than that.

As an antidote to loose-footedness amongst employees, work-life balance appears to be one of the strongest medicines. Consider some of the evidence:

- An IES study[23] found some correlation between the breadth of work-life options on offer and low employee turnover.

- Shoe retail chain Russell and Bromley sees a link between flexibility over working hours (staff can take hours worked over the norm as time in lieu) and retention, to the extent that some part-time staff – a group notorious for high labour turnover – have progressed with the company to become directors. According to the head of HR, Ann Friday, 'Tired people don't function as well as fresh people, so there is a direct benefit to the business, too.'[24]

- A study by the Women in Cable and Telecommunications Foundation found that companies which invested heavily in work-life balance and, significantly, demonstrated strong top management support for work-life balance, had much higher retention and lower labour turnover than the norm.

- Several studies of women's attitudes to work reveal that quality of family life is the most significant factor – particularly for those with children – in deciding whether to go or stay in a job.

- A study by the London School of Economics in 2001 found that 80 per cent of people in Generation X (ie born between 1963 and 1981) and 93 per cent of people aged 18 to 25 would be more likely to stay in their jobs if they could take greater control over when and how they worked. Surprisingly, it doesn't seem to matter greatly how important extra-work activities are to employees who decide to quit. What matters is that work is intruding too much into their extra-work space.

- The attractiveness of working options that permit work-life balance is increasingly important in the recruitment market. Various studies have found that for a high proportion of potential employees – who are often the most talented – the opportunity to work flexibly, even if they do not want to use it immediately, is a priority in their selection of an employer.[25]

Employee motivation

Says the 2003 Best Companies to Work For survey:[26] 'Companies that allow their staff to work flexibly reap handsome dividends. It is a case of a little going a long way.' Employees who have even one morning or afternoon a week working from home are more content with management, and record much higher scores for fair dealing and personal growth. The increased stress they experience, perhaps as they try to prevent domestic life encroaching while working at home, does not seem to tarnish the overall positive effect.

Although high motivation doesn't always link with high productivity, few companies set out to design low-motivation workplaces and most would see this as a serious problem for long-term competitiveness. Small wonder, then, that claims by Gallup that nearly a fifth of employees are actively disengaged by their work (ie they have no interest in it and regard it as a chore) are causing concern. Gallup relates this disenchantment to lower levels of productivity, greater stress, low loyalty to the company and substantially higher levels of absenteeism.

A study by the Families and Work Institute concluded that the combination of flexible working, dependent care and fringe benefits resulted in employees with more positive attitudes towards the work and their employer. DuPont, in a survey of employees, found that those who used work-life opportunities provided by the company were more committed, both to their job and to staying with the company. Given that other studies demonstrate a close link between employee commitment and shareholder return (companies that have high employee commitment average 60 per cent higher shareholder return), investing in the antecedents of commitment makes good commercial sense.

Absenteeism

The BT survey quoted above also establishes a positive link between flexible work practices and reduced absenteeism. It found that a remarkable 22 per cent had at some time during the previous working month stayed at home and worked, when they felt too ill to travel to work. Many other surveys have found that attention to work-life balance and family-friendly policies reduces absenteeism. As long ago as 1993, Johnson and Johnson in the United States found that people who made use of work-family benefits packages took only half as much sick leave as other employees.

Companies offering positive policies on work-life balance also benefit from shorter absences by people on maternity leave. A US study in 1993 found that these employees started their maternity leave later into the pregnancy and returned earlier.

Creativity

A number of studies in recent years have explored the importance to creativity in the workplace of having supportive networks of family and friends. From these, we know that external support alleviates emotional exhaustion[27] and has a direct and positive impact upon an individual's creative responses.[28,29] What these studies basically indicate is that employees who don't have sufficient time to nurture important social relationships are less creative than those who do. This applies across all types of work, not just those we label as creative jobs. In practical terms, a long-hours culture means less day-to-day practical innovation, less questioning of how and why things are done in particular ways, less pressure from within for progressive change and improvement, because people have not recharged their emotional batteries sufficiently. For me, this is one of the most significant arguments in the business case for work-life balance, perhaps because its effects are less obvious than others we explore here. An interesting, if unoriginal, analogy is suggested by one of the research papers above, which indicates that married employees tend to be more consistently creative than their unmarried colleagues. (This correlates well with other studies which show that married men suffer on average less stress and fewer health problems in general.) The body corporate is the sum of the people in it; it is the collective emotional energy that determines how healthy and creative the organisation remains over the long term.

Customer satisfaction

A variety of studies, including one by PricewaterhouseCooper in 2000,[30] indicate that a major cause of customer dissatisfaction is lack of continuity in the staff they deal with. Some 80 per cent believed that problems with employee retention were a substantial part of the problem.

Lloyds TSB calculates that improving employee retention by a factor of one improves customer satisfaction by 0.48. First Tennessee Bank used a wide array of work-life measures, including an intensive training programme, to make sure managers were sympathetic and supportive to employees in establishing individually appropriate working patterns and a policy to allow full-time workers to cut their hours without losing benefits. The resulting improvement in employee retention was reflected in year-on-year rises in customer satisfaction with the quality of service.

Quality

The nearly 30 per cent of employees (according to a Work and Family Institute study)[31] who feel overworked and overwhelmed by their work volume report that they make more mistakes. Anecdotal evidence from our own studies indicates that these employees become less and less efficient as they work longer. They simply don't have the time to step back and decide what is important or what is the best way to tackle a task.

On the other hand, the Boston College study quoted earlier found that a high proportion of flexible workers and their managers perceived a significant improvement in the quality of work after giving people more control of their time. In companies such as Motorola, Kraft, Honeywell and Bristol Myers Squibb, an average of 87 per cent of employees working flexibly said that the quality of their work had improved. More importantly, 65 per cent of managers agreed.

Equal opportunities/diversity

The Women in Cable and Telecommunications Foundation study[32] found that companies which paid high attention to work-life balance issues also had the highest gender diversity. The connection is obvious – people who want non-standard working arrangements (or think they might want them in the future) are going to look for employers most able and willing to accommodate those needs. While this might not be the only reason for their choice (nature of the work, geographic proximity of the workplace, salary levels and other factors will clearly be weighed in the balance too), it is of sufficient importance to influence the composition of the workforce.

In addition, once these employees have found an appropriate balance between their work and non-work lives, they are much less likely to look elsewhere for work. Comments another *Harvard Business Review* author, Felice Schwartz:

> *opportunity, flexibility, and family support are the keys to retaining the best women and eliminating the extra cost of employing them.*[33]

For many organisations, the requirement to demonstrate good practice in diversity management goes well beyond the legal. Increasingly, customers – particularly in the public sector – expect the organisations they deal with to have an appropriate gender and racial mix. This means more than having Hindi salespeople selling to Hindi communities; it also means having an adequate representation of minorities and women within the management structure of the organisation. While work-life balance policies tend to reinforce gender advancement more than racial minority advancement, the two issues may become linked when, for example, there is a significantly higher proportion of single mothers amongst young black women than amongst their white counterparts.

Health costs

Although UK companies do not normally carry the same burden of healthcare costs that US companies do, the costs of stress to businesses are huge. Cary Cooper, BUPA Professor of organisational psychology and health at the University of Manchester Institute of Science and Technology (UMIST), estimates that:

> *roughly 40 per cent of sickness absence in the UK workplace is stress-related in one form or another. This equates to about £4 billion per year of the £11 billion that the Confederation of British Industry calculates as the total cost of sickness absence to the UK economy.*

Professor Cooper also highlights the growing additional cost to employers of stress-related litigation whereby 'settlements in cases where employees sue their employers for stress are now averaging £250,000'. In addition to these huge financial costs that stress-related absence imposes on British industry, stress at work is further associated with higher levels of accidents and reduced productivity.

Various studies have shown that stress is greatly reduced among employees who have the option to work more flexibly. Although long hours have been identified as the primary cause of stress, a regular e-survey of HR professionals records that only 43 per cent of employees in a survey of 160 UK companies see work-related stress as a major issue in their organisation.[34] Against this, the *Management Today* study above found that six out of ten men believed they were under greater work pressure than their fathers. Says the report's author, Matthew Gwyther, 'In 40 years a profound change has occurred among British men, and it has left a proportion of them reeling.'

The costs of workplace stress are revealed (or some of them at least) by the soaring increase in days taken off due to stress. According to the Health and Safety Executive these rose from 6.5 million days in 1996 to 13.5 million in 2001. It is not surprising, then, that the HSE is introducing standards and a system to penalise employers who fail to address stress issues adequately.[35]

Working smarter

As Marriott Hotels found when it analysed why people were working 50 to 60 hours a week, a good proportion of this comprised low-value activities that acted as 'fillers' in a long-hours culture. Identifying and eliminating these activities, while at the same time telling people to go home when their work was done, cut an average of five hours off people's working week. (Even so, hours still seem excessive!) As part of its Management Flexibility Programme, initially piloted over a six-month period at three hotels in the USA, Marriott took such measures as eliminating unnecessary meetings and procedures that had previously formed part of company tradition. Managers were given more resources, such as Internet access, to perform their jobs more efficiently, and time spent on information exchanges between employees in shift change overlaps was reduced. The scheme was eventually expanded nationwide, and helped to foster a new culture of flexibility and openness within Marriott, as employees were further encouraged to work more flexibly. Speaking on the success of the programme, Bill Munck (Vice-president and market manager at Marriott International) enthused:

> *I can't overstate the effect that it had. . . . People started to realise that we were indeed serious about creating an environment that would enable them to work more efficiently and get home earlier.*[36]

London Borough of Merton

London Borough of Merton Council introduced a range of flexible working options in its housing lettings, revenues and benefits departments in response to substantial problems in sickness absenteeism, recruitment and employee motivation. It offered employees the options of a compressed workweek, working from home, career breaks, jobsharing and special leave.

To make the project work, Merton invested heavily in training managers in the departments concerned, so they assessed employees' performance on output rather than hours worked. Among the benefits Merton reported were:

- 75 per cent reduction in time off for medical appointments among those working from home
- an overall drop of 50 per cent in sickness absenteeism
- Improved productivity and service levels, through reduced backlogs.

IMPACT ON THE COMMUNITY

It is almost certainly no coincidence that companies in the *Sunday Times* 100 Best Companies to Work For[37] which score well on work-life balance tend to have a high level of employee activity in the community. Several potential reasons have been advanced for this:

- Employees have physical, mental and emotional energy to spare for such activities.
- People who feel they are being dealt with fairly and generously are likely to look for ways to reciprocate.
- Good places to work tend to attract people who are naturally supportive.
- Employees are more likely to support company initiatives to promote community causes, if they feel their own reputation is enhanced by that of their employer, and if they feel the employer shares the same values, with regard to community involvement.

Whatever the reasons, the case for businesses to be seen as positive contributors to their communities has had a substantial airing in a variety of forums, including the Tomorrow's Company enquiry.[38] It is also a theme I have explored over the years in a number of books.[39] The primary benefits to the organisation appear to be:

- maintenance of a positive corporate reputation – this appears to correlate strongly with employer brand (and hence recruitment of talent), customer loyalty, investor confidence (although only up to a point: ethical businesses such as The Body Shop may perceive their stock to be undervalue by the City) and the ability to hold sway on issues such as planning applications
- fewer problems arising from employee dishonesty (eg shrinkage in retail)
- wider perspectives brought to bear on difficult business decisions – because people have lives in other kinds of organisations, they are able to bring more than one set of views to an issue

- the active resolution and/or alleviation of social problems that may impact upon the business (again, taking a retail example, involvement in urban regeneration has a marked positive impact on trade turnover).

For the community, benefits include having the commitment of a company to allow and encourage its employees to take an active role in charity fundraising, serving as school governors, or assisting in the management of voluntary organisations. Rural or economically depressed communities may also benefit from flexible working policies that encourage teleworking. In essence, companies can transfer work to these areas by seeking virtual employees there.

On the other hand, a culture that stimulates a poor work-life balance may actually harm the community. According to Jody Heymann, author of a book on the impact of long working hours,[40] parents who consistently work long hours damage the education of their children. For every hour the parent works between 6 pm and 9 pm, his or her child is 16 per cent more likely to score in the lowest quartile on maths tests. Children of permanent night workers were 172 per cent more likely to drift into crime and be suspended from school.

A growing dilemma for dormitory towns is that people quite literally just come home to sleep. A long-hours culture makes it very difficult to engage in community activities, especially if you are tired.

To what extent are these issues that an employer should care about? It is unlikely that many people would want to go back to the days when large employers ran every part of the life of the communities in which they were located – from the swimming pool to the pub and the taxi service. But it does seem appropriate that companies a) should not prevent employees from contributing to their local communities by demanding too much of their time and attention, and b) should seek ways in which they can support employees in such contributions. Indeed, several writers conclude that there are strong benefits to companies in terms of raising employees' self-esteem and sense of well-being. For example, a *Harvard Business Review* overview of the role of work and men's identity[41] concludes:

> *Rather than simply retreating into family life as a way to avoid the disappointments of the current workplace, today's men can find meaning through the larger world as well. A balance of career, family and community suggests more than a hierarchy in which one occupation takes precedence over everything else; a life focused on more than just work – or family – can provide a stable foundation for every man's personal definition of success.*

Although it is now commonplace for large employers to match employees' cash donations to eligible charities, it is still relatively rare for them to match, or even part-match, contributions of time. Yet the feedback from charities is most often that the most valued contribution from companies is in terms of specialist skills and transfer of expertise.

WHO TO MAKE THE CASE TO

Part of the problem is that there are at least five audiences to whom the case must be made:

- *Top management* has to sign on to the benefits, to demonstrate the advantages of WLB by providing positive role models and to make the link between success and WLB constantly in their communication with employees.

- *Managers* have to believe that the business genuinely wants them to institute good WLB practice, and that failure to deliver a culture of WLB is a black mark on their advancement prospects; and that they, too, can have a better WLB without damaging their career prospects.

- *Employees* in general have to recognise that WLB is a valued part of the social exchange or psychological contract between them and the organisation; that top management genuinely wants them to be successful in both parts of their lives; and that success outside work is regarded by the company as a positive factor in achieving success within work.

- *Potential employees* must be convinced that the company means what it says when it promotes family-friendly policies and flexible working; that the promised environment is what they will actually experience.

- *Investors* have to accept that the business will be more profitable and create greater shareholder value from the investment in WLB.

Each of these audiences may be looking for different paybacks from investment in work-life balance. While making the case for work-life balance to one group might require a different emphasis from making the case to another group, the essence of an effective work-life balance strategy is that it creates win-win situations for all three.

Let's take these audiences one by one.

Top management

Top management often starts off with two major barriers to understanding the issues of work-life balance. The first is that in order to get to their elevated positions in the organisation, they have frequently adopted a life-style where long hours are normal and expected. Their peers live similarly. So it is sometimes difficult to accept that what they enjoy (as typically they do) may not be enjoyable, appropriate or even possible for others. The second is that being at the top of the tree, they are the ones who have most choice over where and how they work, even if they don't always exercise that choice very wisely. In his book *Beating the 24/7*,[42] Winston Fletcher interviewed 16 business leaders who felt they had got their work-life balance about right. Common factors amongst these leaders were that they had all sacrificed their families too much earlier in their careers, that they had highly supportive (and, one suspects, long-suffering) spouses, and that they were able to insulate themselves from weekend and out-of-hours intrusions from telephone calls. They were all also masters of delegation. The obvious conclusion from these interviews is not that they have become smarter at managing their work-life balance, but they have learned, and have earned the power to pass on the problem to someone else!

A major part of the problem is that senior and middle managers are simply not convinced intellectually of the business case. In a recent study of alumni of Henley Management College,[43] less than a third said they thought that attention to work-life balance issues had any significant effect on productivity, retention, recruitment or motivation. Most regarded the topic as a distraction from tasks that really mattered.

Critical questions from top management include:

- What is the impact on the bottom line?
- How will this help or hinder us in delivering our key strategic objectives?
- How can we measure the impact of our investment?
- Who else is making this kind of investment, and what have the returns been for them? How reliable is that data?
- What will have to change in the organisation? In our own behaviour?
- Will this create extra burdens for us? Or will it reduce some of our existing burdens?

None of these is unreasonable to ask. Some of the data earlier in this chapter may help provide answers.

From the beginning of writing this book, I have had the image in mind of the accountancy-bred chief executive presented with a copy by his HR director. Leafing through the pages, his first question is 'How on earth are we going to afford that lot?' Answering him is relatively easy. Each investment in work-life balance can be measured, and, of course, the full portfolio can be assembled gradually, over years. Moreover, a policy of flexibility means that employees will be able to make use of various requirements as they need them – it's unlikely that anyone would seek to access them all at once. If there is such a risk, then establishing a cafeteria of benefits and a limit on what people can access at any one time has proved an effective cost control for many organisations.

Another common objection is 'How can we justify interfering in people's lives in this way? Surely we should treat them as adults and let them sort their own problems out?' The simple answer is that WLB is exactly about treating people as adults – offering them the information and control to organise their lives in ways that deliver what the company expects and what they seek for themselves and their dependents. It sometimes takes a while for the penny to drop. I recently had a conversation along these lines with a very sceptical HR director. He was not convinced until I asked him what was happening in how the company dealt with its customers. They were, he explained, much more sophisticated in their buying habits and expected a much higher level of customisation. 'What's the difference between your customers and your employees then?' It turned out that many employees were also customers. He soon conceded that it simply wasn't logical to impose one-size-fits-all rules on them as employees but a 'we pride ourselves on fitting the product to you' approach as customers.

An additional reason for being proactive in WLB is that many of the policies and processes detailed in Chapter 3 are now legal requirements, and we can expect the trend towards legislative support in this area to continue. Being seen to work willingly with the spirit of these changes and, if practical, always to be a step ahead of them, is much better for the organisation's reputation as an employer than being dragged reluctantly along.

Managers

Managers often feel like piggy in the middle. Especially with the implementation of the Employment Relations Act 1999, they are under pressure from HR and top management not to make decisions that might result in employee appeals, with all the attendant cost, damage to corporate reputation and undermining of trust between employees and the company. They are also under pressure from employees to give them special treatment, and from line managers to deliver results – two potentially conflicting demands.

The case for line managers has to be built around convincing them that they can have the best of both worlds. That by thinking flexibly and working with the team as a whole, they can develop more effective ways of working that will benefit the employee, the company and themselves. Consultant-speak and exhortation won't work. Nor, in most cases, will the big stick. What does seem to have worked for companies such as P&O Ferries is patient demonstration of what is possible. This means:

- having a portfolio of relevant, practical examples of how managers in similar environments have tackled the issues successfully

- using specific cases to work through alternative approaches, so managers can convince themselves

- engaging line manager converts to take the message to their peers

- making sure that they feel fully supported, both with information resources (eg websites) and HR/line manager colleagues to guide and advise.

Many line managers will find it hard to give up the habit of 'face time mentality' – expecting to see people working. It may require patience and the experience of small-scale trials to convince them they can afford to let go. Many may also have poor skills of delegation, project management and leadership – these will need to be addressed as part of the 'sell'. They may also need support in developing the skills of systems thinking – being able to come up with creative and viable win/win solutions.

A frequent objection from managers is: *If I make an exception for one person, they'll all start demanding individualised working patterns.* It is tempting to respond with *So?* More likely to begin to win their minds over, however, is to help them understand that it is often easier to work out alternative work arrangements for the whole team than for one individual. In other words, don't deal with the issues piecemeal – look at the bigger picture.

Employees

Employees have their own set of attitudinal barriers and fears as well. More than one in three employees believes that it is not their employer's responsibility to help them balance work with other aspects of their lives.[44] Many men perceive work and family as a women's issue. Both men and women may even be reluctant to talk about work-life balance in case they are seen as disloyal, or uncommitted.

Employees need to be convinced that:

- the company is serious about its work-life objectives

- they will not be penalised in their career, in the assignments they receive, in their status or in any other way, from making use of alternative working options

- they can seek help in working out how best to balance their work and non-work lives, should they require and desire it

- their line managers and colleagues will be supportive

- they have the option to revert to 'standard' working arrangements at a future date of their own choosing, or to fashion a different set of arrangements as their circumstances change.

Once again, this is not an easy sell. Perceptions and prejudices may be deeply ingrained and fear can be a very difficult barrier to overcome. Observation of role models – people against whom they can benchmark – is probably the most effective means of helping them overcome their concerns and suspicions. Having top management who appear to have a good work-life balance is not necessarily an answer, unless that same behaviour is echoed amongst line managers at lower levels. For reticent employees, the proof of the pudding lies in what happens to those people, in terms of their career progression, their continued status as rising stars, and who gets laid off when redundancies occur.

Potential employees

Potential employees will be influenced by what they see and hear about the company and its employment practices. There are three main routes for this information to reach them: what they hear from existing employees and their families; what they read in the press; and what they learn from the company's advertising and other recruitment activities. It's not just what you tell people about the job opportunities at your company that matters; it's also where and how you reach them. For the what, including examples of employees working non-standard hours, or working from home, in your brochures and on the recruitment website is not difficult. However, companies make a wide variety of excuses for not doing so, most of which boil down to concern that they will attract a flood of applications from people with unrealistic expectations. While that fear is understandable, if the company is serious about encouraging employees to work more flexibly, few symbols are as powerful as an influx of new recruits who are doing just that.

With regard to the how and where, traditional routes may not always be the most effective in attracting people who have different life circumstances from the norm. Employers who actively research and make use of networks – for example, the register of carers held by a local authority, or associations for new or single parents – can tap into reservoirs of potential employees they would otherwise miss.

Investors

Investors are not normally an audience HR would be directly concerned with. The case to investors has to be made by the externally-facing directors of the organisation – in particular, the CEO, chairman and finance director. However, HR can and should help by providing the evidence that investment in work-life balance increases competitive advantage and contributes to the value of the business. For public sector organisations, a different set of data may be needed, based upon how work-life balance policies and activities are contributing to key internal goals, such as diversity and equal opportunity, and to broader societal objectives.

Making the business case

Experience in making the business case suggests a number of truisms:

- It's difficult for HR to do it on its own.
- This is a long haul; real change (and therefore the full benefits) won't happen overnight.
- It is neither necessary nor desirable that everyone should embrace the same view of work-life balance.

Where HR has succeeded in creating a groundswell for change, it has almost always done so hand in hand with other champions of good working practice. Engaging representatives of all the internal audiences above in initial discussions and getting them into dialogue with each other provides a platform of informed opinion upon which to begin to construct both the case and the policies to respond to it. Building this initial consortium for change can be a slow business, but there is little point launching work-life balance initiatives without at least some clusters of support and encouragement in the organisation.

It's a long haul, too, to build sufficient momentum to demonstrate significant benefit to the business. HR needs to overcome ingrained perceptions and attitudes that may colour behaviour even when people say the right words. While waiting for the benefits to become sufficiently evident that they make the case on their own, HR needs to remind people frequently of the reasons for work-life policies – in other words, to keep making the case.

It is also critical not to alienate those people whose view of work-life balance is very different from that being proposed. Managers who enjoy working all hours and gain their sense of identity and self-worth from their work, who have little interest in life outside work, should not be made to feel they are now a subspecies. Inclusivity and flexibility applies to them, too. They have as much right to choose how they want to parcel out their time and attention. Supporting these people in their choices, while making them aware of the broad medical and other implications of that choice, is as important as ensuring that they do not impose their choices on other people. The message that *everyone, including themselves* is an exception will generally make it much easier for them to accept the wider changes.

Case studies

Evidence of the business case for work-life balance and flexible working programmes can be seen across several industries . . .

At Acme Whistles, a small manufacturing firm with 50 employees in the West Midlands, the promotion of work-life balance has had a large positive impact on recruitment and retention. Staff are allowed time off freely for personal reasons, and the needs and culture of the largely ethnic-minority staff are taken seriously, even if they aren't fully understood or shared by management. The impact such liberal flexible working policies have had on recruitment and advertising costs are extremely significant: 'We are saving on every aspect on employing people,' enthuses Simon Topman, chief executive of the company. 'We have a large pool of people who would love to work for us, and we call on them when positions become available. We recently took on two new employees through this method, which could have cost up to £2,000 had we needed to advertise.'

Similarly, at Farrelly Facilities and Engineering, a small engineering firm of 50 staff based in the West Midlands, flexible working has had a favourable business impact. In 1998 the owners decided to cut the working week from the traditional 50 to 60 hours, to an average of 37 hours. Gerry Farrelly, company director, highlights the success of this programme: 'Over a two-year period after we made the culture change, our turnover doubled and profits tripled.'[45]

Yorkshire Building Society presents another example of successful work-life balance initiatives. Policies including jobsharing, flexitime, career breaks and compressed hours (such as the nine-day fortnight) have impacted greatly on the success of the business: 'In one year the cost of stress-related absence dropped from £120,000 to £105,000,' states Susan Hibbert, HR projects manager.[46]

SAP offers a broad portfolio of work-life balance initiatives for its staff. According to Stuart Affleck, HR and senior recruitment consultant for SAP UK and Ireland, a positive stance on work-life balance has had a huge effect on recruitment and retention: 'Work-life balance essentially helps us to become an employer of choice. Through our initiatives in this area, we are successful in employing upper-quartile performers who make up a committed and motivated workforce.'

THE PSYCHOLOGICAL CONTRACT

The 'psychological contract' is a term that has come to describe the mutual but usually unwritten expectations between employees and employer. There are also similar sets of expectations that define the relationship between the organisation and its customers, pensioners, investors, suppliers – indeed, all its key stakeholders. When the psychological contract breaks down between one stakeholder group and the organisation, there is likely to be fallout in other key relationships. For example, a dispute between a major airline and its staff had an almost immediate effect on customer loyalty; a consultancy that was found to be cheating its customers was rapidly deserted by key staff, who felt top management had betrayed them as well as the customers; and a manufacturing company whose overseas investors cancelled a major investment in plant saw the results first in reduced motivation, then in productivity. Similarly, a culture which requires junior doctors to work 60 or 70 hours a week almost inevitably damages the psychological contract with patients, who rightly fear that the promise of best possible care is being broken.

In the psychological contract between employees and the organisation, there are many elements, only some of which will be the subject of specific promises. All the key elements fall into three categories, however, based on the concept of *value*. In any transaction, the satisfaction of each side depends upon whether it feels the exchange that has been made is fair and that each side values what it receives. Table 1 illustrates the three meanings of value.

For value in the sense of 'worth', the equation as regards work-life balance is determined by a perception of what is reasonable in terms of the rewards and the costs of employment. The rewards include monetary return, in a variety of forms, job satisfaction and a sense of personal growth and marketability. The costs include wear and tear from stress or hard mental/physical effort, and the degree to which the job prevents employees from spending time and energy on other parts of their lives that they value. Whereas working 50 hours a week might not seem a

Table 1 The meaning of value

Meaning of value	What the employee expects of the organisation	What the organisation expects of the employee
Value = Worth	*In addition to a reasonable wage:* • *contribution to a secure retirement* • *other benefits, such as health insurance* • *training and development that will maintain or increase his or her value on the job market* • *opportunities for advancement*	*Contribution to:* • *the creation of value for shareholders* • *maintaining the reputation of the organisation*
Value = Respect	*To demonstrate that it values the employee through:* • *recognition/ praise* • *listening to his or her ideas and opinions* • *accepting and accommodating his or her individuality (eg having policies that allow for different personal circumstances)*	*To be a positive ambassador for the organisation* *To demonstrate pride in the organisation*
Value = Beliefs	*Having and demonstrating a set of personal values and beliefs that align closely with those of the organisation*	*Having a clear and consistent set of values that align with or transcend societal norms; ensuring that leaders demonstrate those values and that policies and procedures support them*

problem to one person if he or she is well-paid and has relatively few other calls on his or her time and thus is able to engage in most of the other activities he or she values, to someone with a different set of obligations and priorities it can seem a heavy imposition.

Value in the sense of 'respect' includes employees' perception that the organisation recognises their need for a life outside work and values the benefits that it brings to the working environment. A feeling that the organisation does not care about employees' non-work needs and priorities is likely to create a psychological contract by which it becomes morally acceptable for the employee to work the system to gain extra time off. While the link between well-designed work-life policies and employee attitudes to cheating on time has not been proved, it has at least an intuitive validity.

Value in the sense of 'alignment of beliefs' is again related to the attitude which employees ascribe to the organisation in terms of work-life balance. In a workforce that increasingly values non-work aspects of life at least as much as work-related aspects, for the organisation to present a conflicting set of values is highly likely to undermine the psychological contract. Values in this sense are assessed not by what the organisation says (ie its policy statements, or the visions and values charter) but by what it is perceived to do. This perception will be created by a mixture of role models (eg senior managers who demonstrate that they care about employees and their families), by who the company rewards and how it rewards them, and by a host of other systems that give clues to the underlying assumptions about what matters.

Underlying all the assumptions in the psychological contract is the understanding that, to the employee, perception is reality. If the employee perceives the exchange to be unfair, he or she will be less motivated, less loyal, less engaged with the organisation and (sometimes) with his or her work, and vice versa. However, because perceptions are built upon the employee's values, his or her *values about work-life balance* will also colour how he or she feels. For many people, acquiring sufficient capital to have financial security is so important to them that they are prepared to sacrifice other parts of their lives to achieve that goal. For them, a psychological contract that offers financial security at a relatively early age, in exchange for long hours and perhaps even for work they do not greatly enjoy, is equitable. Such contracts are sometimes very fragile, however; a contract based primarily upon financial reward tends to emphasise loyalty to one's career rather than to one organisation.

The business case needs to be made, then, in the context of a clear, coherent and consistent psychological contract between the organisation and its employees. The payoff from the investment in work-life balance policies depends to a large extent upon an alignment of expectations between them. Key questions for HR to answer before it embarks on major change related to work-life balance are:

- What does top management think the psychological contract is, especially with regard to work-life issues?

- What do employees think it is? (Different groups and levels of employees may have different views.)

- What do both think it *should* be?

- Are there major gaps in expectation, and if so, how can we address these?

- How flexible does the psychological contract itself need to be? (In other words, do we need to offer a different contract to different groups who have different expectations?)

- What policies with regard to work-life balance would best support the psychological contract(s)?

One final comment on the psychological contract: while it may seem obvious that it is not the same as the legal employment contract, the disparity between that document and what is actually expected of people will have a significant impact on perceptions of the psychological contract. A 1999 Quality of Working Life study by the Chartered Institute of Management and UMIST concluded that the line between home and work is blurring, and that over 75 per cent of people surveyed work beyond their contracted hours. In general, employees accept that a little give and take over hours is normal and not a cause for resentment. But frequent or consistent expectation by the company that people will work more than their contracted hours sends out subtle but powerful signals about the organisation's (lack of) trustworthiness. If you can't keep to your promises on something that's contractual, why should employees trust promises that aren't underpinned by a legally binding contract?

A PROBLEM WITH SMALL BUSINESSES

In theory, at least, small businesses are more resistant to flexible working practices than large ones. Whether this is really true is debatable. Although fewer small businesses may adopt flexible practices, they may apply them to a much higher proportion of their employees.

Certainly, the weight of evidence available suggests that small firms' concerns that they do not have the numbers of people to make flexibility work, or that it will involve a high extra burden of administration, are misplaced. In practice, the opposite seems to be the case. For example, Classic Cleaners won several awards for a programme that allowed its 11 staff in two outlets to work hours that suited them and the business. Plagued by the cost and time required to cope with staff turnover, the company saw immediate benefits as retention improved radically and absenteeism dropped. In addition, the business saw a 15 per cent increase in turnover.

The Judge Institute in Cambridge has studied small businesses in East Anglia and found that those which try hardest to meet employee needs for flexibility are also those where employees register the highest levels of trust and loyalty. It also found that employers who did not provide flexible working often mistakenly assumed that their staff did not want it, but had never checked their assumptions.[47] Those small employers who had put a significant effort into work-life balance were often more creative and adaptable than larger firms. Without rulebooks or policy guidelines to refer to, they simply treated people as individuals and tried to find practical solutions that met the needs of both the employee and the business.

Far from creating bureaucracy, then, flexible working seems to make life a lot easier for smaller businesses and their owner-managers. Indeed, the idea of the life-style business – one where profit is a secondary or equal consideration to enabling people to live a more complete life – is almost exclusively a small business phenomenon.

More problematic is the small business owner. He or she works an average 50-hour week, with nearly a quarter of such owners putting in between 56 and 70 hours. One in four takes less than one week's holiday a year; 99 per cent feel stressed at work; and one in five feels stressed more than three-quarters of the time.[48]

Although this book is written primarily with the HR professional in mind, most of the concepts and approaches can be applied with equal and potentially greater efficacy to small businesses that do not have a formal HR function. It may not be necessary to design a comprehensive work-life balance policy – all that is needed is for the small company to make clear that it is open to alternative ways and times of working and to discussing such issues regularly with employees.

REFERENCES AND READING

1 GUEST D. (2002) 'ENOP Symposium on work-life balance: an introduction'. *Social Science Information*. Vol. 41, 2. pp253–254.
2 JOSHI S., LEICHNE J., MELANSON K., PRUNA C., SAGER N., STOREY C. J. *and* WILLIAMS K. (2002) *Work-life Balance ... A Case of Social Responsibility or Competitive Advantage?* Available at : http://www.worklifebalance.com [Accessed 10 July 2003].
3 STURGES J., GUEST D. *and* MACKENZIE DAVEY K. (2000) 'Who's in charge? Graduates attitudes to and experiences of career management and their relationship with organisational commitment'. *European Journal of Work and Organizational Psychology*. Vol. 9, 3. pp351–370.

4 SODEXHO (2002) *Survey.* February.

5 GALPIN M. 'Helping high flyers to fly high'. *Insights.* Vol. 4. p3. Available at: http://www.pearnkandola.com [Accessed 14 July 2003].

6 GALINSKY E., JOHNSON A. A. *and* FRIEDMAN D. E. (1993) *The Work-Life Business Case: An Outline of a Work in Progress.* New York, Families and Work Institute.

7 BRADLEY H. K., FENTON C. S. *and* WEST J. A. (2003) Winners and losers. *ESCR Research Report.* Swindon, Economic and Social Research Council.

8 KIMMEL M. S. (1993) 'What do men want?' *Harvard Business Review.* Vol 71, 6. pp50–63.

9 CECR (1994) *Across the Board.* July/August; p21.

10 GWYTHER R. (2003) 'Working dads who want it all'. *Management Today.* April. pp44–53.

11 WEISS R. (1990) *Staying the Course.* London, Collier Macmillan.

12 KIMMEL M. S. (2000) 'What do men want?' in *Harvard Business Review on Work and Life Balance.* Boston, HBS Press. pp135–163.

13 HEWITT ASSOCIATES (2002) *Work/Life Benefits Provided by Major U.S. Employers in 2001–2002.* Lincolnshire, Illinois, Hewitt Associates.

14 See reference no. 8 above.

15 CONNOR M., HOOKS K. *and* MCGUIRE T. (1997) 'Gaining legitimacy for flexible work arrangements and career paths'. in Parasuraman, S. and Greenhaus, J . (eds.), *Integrating Work and Family: Challenges for a Changing World.* Westport, CT, Prager, pp154–160.

16 DONKIN R. (2003) 'Why employers don't really want happy workers'. *Human Resources.* January. p16.

17 HOPKINSON P., JAMES P. *and* MARUYAMA T. (2002) *Teleworking at BT – The Environmental and Social Impacts of its Workabout Scheme.* University of Bradford/UK Centre for Economic and Environmental Development.

18 PRUCHNO R., FRIED M. *and* LITCHFIELD L. (2000) *Measuring the Impact of Workplace Flexibility.* Boston, Boston College Center on Work and Family.

19 THE WORK FOUNDATION *Work-life Balance Boosts the Bottom Line,* research paper. www.the-workfoundation.com.

20 TOWERS PERRIN (2001) report.

21 MICHAELS E., HANDFIELD-JONES H. and AXELROD B. (2002) *The War for Talent.* Boston, Harvard Business School Press.

22 www.reed.co.uk.

23 KODZ J., HARPER H. *and* DENCH S. (2002) 'Work-life balance: beyond the rhetoric'. *IES Report*, No 384. Brighton, Institute of Employment Studies.

24 WATKINS J. (2002) 'The hard sell'. *People Management.* Vol. 8, 25. pp12–13.

25 TOWLE R. L. (1999) *Audit Checklist of Research, Search, Recruitment and Selection Alternatives.* Alexandria, VA, Society for Human Resource Management.

26 MCCALL A. (ed.) (2003) '100 best companies to work for'. *Sunday Times Supplement.* 2 March.

27 RAY E. B. *and* MILLER K. I. (1994) 'Social support, home/work stress, and burnout: who can help'. *Journal of Applied Behavioural Science.* Vol. 30, 3. pp357–373.

28 KOESTNER R., WALKER M. *and* FICHMAN L. (1999) 'Childhood parenting experiences and adult creativity'. *Journal of Research in Personality.* Vol. 33, 1. pp92–107.

29 MADJAR N., OLDHAM G.R. *and* PRATT M.G. (2002) 'There's no place like home? The contributions of work and non-work creativity support to employees' creative performance'. *Academy of Management Journal*. Vol. 45, 4. pp757–767.

30 PRICEWATERHOUSE COOPERS. (2001) *Sustaining the Talent Quest*. Conference Board Research Report. London, PriceWaterHouse Coopers. Available at: http://www.pwcglobal.com [Accessed 15 July 2003]

31 GALINSKY E., KIM S. *and* BOND J. (2001) *Feeling Overworked: When Work Becomes Too Much*. New York, Families and Work Institute.

32 WOMEN IN CABLE AND TELECOMMUNICATIONS FOUNDATION. (2001) *Diversity Through Investment: Findings of the Women in Cable and Telecommunications Foundation's Best Practice Initiative*. Chantilly, VA, Women in Cable and Telecommunications Foundation. Available at http://www.wict.org/foundation/bestpractices/bpwhitepaper.pdf [Accessed 15 July 2003]

33 SCHWARTZ F. N. (1989) 'Management women and the new facts of life'. *Harvard Business Review*. Vol. 67, 1. pp65–76

34 www.hrprofessionalspanel@orc.co.uk.

35 WILLMOTT B. (2003) 'Stress standards to put pressure on employers'. *Personnel Today*. 14 January. p 1.

36 GANESAN S. (2002) 'Marriott International: the spirit to serve'. *Global CEO*. October.

37 See reference 27 above.

38 RSA Enquiry (1995) *Tomorrow's Company: The Role of Business in a Changing World*. Hampshire, Gower. http://www.tomorrowscompany.com

39 CLUTTERBUCK D. (1981) *How to be a Good Corporate Citizen: A Manager's Guide to Making Social Responsibility Work – and Pay*. London, McGraw-Hill. CLUTTERBUCK D., DEARLOVE D. *and* SNOW, D. (1992) *Actions Speak Louder: A Management Guide to Corporate Social Responsibility*. 2nd ed. London, Kogan Page. CLUTTERBUCK D. *and* SNOW D. (1990) *Working With the Community*. London, Weidenfeld and Nicolson.

40 HEYMANN J. (2000) *The Widening Gap: Why American Families Are in Jeopardy and What Can Be Done About It*. New York, Basic Books.

41 KIMMEL M. S. (1993) 'What do men want.' *Harvard Business Review*. Vol. 71, 6. pp50–63.

42 FLETCHER W. (2002) *Beating the 24/7: How Business Leaders Achieve a Successful Work/life Balance*. Chichester, Wiley.

43 BIRCHALL D. (2001) *Work-Life Balance Policies: Management Views on the Impact: A Report from the Future Work Forum at Henley Management College*. Henley-on-Thames, Henley Management College.

44 KODZ J., HARPER H. *and* DENCH S. (2001) *Work-Life Balance: Beyond the Rhetoric*. IES Report No. 84. Brighton, Institute for Employment Studies.

45 DEPARTMENT OF TRADE AND INDUSTRY. (2003) *Flexible Working: The business case – 50 success stories*. London, Department of Trade and Industry. Available at http://www.dti.gov.uk/work-lifebalance/publications.html [Accessed 15 July 2003]

46 See reference 46 above.

47 DEX S. and SCHEIBL F. (2002) *SMEs and Flexible Working Arrangements*. Bristol, Policy Press.

48 BUSINESS JOURNAL (THAMES VALLEY). (2002) 'Balancing life and work'. 18 July. Available at http://www.businessmag.co.uk/news/2002july/n0702011.html [Accessed 15 July 2003]

2

The legal perspective

HR has three basic choices with regard to the increasing tide of legislation affecting work-life balance issues:

- the ostrich approach (ignore it until it bites you)
- the 'just in time' approach – implement on or near the date at which a new law becomes active
- the proactive approach – getting well ahead of the game.

Those organisations which opt for the proactive approach gain the benefits of high credibility with employees and some level of resulting competitive advantage. Whichever option a company decides to go for, however, the cost of transgression is increasing, both in financial and in reputational terms. Before embarking on a strategic plan for work-life balance (WLB), the HR professional should ensure that he or she has a clear grasp of the implications of current and emergent legislation. The reality is that many practices which have simply been 'part of the culture' till now may become embarrassing and costly in the future. Holding key meetings when parents or carers cannot attend, investing millions in telecommunications systems but not building in a capacity to work from home, ignoring suggestions from employees for different ways of managing work tasks – these are all potential causes for employees to seek legal redress.

HR has a massive job ahead, examining many aspects of working practice to ensure that company policies do not conflict with legislative intent or interpretation. It also has to ensure that managers at all levels, from top to bottom, are aware of the impact their behaviour might have. This is not a new problem – it has been a fact of working life since the first anti-discrimination legislation – but the scope for litigable error has just been massively expanded!

In this chapter, Mike Huss of specialist employment law advisers Peninsula looks at the legislative framework in depth and provides broad advice on how to integrate legal considerations into an organisation's strategic approach to work-life balance.

LEGISLATION, CURRENT AND PROPOSED, AFFECTING EMPLOYMENT AND WORK-LIFE BALANCE

An employer is faced every single day with the problem of juggling the needs of the business with the individual and collective needs of the employees and those of the government expressed through legislation. Rarely is there a satisfactory compromise.

Organisations like the CIPD, the CBI, the TUC, etc lobby the government on behalf of their members and their members' interests in an attempt to influence draft legislation, to amend existing legislation or to propose new legislation. Individuals can therefore voice their opinion through and by their membership. Individuals or organisations can also write to government departments directly – most effectively by writing to, say, the DTI or the Home Office, or the Employment Tribunal Service, when draft legislation is in the pipeline and asking to be included on the distribution list of the draft legislation. They will then receive a copy of the draft legislation and notification of the closing date for comments. Comment away!

You might also seek to influence via your MP, or by writing to the prime minister, the minister responsible, the newspapers, radio, television, etc. Although you might consider that one voice will not be heard, from the writer's own experience of research in the DTI's library only 169 replies were received in response to a major, national consultation exercise which has resulted in, among other things, the new Statutory Disputes Resolution Procedure! Small numbers vociferously presenting well-argued cases do and will influence legislators.

Legislation will evolve, and some you will personally agree with, some you will not. You will have to obey all of it. As HR practitioners, it is a major part of your responsibilities to ensure that your organisation complies with all of the law all of the time – an unlikely scenario! The first problem with that is knowing that the law exists. The second is understanding it – much is badly drafted and ambiguous. And the third is obeying it!

Let us start with the question of how much there is. Answer: an enormous amount. It is not possible even to quantify it, since it will change during the time it takes to read this article either by a new law passing or, more likely and more difficult to keep track of, by a precedent decision of an appellate court somewhere – ie the Employment Appeal Tribunal, the Court of Appeal (the Court of Sessions in Scotland), the House of Lords or the European Court of Justice. Anyone remotely knowledgeable about the Transfer of Undertakings (Protection of Employment) Regulations 1981 will know how true this statement is!

In the panel is a list of the major pieces of legislation currently in force. It is not exhaustive – even if it is exhausting to read! Consider also that each piece of legislation contains many sections. For example, the Working Time Regulations 1998 cover the 48-hour week, night working and the right to transfer to day working if ill with an illness associated with night working, minimum daily rest, minimum weekly rest, minimum rest breaks, and statutory holiday entitlement and pay for it.

And even these subdivisions have subdivisions of their own. How many employers are aware that any overpaid holiday pay to a leaver cannot be deducted from any leaving pay, unless there is a relevant agreement in force? A simple 'right to reclaim/deduct clause' in a contract of employment statement or job-offer letter is not enough!

Some relevant items of legislation

1975	• *Sex Discrimination Act*
1976	• *Race Relations Act*
1977	• *Unfair Contract Terms Act*
1981	• *Transfer Of Undertakings (Protection of Employment) Regulations*
1982	• *Statutory Sick Pay (General) Regulations*
1983	• *Equal Pay (Amendment) Regulations*
1988	• *Employment Act*
	• *Access to Medical Reports Act*
1989	• *Employment Act*
1990	• *Access to Health Records Act*
1992	• *Trade Union & Labour Relations (Consolidation) Act*
	• *Social Security Contributions & Benefits Acts*
1993	• *Trade Union Reform & Employment Rights Act*
1994	• *Deregulation and Contracting Out Act*
	• *Statutory Sick Pay Act*
1995	• *Disability Discrimination Act*
1996	• *Asylum & Immigration Act (Section 8)*
	• *Reserved Forces Act*
	• *Employment Rights Act*
	• *Employment Tribunals Act*
1997	• *Protection from Harassment Act*
1998	• *Human Rights Act*
	• *Deregulation (Deducting from Pay of Union Subscriptions) Order*
	• *The Children (Protection at Work) Regulations*
	• *Employment Rights (Dispute Resolution) Act*
	• *Working Time Regulations*
	• *National Minimum Wage Act*
	• *Data Protection Act*
	• *Teaching & Higher Education Act (Part III Right to time off for study or training for young employees)*
	• *Public Interest Disclosure Act*
1999	• *Contracts (Rights of Third Parties) Act*
	• *The Immigration & Asylum Act - Code of Practice for Employers to avoid Race Discrimination*
	• *Employment Relations Act*
	• *Tax Credits Act*
	• *Collective Redundancies & Transfer of Undertakings (Amendment) Regulations*
	• *Maternity & Parental Leave, etc., Regulations*
2000	• *Stakeholder Pension Scheme Regulations*
	• *Part Time Workers (Prevention of Less Favourable Treatment) Regulations*
2002	• *Fixed Term Employees (Prevention of Less Favourable Treatment) Regulations*
	• *The Employment Act*
	• *The Maternity and Parental Leave (Amendment) Regulations*
	• *The Paternity and Adoption Leave Regulations*
	• *The Flexible Working (Procedural Requirements) Regulations*
	• *The Flexible Working (Eligibility, Complaints and Remedies) Regulations*

Clearly, if you do not know it, you are very unlikely to be complying and your organisation is vulnerable. You must either set up a system whereby your organisation does know and does comply, or you must 'hook into' someone who will at least keep you informed and up to date to enable you to comply.

One area of employment law high on the agenda for the current government is family-friendly legislation aimed at a proper work-life balance for working parents. Put into force, or amended in some way, on 6 April 2003 are six pieces of policy dealing with this area. They do not come about through one piece of legislation, rather by way of a steady evolution commencing with the Equal Pay Act 1970, through the Sex Discrimination Act 1975, to the latest, the Employment Act 2002. Undoubtedly they will continue to evolve – but for now they concern:

- statutory maternity leave and pay
- statutory adoption leave and pay
- statutory paternity leave and pay
- statutory parental leave (unpaid)
- time off [to care]for dependants (unpaid)
- the right to request flexible working.

Some are updates and modifications. Others are brand new. All will affect the employment contract potentially, if not actually, depending on where in the parenthood cycle an employee is. Briefly described below are the six provisions – but in that you will be reading this sometime after 6 April 2003, beware – they may have changed!

STATUTORY MATERNITY LEAVE

Provisions regarding antenatal care, compulsory maternity leave and 'ordinary' maternity leave and 'additional' maternity leave have been around for a while. The same basic principles largely apply, but changes in 'numbers' are probably the most significant.

Antenatal care (this includes relaxation classes and parentcraft classes) remains unchanged.

Compulsory maternity leave remains as it was.

Ordinary Maternity Leave (OML)

All pregnant employees become entitled to 26 (previously 18) weeks' maternity leave irrespective of length of service or hours of work. Employees can commence leave at any time after the 11th week before the expected week of childbirth (EWC) – as previously.

Additional Maternity Leave (AML)

Basically the changes here relate to numbers – employees with at least 26 weeks' continuous service, at the end of the 15th week before the EWC (previously at least one year's continuous service at the beginning of the 11th week before the EWC) now have the right to up to 26 (previously 29) weeks' Additional Maternity Leave. This effectively means a woman who is entitled to Additional Maternity Leave will be able to take a maximum of 52 weeks' maternity leave in total. During the whole of this period, the contract of employment continues (with the exception of pay).

Notification requirements and returning to work

There are considerable changes to the notice requirements but no space to detail them here. Suffice it to say they are different, important, and costly if you get them wrong.

The overall effect of the changes is to extend slightly the total length of maternity leave, whether for OML or AML, and to give returners from OML the right to return to the same job (previously it could be to the same job or one not less favourable).

For rates of Statutory Maternity Pay (SMP) see below.

STATUTORY ADOPTION LEAVE (SAL)

For the first time a new right to SAL came into force on 6 April 2003. Although the provisions broadly shadow those for SML, there have to be modifications to cope with the differences between the processes of adoption and giving birth!

The adopter must have at least 26 weeks' continuous service leading into the week he or she is notified of having been 'newly matched' with a child.

The leave must relate to being 'newly matched for adoption' – it would not apply to, for example, a step-parent adopting. If two parents adopt the child, only one period of adoption leave is available. (If children are adopted at different times under separate arrangements, then the employee(s) could qualify again.)

Adoption leave

As with maternity, there are two categories of adoption leave available: 'ordinary' and 'additional'. Each is for 26 weeks, with additional adoption leave following on immediately after ordinary adoption leave, giving 52 weeks in total. Unlike ordinary and additional maternity leave, once an employee has qualified for ordinary adoption leave, he or she automatically becomes qualified for additional adoption leave.

Commencement of adoption leave differs compared to maternity, in that as everything works from the date the child is placed with the adopter, the rules operate around that date. So the options open are: to start the leave on the date of the child's placement (whether this is earlier or later than expected) or to start the leave on a predetermined fixed date no earlier than 14 days before the expected date of placement and no later than the actual date of placement.

Notification requirements, returning to work, unexpected difficulties

As you would expect, there are rules regarding notification requirements and returning to work. There are also rules to deal with the situation where a parent may have commenced the adoption leave but the subsequent adoption does not go ahead, where for one reason or another the child is returned to the agency, or where the child dies.

Although there are only in the region of 4,000 adoptions per annum, the need for time to be able to balance work and life is perhaps more important in adoption, especially for an older child with a troubled history. The Government's new legislation is designed to reflect this.

STATUTORY PATERNITY LEAVE

Reflecting the Government's concerns that a new mother needs as much help and support as possible, especially at the time of birth or shortly thereafter upon leaving hospital and returning home, paid paternity leave has been designed to assist during this crucial period.

To qualify, an employee must be the father of the child, or be married to, or the 'partner' of, the child's mother or adopter. A 'partner' means a person of the same or different sex who lives with the mother, or adopter, and the child in an enduring family relationship. (The 'partner' cannot be a 'relative' of the mother, or adopter, defined as a parent, grandparent, sister, brother, aunt or uncle.) The employee must also have, or expect to have, responsibility for bringing up the child. Only one period of leave is available irrespective of how many children are born as a result of the same pregnancy or adopted as part of the same arrangement.

The employee must have been continuously employed for at least 26 weeks by the end of the 15th week before the EWC, or in the case of an adopted child, for at least 26 weeks leading into the week in which the adopter is notified of being matched with a child.

Taking the leave

Leave may only be taken in a block of one week or two weeks. It is not permitted to take two one-week leaves. It can only be taken during the period beginning with the date of the child's birth, or placement, and ending 56 days after that date or, in a case where the child is born before the first day of the EWC, 56 days after that day.

Subject to this, the leave can begin (at the employee's choice) on the date the child is born/placed with the adopter, on a specified number of days or weeks after the date of the child's birth/placement (whether this is earlier or later than expected), or on a specified predetermined date which is later than the first day of the EWC or expected date of placement.

Notification requirements and returning to work

Again there are rules – wouldn't you just expect it! – regarding notification requirements and returning to work.

STATUTORY MATERNITY PAY (SMP), STATUTORY ADOPTION PAY (SAP) AND STATUTORY PATERNITY PAY (SPP)

Conditions and rules apply! Although it is possible for a woman to qualify for SPP, it is not possible for a man to qualify for SMP. Careful examination of the rules is therefore advisable. Employees who do not qualify for SMP, SAP and SPP may nevertheless qualify for similar allowances from the DWP. Only the main rules are described below.

SMP, SAP and SPP are paid in a similar manner to Statutory Sick Pay (SSP) – through the payroll – and it may be possible for the employer to reclaim part of the costs, which may not be the case with SSP.

Rates of SMP/SAP/SPP

There are two weekly rates of SMP/SAP/SPP that may apply: the earnings-related rate and the standard rate.

The earnings-related rate

The earnings-related rate is 90 per cent of the employee's average weekly earnings. (Rules, again, specify how the average is to be calculated. There are also rules relating to whether the baby is born before or during the qualifying week; calculations resulting in fractions of a penny; back-dated pay increases and the effect on the lower earnings limit and the effect on increasing an employee's average weekly earnings).

If the average is less than the lower earnings limit for the qualifying/matching week, the employee cannot receive SMP/SAP/SPP but may be eligible for an appropriate allowance from the DWP.

The earnings-related rate is always paid for the first six weeks of the SMP entitlement.

The standard rate

The standard rate is a set flat rate that is reviewed each year. With effect from 6 April 2003 the standard rate is £100.00 per week.

It will normally be paid for the remaining 20 weeks of the SMP entitlement, throughout the 26 weeks' SAP entitlement and throughout the one-/two-week SPP entitlement. However, exceptionally, if the standard rate of SMP/SAP/SPP is greater than the 90 per cent calculation of average weekly earnings, then the latter earnings-related amount should be paid throughout the SMP/SAP/SPP period. (There is a different rate for where the baby is born before the EWC and the date is before 6 April 2003.).

One of the biggest problems relating in particular to SMP, and to a lesser degree to SAP and SPP, is that the gestation period in pregnancy is quite long, and during this period the world changes, health problems can arise or disappear, intentions and relationships change, and perhaps most unfortunate of all, death can intervene at any time within the process. Consequently, there are quite detailed rules setting out the circumstances and the consequent results of those circumstances. An article such as this is not a suitable vehicle for spelling out all of the minutiae of such rules. But be aware they exist – and check, if appropriate.

SMP/SAP/SPP recovery

The employer can recover a percentage (currently 92 per cent, but please check in your individual circumstances) of the SMT/SAP/SPP paid. This is done by deducting the amount to be recovered from any allowance payments due to the Inland Revenue Accounts Office for the tax month in which the SMP/SAP/SPP was paid. If the amount to be recovered exceeds the contributions due in a month, then the excess due can be deducted from the PAYE income tax due that month. In the event that the SMP/SAP/SPP amount to be paid exceeds the total of NI contributions and PAYE income tax due to be paid to the Inland Revenue, the employer can apply for advance funding.

SMP/SAP/SPP record-keeping

Clearly, paying out money and then 'demanding' almost all of it back from the government is a sensitive operation requiring strict adherence to the rules or it will cost you dear. All sorts of records must be kept, and they must be kept for at least three years after the end of the tax year to which they relate.

STATUTORY PARENTAL LEAVE

The purpose of parental leave is to allow the parents to care for a child. This means looking after the *welfare* of a child, and that includes making arrangements for the good of the child. Thus the definition might include factors like spending more time with the child, accompanying a child to/in hospital, investigating new schools and new childcare arrangements and settling them in, and enabling the whole family to spend more time together.

Should a parent use the leave for some other purpose than to look after the child, it is a breach of trust and honesty and can be dealt with through the normal disciplinary procedures. (Away team matches, shopping sprees and fishing trips thus do not qualify for parental leave!)

Statutory default scheme

The right is a statutory one and applies to both parents for each individual child. The birth of twins therefore entitles both parents to twice the entitlement, triplets thrice, and sextuplets do not bear thinking about! Statutory parental leave is unpaid, although it is open to employers to enter into contractual agreements to make some or all of this leave paid. (Research in other EU states shows overwhelmingly that there is a greater take-up of parental leave, particularly by men, when the leave is paid. The Government would be keen to see more employers giving paid parental leave. Indeed, it might be argued that the introduction of paid paternity leave, introduced after the introduction of parental leave, is a step in that direction. Clearly, many people believe that a child needs lots of attention from parents, especially at certain crucial periods or times, and only paid parental leave will support this.)

Because of the volte-face regarding children under five on 15 December 1999 there are two sets of rules. It is, perhaps, little comfort to know that with effect from 31 March 2005 one group will have worked itself out of the system.

The basic statutory right is to take up to 13 weeks' unpaid parental leave during the first five years of the child's life. In the case of adopted children the right is still to 13 weeks' unpaid leave but, in this instance, to be taken up to five years from the date the child was placed for adoption or until the child's 18th birthday, whichever is the sooner.

Parents become entitled to statutory parental leave once they have completed one year's continuous employment with the employer.

At least 21 days' notice of intention to take leave must be given, and the exact date of its start must be stated. (The exception to this is for fathers who wish to take leave straight after the baby is born, or prospective adoptive parents from a date straight after the child is placed with them, where in either case the precise date of the event cannot be foretold.) In these cases at least 21 days' notice of the EWC or expected week of adoption must be given. It is also possible that employees might opt for statutory paternity or adoption leave in these circumstances, since these rights are now open to them (with effect from 6 April 2003) as they were not open previously (when the only option was statutory parental leave).

Parents cannot take more than four weeks per annum. Any leave taken is deemed to be in *weeks*, so if an employee takes two days' leave in one week, that will count as *one week's* leave taken. If he or she takes two separate days in succeeding weeks, that will count as *two weeks* of his or her entitlement used up.

Postponement of leave

The employer may postpone statutory parental leave where, in the employer's view, to take such leave would unduly disrupt the business. The employer can also do so if proper notice is not given.

In cases where a father wants leave immediately following the birth, or adoptive parents immediately after the adoption placement date, the employer cannot postpone the leave.

Where employers do postpone a period of leave, they can only do so where it is agreed to permit the employee to take an equivalent period of leave on a date agreed with the employee, following consultation, which must not be later than six months after the would-be commencement date of the previously postponed period. The employee must also be given the reasons for postponement in writing within seven days of receipt of the employee's notice to the employer.

Record-keeping

Although there is no statutory requirement for record-keeping, it would be a foolish employer who did not ensure at least that any requests are recorded, and especially details of why any request was refused and of when the subsequent 'replacement leave' was taken.

You can ask for evidence to support a request for the parental leave. If you do so, do it for everyone applying!

Conditions, and return to work

Such leave is an individual right and is not transferable – ie one parent cannot transfer his or her 13 weeks to the other parent.

An employee returning to work after an isolated four weeks or less is entitled to return to the same job. Returning after a period of more than four weeks, or immediately following a period of additional maternity or additional adoption leave, an employee is entitled to return to the same job, or if that is not reasonably practicable, to return to another job which is both suitable and appropriate for him or her in the circumstances.

Variations

Described above are the basics of the statutory default scheme. Some exceptions apply. Chief amongst those are:

Children born or adopted between 15 December 1994 and 14 December 1999

The 13 weeks' unpaid parental leave entitlement is to be taken between 10 January 2002 and 31 March 2005, and is to be taken on the basis of four weeks per annum maximum, and the remaining week in the first three months of 2005. Parents who adopted between the above dates are equally entitled to 13 weeks but, in their case, leave is to be taken before 31 March 2005 or the child's 18th birthday, whichever is the sooner.

Although the normal requirement is for a parent to have been continuously employed for one year before becoming entitled to parental leave, parents of these children, if they worked for a previous employer during this time for more than a year, do not have to have worked for the current employer for more than a year before qualifying. The service with the previous employer counts.

Disabled children (where the parents are entitled to disability living allowance)

Parents of disabled children may take 18 weeks' unpaid parental leave prior to the child's 18th birthday.

Parents of disabled children have the flexibility to take statutory parental leave a day at a time if they wish, and not to have a week deducted on each occasion.

Such parents are entitled to parental leave if they have completed one year's continuous employment with the current employer, or with a previous employer during the period between 15 December 1998 and 9 January 2002.

Contractual/collective/workforce parental leave schemes

It is open to employers and employees to agree their own rules relating to parental leave. Such agreements cannot offer less than the key aspects of the statutory parental leave. They can vary any aspect of the scheme to allow paid parental leave, either at normal pay or some lesser rate; to be taken in days (and not lose a whole week each time); to take any amount per annum; to accommodate arrangements for postponing leave; etc.

TIME OFF TO CARE FOR DEPENDANTS

When the rules for this right were being drafted, someone who should have known better did not notice that by 'cutting and pasting' across existing similar paragraphs in the parental leave drafts he or she had entered a requirement to give at least 28 days' notice of the impending emergency! Subsequently, however, the final legislation did not contain that requirement.

Employees have dependants. Dependants have emergencies. Dependants are not necessarily only children. Emergencies, by their very nature, cannot be foreseen. The time it will take to deal with the problem cannot always be accurately forecast. Consequently, the regulations are written so that employees can take unpaid time off to deal with such a situation without the fear of losing their job.

The right only applies if the employee, as soon as is reasonably practicable, tells the employer why he or she is absent and for how long the absence is likely to last.

A dependant is defined as a parent, wife, husband or child, someone who lives with the employee as part of the family (not an employee of the family), attendant, lodger or boarder. The regulations also allow someone to be a dependant who relies on the employee in particular circumstances of an illness, injury or assault until resumption of normal care arrangements.

No predetermined maximum amount of leave that can be taken is set out in the regulations. However, they do state that it is anticipated that time off in such circumstances is to deal with *immediate* issues – eg to deal with rearranging care for an ill or injured dependant, not to care for the dependant personally long-term. Such absences should therefore not be for more than one or two days.

There is no length of service requirement to qualify for this right.

Again, as with parental leave, any employee taking such leave but using it for anything unconnected with an emergency regarding the dependant, could be subject to disciplinary action if found out.

THE RIGHT TO REQUEST FLEXIBLE WORKING

The important point to note with this legislation is to note that it is a right to *request*, not a right to be given, flexible working. The employer must not treat such a request lightly, but it is legitimate to refuse the request, having followed proper procedures, if there is a genuine commercial reason why such a request should be refused.

The right is to request a contract variation to be able to care for a child.

No further application can be made before the end of a period of 12 months beginning with the date of submission of the first application. This means that a parent could request such a variation a number of times up until two weeks before the child's 6th birthday (18th in the case of a disabled child).

What the regulations do *not* do is give the employee the statutory right to return to the original pattern of working. Once the contract has been varied, it stays that way unless a further 'flexibility' variation is requested. (It is always open to employers to agree to any variation 'contractually' if they wish to do so.)

Eligibility

The eligibility criteria are that the employee must have at least 26 weeks' continuous employment at the date the application is made; must be the mother, father, adopter, guardian or foster-parent of a child under the age of six (18 for a disabled child), or be married to, or the partner of, such a person; must have or expect to have responsibility for the child's upbringing and be making the application to enable him or her to care for a child; must make the application no later than two weeks before the child's sixth birthday (or 18th for a disabled child); and must not be an agency worker or a member of the armed forces.

The scope of the request

An employee may make a request regarding hours of work, times of work, and/or the place of work as between the employee's home and a place of business of the employer. Such a request could encompass changes to do with annualised hours, compressed hours, flexitime, job-sharing, staggered hours, shift- or term-time working.

The form of application

An employee must apply in the correct format: that is, it must be made in writing and state that it is such an application; state whether a previous application has been made, and if so, when; specify the change applied for and the date the change is to happen; explain what effect, if any, the employee thinks making the change would have on the business and how any such effect might be dealt with; explain how the employee's relationship with the child meets the conditions; and be signed and dated.

It is important that the employee completes the application in the correct format or he or she will have not statutory right to request a change.

The procedure for dealing with applications

A meeting between employer and employee must be held within 28 days of receipt by the employer of the application unless the employer notifies the employee, in writing, of agreement to the variation within that time period. (There are rules to cover absences of the decision-maker.)

Within 14 days after the date of the meeting, the employer must give the employee written, dated, notice of the decision. Where the decision is to agree the application, the notice must specify the variation agreed and state the date on which it is to take effect. Where the decision is to refuse the application, the notice must state which of the specified grounds for refusal (see below) are considered to apply, with an explanation of why they apply in relation to the application, and set out the appeal procedure.

Specified grounds for refusal of the application

There are only eight grounds upon which an employer can rely to justify refusing a request. They are:

- the burden of additional costs
- a detrimental effect on the firm's ability to meet customer demand
- an inability to reorganise work amongst existing staff
- an inability to recruit additional staff
- a detrimental impact on quality
- a detrimental impact on performance
- an insufficiency of work during the periods the employee proposes to work
- planned structural changes.

If the refusal is not based on one or more of the above, it will be illegal.

The right of appeal

An employee wishing to appeal against a refusal must do so in writing, set out the grounds for appeal and date it, and do so within 14 days after the date on which the refusal notice was given.

The employer must then hold an appeal meeting within 14 days of receipt of the appeal, unless within that time the employer gives the employee written notification that the original decision has been overturned, in which case the notice must specify the variation that has now been agreed and the date on which it will take effect. If the appeal is held, it must be at a time and place convenient to both the employer and the employee.

The employer must give the employee written, dated notice of the decision regarding the appeal within 14 days after the appeal meeting.

Where the employer upholds the appeal, the notice must specify the contract variation agreed and state the date on which it is to commence. Where the employer dismisses the appeal, the notice must state the grounds for the decision and contain sufficient explanation as to why those grounds apply.

Extension of time periods, rights to be accompanied, and withdrawal of application and remedies for breach

These are rules relating to reaching agreement to extend time periods. There is a right to be accompanied by a single companion who is a worker also employed by the employer, and rules regarding how they may be involved, including time limits if the companion is not available for the proposed meeting date. An employer can treat the application as withdrawn in some circumstances where the employee has not actually withdrawn it.

Complaints of alleged breach by an employer can be brought before an employment tribunal by the employee. Depending on the precise nature of the breach, tribunals have a number of options open to them if they find there was a breach; these options range from a declaration on the matter to an order for the application to be reconsidered by the employer, or to an award of up to two weeks' pay for some breaches, up to eight weeks' pay for another.

The 'week's pay' is subject to the statutory maximum level of a week's pay, and the claim to the tribunal must be submitted within three months of the date on which the application was refused, or from the date of the breach, if applicable.

It is important for employers that they follow the procedural steps laid down by the regulations. Infringement of the procedures will certainly lead to conviction in the tribunal if a complaint is made. Refusal of the request, if it has been considered properly and thoroughly and rejected for an authorised reason, will *not* lead to conviction.

The employee has the right to *request*, not the right to *have*, a variation to his or her contract of employment. Leaving aside statute (for the moment!), is it not common sense and good practice to consider properly any request from any employee for a change to his or her contractual terms? It is unfortunate that the Government, when it legislates, never uses one rule or procedure when ten will do, but that in reality is what this legislation seeks to do. Do not reject it out of hand – think about it; consider all the factors, and then decide.

The rights described above are designed to enhance the work–family interface. They will undoubtedly do this. They will also cause problems. Life is just a succession of problems. They will not go away in the future – they will change, sometimes for the better, sometimes for the worse, but they will change.

The remainder of this chapter highlights some of the legislation heading our way, some of it home-generated and some Europe-generated.

FORTHCOMING LEGISLATION

On 27 February 2003 the Government published the White Paper review of the entirety of operation of the Employment Relations Act 1999, which concluded that no major changes are needed to protect workers' rights. Predictably, the CBI is pleased and the TUC is not!

There are, however, still some changes proposed. These include:

- to provide earlier access rights to unions in recognition claims
- to expand the law on the right to be accompanied in disciplinary or grievance hearings so that the companion can contribute
- to establish a new legal right for workers to access their union's services.

There is also news of some moves regarding four areas of the Employment Rights Act 1999 which have yet to be implemented:

- the blacklisting of trade unionists – In an announcement on 27 February 2003 the Government announced it was moving to full public consultation on the basis of its review findings so far. Comments were to have been received by 22 May 2003
- collective agreements, detriment and dismissal – No proposals have yet been announced, but it is likely that there will be a consultation exercise embarked upon before regulations come into effect
- an extension to the definition of 'worker' to confer a range of employment rights
- the conduct of employment agencies and businesses.

The definition of 'worker'

This aspect has had some movement recently in that the DTI in July 2002 issued a Consultation Document with responses due back by 11 December 2002. The background circumstances are that the concept of worker, being a halfway house between truly self-employed and employees, has been around for some time now in respect of such individuals who are not employees but who do enjoy some – limited – protection afforded to employees. This is in respect of trade union membership and activities and unlawful discrimination on the grounds of sex, race, disability, etc. Furthermore, there are seven pieces of legislation which specifically allow rights for workers as well as employees:

- the right not to have unlawful deductions taken from pay

- restrictions on hours of work and the right to breaks, and the right to paid holidays under the Working Time Regulations

- the right to the National Minimum Wage

- the right to make a complaint to an employment tribunal if dismissed or treated less favourably for whistle-blowing under the Public Interest Disclosure Act 1998

- the right to take part in, and be counted towards, the numbers involved in compulsory trade union recognition

- the right to enjoy part-time equivalent pro-rata rights to comparable full-time workers

- the right to be accompanied at disciplinary and grievance hearings.

Currently, therefore, there remain a number of rights that relate to employees only, and not to workers. The definition of a worker is as an individual such as a temporary or casual worker, who works either under a contract of employment or under any other contract (whether express or implied, and if express, whether oral or in writing) whereby the individual undertakes to do, or perform personally, any work or services for another party to the contract whose status is not, by virtue of the contract, that of a client or customer, of any professional or business undertaking carried on by the individual.

Section 23 of the Employment Relations Act 1999 conferred the power on the Secretary of State to extend the scope of statutory employment rights to categories of persons not currently covered. It has been known for some time that the Government has been considering whether to utilise this power, and if so, how. Now the DTI has published a Discussion Document explaining the issues surrounding employment status and the arguments – both pro and con – for extending statutory rights.

The Government acknowledges that this 'targeted' approach inevitably means that the coverage of rights varies, and that this, together with the different definitions dealing with employment status, may be confusing for all concerned. It therefore invites views as to what changes, if any, are appropriate – views on:

- whether the current targeted system and the definitions used are easy to understand

- what the costs and benefits of extending the scope of some, or all, rights may be for small businesses, other organisations and the working people affected

- what non-legislative approaches could be used to address problems arising from lack of clarity in employment status

- whether there are ways to overcome practical difficulties in extending some or all rights to certain working people where a third party (such as an agency) is involved in the employment relationship.

Clearly, this issue has a potentially major impact for organisations who utilise the services of workers and self-employed subcontractors to operate their business.

Employment agencies and employment businesses

The Government carried out further consultations regarding the Conduct of Employment Agencies and Employment Businesses Regulations 2001, with the closing date for comments on the consultation documents as at 1 November 2002.

One aim of the reforms is to clarify terminology and contractual relationships within the sector, so that workers and hirers know who is contracting with whom. Terms such as 'employment agency', 'employment business' and 'employment bureau' have been used somewhat loosely in the past, resulting in a good deal of confusion. In law, employment *agencies* are organisations that match job-seekers to employers, and employment *businesses* are organisations that hire out their own staff. The new regulations use only these two terms, and organisations will have to be clear about in which capacity they act. The term 'bureau' has been dropped altogether.

The new regulations therefore provide that bodies offering work-finding services will have to make it clear whether they are operating as *employment agencies* or *employment businesses* or, if they offer both services, whether they are acting as an agency or a business in relation to a particular transaction.

Since employment businesses are subject to stricter controls than agencies, and since they often offer agency services as well, it is fairly common for employment businesses to purport to be agencies when it suits them. This can lead to confusion as to what employment rights a worker – particularly a temporary worker – has, and how they should be asserted. The new regulations should clarify the position.

Another important change relates to the imposition by employment businesses of excessively high fees in circumstances where a hirer wishes to employ a worker on a permanent basis. The revised regulations prevent employment businesses from imposing transfer fees unless the hirer is first given the option of hiring the worker for an extended period on the business's terms. When that period has ended, the hirer is free to employ the individual without having to pay a fee. This provision allows employment businesses a guaranteed return and hirers to employ temporary staff on a permanent basis without incurring a penalty.

The draft regulations also tackle the practice of imposing financial penalties on hirers who, during a specified 'quarantine' period (sometimes lasting six months or more), employ the worker directly. Limits are imposed on the length of this quarantine period to the effect that when a hiring has ceased, no contractual term can be enforced after the later of either eight weeks from the day after the last day of hire or 14 weeks starting from the first day of hire. Furthermore, the quarantine period during which a hirer is prevented from employing the worker through another employment business, or assisting him or her to find another employer, is limited to four weeks.

Other specific changes include:

- a ban on charging models and entertainers fees before work is arranged
- stronger protection for parents using nanny agencies

- ensuring that agents use properly controlled client accounts when handling workers' earnings

- protecting workers from having their CVs circulated indiscriminately either on the Internet or by other means

- tougher controls on bogus advertisements, in print and on the Internet, such as those that advertise non-existent jobs.

The Conduct of Employment Agencies and Employment Business Regulations 2001 are intended to replace the Conduct of Employment Agencies and Employment Businesses Regulations 1976, the Employment Agencies Act 1973 (Charging Fees to Workers) Regulations 1976 and the Employment Agencies Act 1973 (Charging Fees to Au Pairs) Regulations 1981.

The latest consultation follows three previous consultation periods on draft regulations. The proposed changes update Regulations that date from 1976 and have been introduced with the stated aim of providing workers with greater protection from exploitation and enabling them to move more easily from temporary work into permanent employment. The DTI estimates that the new Regulations will benefit more than 700,000 temporary workers ranging from office staff to models and actors. (Readers should, however, be aware that all of the foregoing are proposals and may alter as a result of the latest consultations.)

Amendments to the Transfer of Undertakings (Protection of Employment) [TUPE] Regulations 1981

On 13 February 2003 the Government announced the publication of a new Code of Practice relating to contracts involving transfers within and outside public administration.

Transfers within public administration

The Government intends to apply the Cabinet Office Statement of Practice *Staff Transfers in the Public Sector* to all such transfers to ensure, where there may be doubts as to whether the Transfer Regulations apply, that staff transferring are treated as being covered by the Transfer Regulations, where appropriate, and by regulations on an ad-hoc basis for cases outside the Acquired Rights Directive's scope.

Occupational pensions

The current uncertainty regarding the transferring of pension schemes is undesirable. The Government therefore intends that transferees will have to provide equivalent pensions to those in place prior to the transfer. (This is likely to be prohibitively expensive for a private contractor given the value of public service pensions.)

The maintenance of terms and conditions of employment after the transfer

Staff recruited after the transfer are not protected by the Transfer Regulations and consequently have often been recruited on considerably less favourable terms. This has led to a two-tier workforce. In future, 'best value' authorities will be under an obligation to ensure that contractors employ 'new starters' on no less favourable terms than those of the TUPE-protected transferred staff.

Other changes

On 14 February 2003 the Government announced its intention to carry out yet further public consultation on draft revised regulations in the first half of 2003, so that new regulations can be laid before Parliament sometime in the autumn with the intention that they should come into effect early in 2004. They are likely to be concerned with:

- the contracting-out of services
- requiring the transferor to tell the transferee of the employment liabilities that will transfer
- introducing new flexibility to insolvent businesses
- clearer rules relating to dismissals arising out of a transfer
- clearer definitions as to how valid changes to terms and conditions as a result of a transfer can be made
- the application of the regulations in insolvency situations
- hiving down
- the continuity of employee representation
- the employer's liability insurance
- the employer's territorial extent.

An amendment to the Rehabilitation of Offenders Act 1974

As part of the changes arising out of the setting up of the Criminal Records Bureau it was realised that although convictions could become spent, under certain circumstances cautions, reprimands and final warnings could not. Because cautions for recordable offences, reprimands and final warnings for recordable offences are entered on the Police National Computer, they would show up in any search. Consequently, the Government intends to deal with this by proposing that there should be a nil rehabilitation period for the records of these events.

More generally, a fundamental review of the ROA 1974 was announced recently. The terms of reference of the review are:

> *To review the scope and operation of the Rehabilitation of Offenders Act 1974 (including the Exceptions Order and how it works). To consider whether it adequately achieves the policy goal of reducing crime by facilitating the rehabilitation of offenders and the protection of the public, or whether any other arrangements might better deliver this objective.*

The review will start from fundamental principles about what the Act is designed to achieve. It will not, for example, simply be an opportunity to extend the range of exemptions.

The review will be conducted in accordance with the Home Office statement of purpose: *to build a safe, just and tolerant society in which the rights and responsibilities of individuals, families and communities are properly balanced, and the protection and security of the public are maintained.*

It will contribute to the following Home Office aims:

- the reduction of crime, particularly youth crime, and the fear of crime; and the maintenance of public safety and good order

- the delivery of justice through effective and efficient investigation, prosecution, trial and sentencing, and through support for victims

- the effective execution of the sentences of the courts so as to reduce reoffending and protect the public.

It will aim to produce proposals which:

- deal honestly, fairly, sensitively and openly with people

- ensure the best possible contribution to the Government's strategy of crime reduction, alongside other initiatives such as the Sentencing Review and the Review of Barriers to Employment and Housing undertaken by the Social Exclusion Unit

- provide a coherent and clear balance between the interests of those who have been convicted of a crime but now want to lead constructive and law abiding lives, and those vulnerable people who legitimately deserve reasonable protection against offences being committed against them

- contribute to a proportionate, efficient and cost-effective system of criminal record disclosure

- comply with the Human Rights Act 1998 and relevant legislation designed to ensure equality of opportunity in the workplace.

Once again, however, the review process will be protracted and any changes resulting from the review will not come into effect for some time – the review process was meant to conclude in May 2001. Proposals then had to be worked up and Parliamentary time sought. It will be a matter of years, rather than months, before the process is concluded.

A review of the regulations on the employment of children

To ensure that children who work enjoy the best possible protection, a review of the law is being undertaken by a group of officials from the departments of Health, Trade and Industry, Education and Employment, the Cabinet Office and the Health and Safety Executive.

Expert practical advice will be provided by the National Child Employment Network. (The Network provides a forum for people working in the field of child employment to exchange best practice information.)

The terms of reference of the working group are to:

- consider the present arrangements for protecting children in relation to employment, including regulatory arrangements, levels of protection and enforcement

- examine any research, or other evidence it considers necessary, from any source including interested organisations and individuals

- make any necessary investigations

- draw up any proposals necessary to ensure that children's health, safety, welfare and development is strictly protected, and that they are shielded from exploitation

- report jointly to relevant ministers at the Department of Health and the Department of Trade and Industry.

It is understood that the review body reported to ministers in the autumn of 1999 and ministers accepted the recommendations in the review and will seek to implement them when parliamentary time allows.

In the meantime, however, the Children (Protection at Work) Regulations 2000 came into effect on 7 June 2000 (England and Wales) and 9 June 2000 (Scotland), and give further effect, retrospectively, to the European Directive on the Protection of Young Workers.

The Regulations raised to 13 the minimum age at which children may be allowed by local authority by-laws to be employed in light agricultural or horticultural work. They require such by-laws, authorising children to take part in street trading, to contain provisions and to determine the days and hours during which, and at the places of which, they may do so.

They also ensure that only those aged at least 16 and who are also over compulsory school-leaving age may take part in performances of a dangerous nature.

Other legislation

Throughout 2003 and 2004 a string of new European legislation affecting discrimination comes into effect:

- Legislation banning religious discrimination (apart from the obvious exceptions) must be in force by December 2003.

- Legislation banning discrimination against someone because of their sexual orientation must be in force by December 2003.

- Legislation banning race discrimination must be in force by July 2003. (This extends discrimination to areas like goods and services.)

- Legislation banning discrimination against disability is updated in 2004 (although it does not have to be until December 2006).

- Legislation banning age discrimination must be in force by December 2006. (Currently it is only a voluntary code.)

NEW EUROPEAN DIRECTIVES

Equal Treatment Amendment Directive

The European Equal Treatment Directive (No. 76/207) will provide, among other things, a pan-European definition of unlawful sexual harassment in employment, and an indication of what employers are expected to do in order to prevent such harassment occurring in the first place.

Agreement on amendments to the Directive has been reached after a period of conciliation between the European Commission and the European Parliament, and the changes will come into effect in 2005.

The Commission proposes the changes in the light of evidence that between 40 per cent and 50 per cent of women and 10 per cent of men have experienced sexual harassment at least once in their working lives. The problem is at times compounded by a lack of clarity as to what exactly constitutes harassment and what an employer's responsibilities are to take preventive steps. It is hoped that the changes will make these issues more straightforward.

The definition of 'harassment' to be found in the amendments to the Directive will be familiar to those who have been following the development of harassment law over recent years. Harassment is to be defined as *unwanted conduct of a sexual nature with the purpose or effect of violating the dignity of a person, particularly when creating an intimidating, hostile, degrading, humiliating or offensive environment.*

This broad definition is very similar to that already to be found in the European Commission's Code of Practice on measures to combat sexual harassment, annexed to the recommendation on the protection of the dignity of women and men at work (No. 91/131), a definition that has been both expressly and implicitly adopted by the EAT in decisions like those in *Wadman* v *Carpenter Farrer Partnerships* [1993] IRLR 374 and *Reed and another* v *Stedman* [1999] IRLR 299. Things should therefore not be expected to change that much in the way in which the law on harassment is applied in the UK. The introduction of specific rules on harassment will be felt most in countries such as Greece and Portugal, where there is no existing legislation on the matter.

Another matter worthy of comment is the changed definition of what constitutes indirect discrimination. The Directive's future has been anticipated by changes already made by the Sex Discrimination (Indirect Discrimination and Burden of Proof) Regulations 2001 SI 2001/2660.

There are, however, one or two other aspects of the amendments that may have a greater impact in the UK. The first is that the amended Directive, albeit in the recital rather than the substantive body of the text, will state that the right to judicial protection applies even after employment has ended, which may lead to a rethink on post-employment discrimination in the UK. The Directive will also introduce obligations on employers to take 'preventive measures' against all forms of discrimination, especially sexual harassment, as well as introduce enterprise level 'equality plans' which are to be made available to workers and their representatives. Such proactive elements are a growing trend in modern equal opportunities practice and constitute a form of law that we shall all have to come to terms with in the future.

Extension of Working Time Directive

The original Working Time Directive excluded workers in 'the transport sector'. The DTI originally fudged this area by describing the Working Time Regulations 1998 as applying to 'mobile' workers, so that those not 'mobile' in the industry could benefit from the Regulations. The Department went further and implied that the transport workers – ie mobile workers – in other sectors would not be covered by the Regulations.

A European Court of Justice case involving Tuffnells (*Tuffnells Parcels Express Limited* v *Bowden* C-133/00 [2001] IRLR 838 ECJ and [2000] 560) pointed out the error of this. Part of the reasoning for the decisions was that the EU had already recognised the deficiency in the original Directive and had started an amendment Directive 'on its way' – something the DTI should have recognised.

Member states have until 1 August 2003 (1 August 2004 for junior doctors) to implement the changes. They are being enacted through 'Horizontal Amending Directives' (whatever happened to plain English?), five in all. They cover road workers, rail workers, air workers, sea workers and junior doctors.

Each one is different from every other, and here is not the place to describe the relevant details. Suffice it to say that if you come under any of these sectors, find out!

Young Workers' Directive – the end of UK opt-outs

The Government issued a consultation document on 19 December 2000 in respect of amending the Working Time Regulations 1998, following the ending of the UK's specific opt-out on certain provisions of the EC Directive on the Protection of Young People at Work (94/33 EC) – the Young Workers' Directive.

Responses to this consultation document were due to be received by 30 March 2001. Consequently, the Government has introduced – with effect from 6 April 2003 – new rules affecting young workers.

The Regulations make a number of amendments to the Working Time Regulations 1998 with regard to maximum hours of work, and night work, for young workers.

Maximum hours of work

The working time of young workers is limited to eight hours a day and 40 hours a week, with normally no provision for averaging over a period of weeks or for individual opt-outs. (There will be some exceptions available in some narrowly defined areas – see below.)

Night work

The regulations will generally prohibit young workers from night working:

- between the hours of midnight and 4 am (with very limited exceptions)
- between the hours of 10 pm and 6 am (or between 11 pm and 7 am if the worker's contract provides for him or her to work after 10 pm), with more exceptions.

Exceptions for young workers

The above limits on maximum working time *do not apply* where specified objective grounds are met – namely, where the employer requires the young worker to undertake work necessary either to maintain continuity of service/production or to respond to a surge in demand for a service/product, *provided* that no adult worker is available to perform the work, and *provided* that performing the work will not adversely affect the young worker's education or training.

Exemptions from the night work restrictions only apply in specified sectors:

- midnight to 4 am – only young workers who are employed in the armed forces, in hospitals or similar establishments, in fisheries, or in connection with cultural, artistic, sporting or advertising activities are permitted to work in the period from midnight to 4 am

- 10 pm to midnight and 4 am to 6 am (or 11 pm to midnight and 4 am to 7 am) – only young workers who are employed either in the above sectors or in agriculture, hotels, catering (including bars and restaurants), retailing, postal or newspaper deliveries or bakeries are permitted to work in the period from 10 pm to midnight and 4 am to 6 am (or 11 pm to midnight and 4 am to 7 am). In addition, the work must be necessary either to maintain continuity of service/production or to respond to a surge in demand for a service/product; *provided* that no adult worker is available to perform the work, and *provided* that performing the work will not adversely affect the young worker's education or training.

Where, by virtue of the above exceptions, a young worker is required to work during a period which would otherwise be a rest period or rest break, the young worker must be supervised by an adult worker where such supervision is necessary for the young worker's protection. In addition, the young worker must be allowed an equivalent period of compensatory rest.

Force majeure

The restrictions on maximum working time and night working do not apply in relation to a young worker where the employer requires him or her to undertake work which no adult worker is available to perform and which

- is occasioned by either unusual and unforeseeable circumstances beyond the employer's control, or exceptional events, the consequences of which could not have been avoided despite the exercise of all due care by the employer

- is of a temporary nature, and

- must be performed immediately.

Where, by virtue of this exception, a young worker is required to work during a period which would otherwise be a rest period or rest break, the employer must allow the young worker to take an equivalent period of compensatory rest within the following three weeks.

Records

The existing obligation to keep records contained in the Working Time Regulations 1998 have been extended to require employers to also keep records adequate to show that the above new limits have been complied with.

Special note

'Young workers' are defined as those who are over school-leaving age and under 18. These new Regulations do not change the previously existing restrictions on the employment of those who are under school-leaving age.

At present, young workers are entitled to 12 consecutive hours' rest between each working day, two days' weekly rest, and a 30-minute in-work rest break when working longer than four and a half hours.

The entitlement to four weeks' paid annual leave is the same for young workers as for adult workers.

The Government expects that the Regulations will have been drafted such that employers will need to satisfy themselves that objective grounds apply in their particular circumstances and at the particular time, although this does not mean that occurrences which are routinely repeated need be considered on every occasion.

Health and safety guidance

Existing legislation places a responsibility on an employer to ensure that young workers employed by the organisation are protected against risks to their health and safety.

The Government sought the views of consultees on whether new guidance on this requirement should be integrated with guidance on these provisions on working time.

In particular, this new guidance might cover some specific areas of concern affecting young workers, such as their safety when travelling to and from work at night and accommodating the demands on them during examination periods.

The Government envisages that such guidance would be developed in consultation with the Health and Safety Commission, and disseminated through the usual enforcement channels.

Information and Consultation Directive

On 11 March 2002 the EC Directive establishing a general framework for informing and consulting employees in the EC (No. 2002/14) was formally adopted.

Although most member states have existing arrangements obliging employers to inform and consult their employees, the main thrust of the Directive is to encourage both to take a more proactive approach to developments within their companies.

The new Directive will place public and private sector employers under an obligation to inform their staff, on an ongoing basis, about matters such as company performance and strategic planning, with additional duties to inform and consult employees with regard to actions that could affect job security, work organisation and terms and conditions.

Workplace bodies comprising elected representatives must be established and any consultation will have to be carried out in such a way that employees can influence management decisions. This means that employer's business decisions are, in theory, going to be open to greater scrutiny by employees. In addition, the information provided must be sufficient and given early enough to enable representatives to 'conduct an adequate study and prepare for consultation'.

The Directive is being introduced into the UK in phases; employers with more than 150 employees have until 23 March 2005 to set up information and consultation procedures; employers with 100 employees must comply by 23 March 2007; and employers with more than

50 employees will be covered from 23 March 2008. Early indications suggest that draft regulations are likely to appear in 2003.

Agency Workers Directive

The objective of the proposal is to provide a minimum level of protection for temporary agency workers, and seeks, in those member states where the sector is still underdeveloped, to review present restrictions on the sector.

The proposal establishes the principle of non-discrimination in working conditions, including pay, between temporary agency workers and comparable workers in the user undertaking as soon as the temporary agency worker has completed six weeks' work in the same user undertaking.

Considerable flexibility is available since exceptions to the general principle of non-discrimination are possible a) for objective reasons (non-discrimination only applies where one is comparing like situations); (b) where a collective agreement exists; (c) where the temporary agency worker has an open-ended contract with the agency; (d) where no comparable worker nor any collective agreement exist, either applicable to the user undertaking or to the temporary agency.

A 'comparable worker' is defined as a worker in the user undertaking who occupies an identical or similar post to that occupied by the worker assigned by the temporary agency, taking into account seniority, qualifications and skills.

This chapter is by no means a complete run-down of the known new law. The proposed list, UK and European, is daunting for employers both by amount and content. Ignorance may be bliss but it is not a credible defence either in the court system or with employees who in many instances may know more than their employer.

If you are not structured, or resourced, to keep up, then consider linking up with a body which will keep you informed and up to date. To do so will cost – but not to do so will cost you more!

3

Worlds at war

Losing control of work-life balance is an insidious process – one that happens gradually. Breaking the cycle is far from easy. Part of the answer is organisational support for employees in planning what they want to achieve in the wider dimensions of their lives.

DEFINING THE PROBLEM

Although some elements of our lives have become easier – convenience foods, washing machines and dishwashers have all saved time, for example – any savings have been swamped by opportunity. How many parents complain about being a taxi service for their kids, dropping them off at ballet classes, swimming, birthday parties, and so on? How much more time do we spend travelling to work than did our Victorian ancestors, who generally worked within half an hour's walk of their labours? How many more visits do we make to distant places because the travel facilities are available? For those of us in the developed world, at least, the increase in richness of the experiences and activities available to us are paralleled only by the increased excesses of our diet. In short, we have become stimulation-obese.

The need for order, structure and a sense of purpose in our lives is fundamental. In previous centuries that order might have been provided by religion. In the early and mid-twentieth century it was often provided instead by the company. In the twenty-first century people increasingly have to provide it for themselves. Self-management, at the individual levels and the family level, is not just a work skill, it is a basic requirement of normal functioning, of emotional intelligence. As such, it should be natural for self-management skills – the habits of being effective – to apply to all parts of our lives.

In practice, of course, this is a lot harder than it sounds. Most of us are too busy living our lives to manage them. As we saw in the Introduction and in Chapter 1, many employees are in danger of being overwhelmed by the multiple obligations upon them, from both the work and non-work areas of their lives. The problem is particularly acute for parents, whose non-work obligations reduce the flexibility they have to accommodate other demands on their time, mental energy and emotional energy. The problems of working mothers (essentially doing two jobs – one at work and one at home, and perhaps a third looking after elderly relatives) are well recognised, and it is they who have been the primary participants in the growth of part-time work. But there are also substantial pressures on fathers. Fathers work longer hours than men who are not fathers.[1] In dual-career families, where the wife does not have or want to work flexible working hours, the father also has to take an increased child-minding role and do more of the household chores. Research indicates that the most consistent family characteristic predicting a feeling of imbalance between work and non-work is being a parent. The most consistent employment characteristic predicting a feeling of imbalance between work and non-work is the length of time worked each week.[2]

Even those who don't have multiple, externally-imposed obligations may feel they lack work-life balance if they have a wide range of other interests they want to pursue.

For both these groups, and indeed for employees in general, it seems that having a positive sense of work-life balance derives from two basic elements: an awareness of what the individual wants and values, *plus* a feeling that he or she is able to exert sufficient control over life to make and implement appropriate choices. Awareness, in turn, has several components: an appreciation of the big picture, a sense of what is happening to one's division of time and energy on a day-to-day basis, and clarity about what one values. Control can be externally focused (being able to decide for oneself how to allocate time and energy) or internally focused (managing one's attitudes and habits to achieve an appropriate balance that reflects what one values).

UNDERSTANDING WHERE YOU ARE AND WHAT YOU WANT

Our survey of companies found that less than a third provided any active help for employees in sorting out what they wanted from their work and non-work lives. Clearly, this is dangerous ground, if the company intrudes too far into people's personal lives. Yet those companies which have provided advice on demand around issues such as parenting, managing elderly dependents, diet management and so forth have almost universally found that employees value and are grateful for the provision. The fact is, this kind of advisory resource is of little practical difference to other guidance that companies make available – for example, pensions planning, retirement planning, or career planning. Nor is it very different from other benefits that companies use to compensate for long hours, such as concierge services. In all of these cases, employees *could* go to a resource they find for themselves. But a major factor in their not doing so, in many cases, is lack of time and energy, resulting from investment in their work. The very fact that guidance is readily available and recommended means that people will take advantage of it.

Figure 4   The work-life balance equation

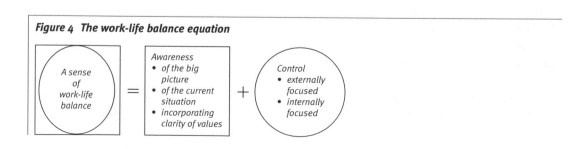

The essence of effective work-life balance guidance is that it enables people to step back from the constant crises of daily existence and evaluate more clearly how they want to live their lives, what is happening at the moment, where they want to make changes, and how they are going to do so. This does not necessarily have to come from a professional counsellor – the most common source of guidance appears to be a sympathetic line manager or mentor. However, to address employees in large numbers, it will normally be appropriate to provide some form of general guidance, which may range from a one-to-one resource to information on a website or in a booklet.

The key, of course, is not to try and manage people's lives for them, but to give them simple tools they can use to work things out for themselves. One of the most useful, which is attributed to Ed Schein at Harvard[3] and has been developed as part of mentor and mentee training around the world over the past 20 years, is the concept of lifestreams.

Essentially, we all have six or more core lifestreams, or continuous areas of attention in our adult lives. For the most part, these operate at the higher levels of Maslow's hierarchy of needs – while we may work to eat and put a roof over our heads, most people in the developed world (at least in North America and Western Europe) work to earn more than enough for the basic necessities. (It is ironic that, in the UK at least, the laws of supply and demand ensure that property prices constantly rise to maintain the proportion of income spent on housing, no matter how much wages rise.)

One of the most useful tools we have developed in helping people think these issues through is the self-diagnostic *Work-life balance: How do you score?* This is based on the concept of six lifestreams, as explained in the box below:

Six lifestreams seem to be important (to varying extents) to most people:

- work (what you do to earn a living)
- career (how you progress and plan to move between one area of work and another)
- domestic/social (how you build and maintain key relationships outside work)
- health (how you maintain physical and mental well-being)
- self-fulfilment (what you do outside work/career to maintain your intellect)
- community/belonging (how you contribute to/participate in society outside your work/career).

How important each of these is to you is a matter of personal choice. However, people who concentrate most or all of their energies into work and career tend to be at higher risk of burnout. They are also much less resilient in the face of career setbacks, because their sense of personal identity is defined very narrowly (by what they do for a living, as opposed to who or what they are as a human being).[4] People who are fulfilled in all or most of their lifestreams tend to be better able to cope with setbacks because they are likely to feel good about other aspects of themselves. Having a supporting circle of family and/or friends, for example, is closely correlated with both resilience and self-esteem, which are in turn associated with overall well-being. If things go wrong in your job, you are much better equipped to overcome them if you have built up emotional capital in other lifestreams.

Most large organisations today have some form of personal development planning. In most cases, the focus is immediate work issues – how you are going to improve performance in your current role. Some organisations widen this to include career planning – how you are going to acquire the skills, track record, experience and networks to advance beyond the current job. Very few also encourage people to think about planning in the other four lifestreams. Of course, the company's ability to influence personal development in those areas is (and should be) very limited. But equally, the organisation has a responsibility *not* to encourage people to think about the different aspects of their lives in isolation – which is what the normal cycle of appraisal and developmental planning discussion almost invariably does. If the objective is to have well-balanced, well-rounded, resilient employees, capable of coping well with change in both their work and non-work lives, then people need time, space and, if appropriate, advice on how to grow in each of the six lifestreams. It is only after people have examined what they value, understood the range of choices available to them and established personal priorities that they can hold an informed dialogue with their managers about the kind of work-life balance they wish to achieve.

I am not here necessarily advocating the provision of life coaching. Even if it were affordable for all, the efficacy of this pseudo-discipline is questionable at both the individual and the organisational level. Most people are fully capable of making their own choices and establishing their own plans of what they would like to achieve in each area of their lives, given simple tools to help them do so. And if they choose not to do so, that must also be respected.

The secret of your success

I couldn't resist this subtitle. It is so redolent of the gung-ho self-help books that promise instant change in life circumstances if only the reader follows a few simple rules. What these books usually forget, however, is that for most people, choices are limited. Once you decide to have children, for example, or you contract diabetes, you have obligations that prevent you from taking choices that might otherwise have been attractive.

However, it *is* worthwhile for employees to examine what success means to them and to use that understanding to make choices within the range their obligations allow. How people define success varies widely, but typically a majority of people suggest phrases such as 'achieving your goals' and/or 'being happy'. A unifying definition is *achieving what you value*. The importance of this distinction is that it is of little benefit achieving things if you don't value them. Becoming rich may be on most people's wish-list, but is that more important to them than having a good family life or being content with themselves?

As with lifestreams, a definition of success that pivots on work alone is limiting, if not flawed. For only a very few people will work be the centre of their lives until the day they die – and many of them may die soon after leaving work because they no longer have anything to live for! Having a big picture of success, as it relates to you and your circumstances, appears to be essential in exerting control over your work-life balance.

A survey by Worklifebalance.com Inc[5] found that the top ten factors people defined as elements of success for themselves were:

1 strength of character – honesty – integrity

2 self-respect

3 personal happiness and contentment

4 meaningful and loving family relationships

5 a positive outlook and attitude

6 wisdom, clarity and confidence about life and what you want from it

7 value and balance from personal and professional life

8 a fulfilling and enjoyable job

9 control and flexibility in the use of time

10 employment stability.

It's interesting that money does not appear in this list at all. Of course, the survey participants may have been idealistic in their responses, but their answers do demonstrate the holistic nature of the meaning of success. Yet employers typically talk of success in only one dimension – what you achieve at work. Even here they can be excessively narrow in their definition. A large IT outsourcing company projected to employees a vision of success that involved working up the grades from junior programmer through programmer through analyst through senior analyst, team leader, manager and ever upwards. Yet it kept losing many of its brightest people at the lower levels. It eventually emerged that many of the most technically talented employees did not share this view of success. Rather than take on more and more management responsibilities, they simply wanted to become better and better techies. As a result, the company introduced dual-career streams, which recognised these different definitions of success.

By depicting success in one dimension and reinforcing that view through the role models it provides, the incentive systems and other aspects of the culture, companies essentially brainwash employees into an acceptance that 'work first' is the natural order of things, and that people should see themselves as successful primarily because of what they achieve at work. To empower employees to pursue a wider definition of personal success, one of the most practical steps companies can take is to change that message. By emphasising that the organisation wants rounded individuals who take an active interest in the community and whose non-work lives can contribute to their effectiveness at work, the company can undo some of the damage that has been done. (It is remarkable how many organisations include such factors in their recruitment criteria at lower levels, but then abandon all those expectations when someone reaches, or applies for, more senior posts. How many CEOs got appointed for having active involvement outside work, I wonder? And even in junior posts, it doesn't take long before employees get the message that all that stuff about leading a rounded life doesn't mean a thing when there is work to be done!)

Attitudinal issues

Many of the most powerful barriers to achieving work-life balance are internal to the individual. For example, men may not fight against perceptions that flexible working and shorter hours are for women because 'deep down, they accept them as reasonable'.[6] They don't want to appear weak, especially to each other. Men still retain:

a deeply rooted commitment to being the breadwinner – even when they have a wife whose earning power equals or surpasses their own. . . . Researchers at the University of Seattle found that instead of working less after the birth of a child, the average man works about 58 hours a year more! They make the time by cutting back on social and leisure activities.

Such increases in work pressure are further evident in a recent study by the Families and Work Institute in the USA, in which 70 per cent of men said that strains on family life were an issue for them, as opposed to 60 per cent five years earlier. Moreover, research shows that men with young children are far less likely to take time off within their parental leave entitlement. According to the US Department of Labor, only a third of fathers with young children take parental leave.[7]

While the vast majority of HR professionals (91 per cent) and employees (96 per cent) agree that people work best when they can balance their work and other aspects of their lives, according to an IES study, this does not mean that managers in general share the same belief. Moreover, there is a significant gap (62 per cent for HR as against 81 per cent for employees generally) in the acceptance that everyone *should* be able to balance work and home lives.

Peer pressure also creates internal barriers: 'People in this organisation have difficulty saying no. When they do, they feel guilty about it.' It all comes down to whether the guilt feelings are stronger about 'letting people down' at work or at home. The downsides of saying no at work are usually immediate; those of not making it to a child's birthday party are longer-term and cumulative. Says a report in *Training and Development* magazine:

When we asked leaders to tell us what the most important aspect of their lives was, more than three-quarters said their families. . . . One leader commented: 'I wish I'd known sooner that if you miss your child's sporting event or play, a year later you'll forget the work emergency that caused you to miss it, but the child won't forget you weren't there.[8]

Another classic comment comes from an IBM salesman:[9]

Even if the company fosters a [positive work-life] environment, the real question is, How well are you doing? One of my teammates is in San Diego, and at lunchtime he goes running on the beach. But he feels guilty that he's out enjoying himself during that part of the day. The company can emphasise the message that as long as it's made up for in some other way and you're still meeting your objectives, it's okay. But the employee has to believe it.

Along with guilt goes fear, in many cases. A survey by Flexecutive for *People Management*[10] found that although marketing and HR people want to work more flexibly, they are concerned what this will do for their careers. Eighty-one per cent believe it will affect their careers negatively; and 83 per cent say that career progression is important to them. It's not surprising that they are experiencing difficulty in achieving work-life balance and that only 32 per cent say they are working flexibly.

One of the most thoughtful scholars on work-life issues is Canadian Professor Norman Amundson.[11] Among his perceptive ideas is the notion of three-dimensional living. The three dimensions he refers to – each of which defines in part how we approach and perceive our lives – are:

- length of life – how much of our awareness and motivation rest with the past, the present and the future
- width of life – the quality perspective
- depth, purpose and meaning of life – the bedrock of resilience.

At the extreme of each of these dimensions are attitudes and behaviours which can be classified as heavily imbalanced. Under 'length of life' Amundson refers to 'skinny living' – where people spend much of their mental and physical energy worrying about their health and how long they are going to survive; and, at the other extreme, 'extreme living' – people who live for the thrill of the moment, engaging in high-risk sports and testing their limits in extreme situations. (The latter isn't limited to young people; my friends see more than a little of this trait in me too!)

Under 'width of life' Amundson refers to 'stubby living', by which he means 'an overabundance of activity, with little regard to the quality and length of life [through] constant motion and workaholism'. At the other extreme is 'sideline living', where unemployment, poverty, disability or other constraining factors prevent people from taking part in activities they aspire to.

Under 'depth, purpose and meaning of life' he contrasts 'false front living' – an overall appearance of purposeful activity on the surface, but with a great emptiness underneath – with 'single issue living', where 'people become fixated on one issue and spend all their time trying to draw others to their cause'. An example of this is an acquaintance who, like me, has a child with Down's Syndrome. Her determination to give this child the best possible start in life has led her to sideline all other relationships and purposes, including her husband and other children. Whether she will ever let the child leave home and become semi-independent is doubtful. Should she do so, it will be hard to fill the hole in her life.

There are also problems with the overall configuration of the three dimensions of living. Some people (described by Amundson as engaging 'antsy living'):

shift their boundaries to accommodate the latest bandwagon or fad. . . . People from this perspective often are very sincere in what they are doing, but cannot be counted on for any sustained action. Their passion is short-lived, and they can adopt seemingly inconsistent positions on any number of life issues. By contrast, 'stuck-in-the-mud living' describes people who can't make any life changes at all. They are dissatisfied with the way things are going but lack the fortitude to change their circumstances.

Amundson's point is that a balanced life requires us to steer between these various extremes. Work-life balance is just one aspect of a wider struggle for personal fulfilment. He proposes five fundamental questions to explore a feeling of imbalance:

- What is the evidence for the imbalance we perceive?

- How has this imbalance changed over time?

- How do other people perceive the level of balance or imbalance in our lives?

- What is the impact of any imbalance on us physically and psychologically?

- How satisfied are we with the situation (and are we sufficiently dissatisfied to do anything about it)?

Addicted to work

Workaholism may not figure prominently in the medical dictionary, but it is a very real and disabling affliction. Although many people who work long hours might be regarded as workaholics, the term really applies only to people, for whom:

- work is the sole significant source of self-fulfilment in their lives

- *not* working (ie enforced idleness) is stressful

- the choice between spending time on work or relationships is almost always settled in favour of work, unless made for them by another person.

The continuum of such behaviour is highlighted eloquently by London Business School's Richard Jolly, when talking of workaholics:

> *These executives build their 'competencies' and CV like a big-game hunter gathering trophies to hang above the mantelpiece ... However, the next trophy, be it a promotion, winning a big contract or getting a company Mercedes, is not the top of the ladder – the reality is that such compulsive behaviour is more like climbing up a hamster's wheel.[12]*

These true workaholics are different from most people working long hours because this is what they *want* to do. And for some people – for example, those with Asperger's Syndrome – this may be a rational and functional choice. Even if it is not a rational choice, a dilemma for Human Resources is how far HR should be prepared to intervene to change the behaviour of workaholics. On the one hand, such people are poor role models for other employees. As long, however, as they do not expect others to follow their example, and, if they are managers, are able to give appropriate encouragement to others to work more flexibly and manage a flexible team, it is difficult to make a strong case for HR to try to make them change behaviour. Indeed, taking the crutch of work away from such people is akin to depriving an alcoholic of liquor – the withdrawal symptoms can be very stressful and there may be no compensating sources of mental stimulation for them to turn to.

In short, it appears that some people become workaholics because they *want* to. According to Arlie Russell Hochschild,[13] work has in recent decades become a substitute for family and community. For people with unfulfilled domestic lives, work affords a comfort and stability they cannot find elsewhere. Relationships at work, shallow as they may be, are more meaningful than those at home. Rather than have long hours imposed on them, many people fabricate the need for long hours so they can avoid the stresses of home life and/or create meaning for themselves.

The CIPD survey *Married to the Job* examined the habits of 291 people who regularly work more than 48 hours a week. Few of these people saw themselves as workaholics, yet:

- One in five took less than 10 days' holiday a year.

- 56 per cent accepted that they had devoted too much of their time to work.

- Two out of five admitted that working long hours had caused arguments at home.

- Nearly one in three found that tiredness seriously affected their sex lives.

Most of these long-hours workers were male, and most were also parents.

Another survey, this time by DuPont, found that one third of Britons sleep six hours or less a night. Sleep deprivation not only affects productivity, it makes people more vulnerable to infection and can lead to memory loss, depression and mood swings.[14]

We can regard most of these people as workaholics by circumstance, even if the circumstances are of their own making, or at least or their own collusion. The key questions for HR are:

- Are these people happy about their work-life balance?

- To what extent do they blame the company for the problems they experience from conflict between work and non-work elements of their lives?

- To what extent is the conflict and its resulting stress reducing their effectiveness?

- Would they welcome or resent a proactive approach by the company in helping them change their work-life balance habits?

The only way to answer these questions is to ask them directly. Based upon the answers received, HR can determine practical policies and support systems to help them overcome the problem.

CONTROL

Losing control over one's time and energy rarely happens all at once. It's a gradual, insidious process in which a multitude of different demands increase over time. Contributory factors may include:

- the rise in volume of e-mails (54 per cent of managers say they are 'deluged with data')[15]

- the need to get work finished before going on holiday, and to catch up when you get back – work doesn't stop because you are not there to do it. The more holidays you take, the more often you are under this kind of pressure

- the increased financial pressure of becoming parents. According to the Equal Opportunities Commission, fathers in Britain work the longest hours in the EU (average of 47.3 hours in 2001). Many increase their hours when a child is born to meet increased financial needs of the family, and fathers who are the sole earner work the longest hours

- continually increasing performance targets — whatever you achieve this year raises expectations for the next

- the more experienced people become, the more they are asked to work outside their stable team (the one in their job description, if they have one) as members of project teams. It seems to be a fundamental law of project teams that they require more time and effort than initially expected. Moreover, project teams have a disturbing habit of peaking at the same time in the demands they make upon members. One manager talked of being 'projected out' (it took a while to work out what he meant, but the description is apt!)

In general, the more control people have over when and how they work, the more they feel that they have balance in their lives. Control over working time – time sovereignty – is as important as working hours,[16] according to research by the Work Foundation. It found that fewer than half of all workers have any control over their hours, and that 54 per cent of those who do are completely or very satisfied with their working hours compared with 42 per cent whose hours are decided by the employer.

However, feeling in control of other parts of one's life is equally important. Although people clearly can compartmentalise their work and non-work lives, it is very hard not to prevent worry in non-work areas from intruding on work. It is not surprising, then, that work-life balance increases with age and with level of education. When children leave the nest, many of the biggest demands from non-work aspects of one's life go with them. Although people may continue to work long hours and to sink their energies into work issues, they feel less pressured.

By contrast, concludes Lotte Bailyn,[17] even when people deliberately choose non-standard working times, to reduce the demands of work, it does not necessarily lead to less conflict between work and home. If they do not control their time, imposed schedules may conflict more heavily with family needs. Working regular evening shifts, for example, might appear flexible, but it often means abandoning any normal social life.

A survey by the DTI suggested five common attitudes towards work and life.

- *Treadmill athletes* have achieved a responsible position and have become locked in to working long hours. While they like the idea of working less, they are not willing to sacrifice their business goals or career and are likely to experience considerable stress.

- *Success-seekers* put their career as top priority, but try to gain some other life as well by being very well organised.

- *Home heroes* struggle to fit in a demanding job and a demanding family, and are often exhausted, but unable to find a better solution.

- *Free spirits* are people for whom their career is not the key defining characteristic of who they are. They work for necessities and/or pleasure, and rarely get stressed about it.

- Finally, *balance masters* are highly competent and committed, but determined not to let their job dictate their lives. Many of them have opted for shorter hours to achieve an appropriate balance.[18]

Three of these categories manage, through different routes, to achieve some level of integration between work and non-work activities. They either give up some of their work aspirations, in favour of greater balance, or exert greater control over *both* aspects of their lives. Those who are not prepared or not able to let go of some of the demands upon them and/or not able to exert greater control are the ones who feel greatest conflict.

The work of Stephen Covey[19] and others reinforces the notion that personal effectiveness is a skill set that extends beyond work and into the social arena. Even if a company decides it is not appropriate to help employees become more effective in their non-work lives, there is much to be gained from helping them acquire the skills of effectiveness – from time management to decision-making – for the impact this will have in their work. Interviews with leaders who are relatively successful in maintaining work-life balance suggests that these individuals have also mastered personal effectiveness to a greater than normal degree.

Achieving effectiveness at work usually involves engaging and gaining the co-operation of colleagues. In the same way, achieving personal effectiveness outside of work may require constructive dialogue and the agreement of different expectations and routines with family and friends. By focusing on improving effectiveness at work, but recommending that employees apply the same principles to other parts of their lives, the company gets the best of both worlds. There is even a case for inviting spouses/life partners to effectiveness training courses – when both parties understand what they are trying to achieve, there is likely to be greater commitment both to the process and the intended goals.

Key to increasing personal effectiveness is the avoidance of procrastination. A study by Carleton University's Procrastination Research Group asked people to what extent procrastination was having a negative impact on their happiness. One in six said it had an extreme negative effect; nearly half answered very much or quite a bit. Procrastination isn't just about not doing things at work. As Fernando Bartolomé[20] reported some 20 years ago, one of the most serious sources of dissatisfaction among married couples is procrastination about when they will have children – 'People who forfeit the present risk the future quality of their private lives,' he concluded.

INTEGRATING WORK AND NON-WORK

One practical approach to managing work-life balance is to accept that both parts of your life are important to you, and that there is much of value that can be transferred from one to the other. I can recall upsetting a rather vocal woman in an audience at a conference, who insisted that women returning to work after several years' absence bringing up children automatically had all the skills required to be a good manager. Being a good parent, she argued, was tantamount to being a good manager. But what, I asked, if you've been a lousy parent? I still think I had a point. Just because someone does a task doesn't mean that he or she does it well, nor does it mean that he or she learns from it. Nonetheless, people who consciously set out to use child-rearing as a learning experience they can apply in other contexts will almost always acquire valuable interpersonal and task management skills.

In the same way, the learning interchange between the work and non-work parts of our lives can – if we choose that it should – be a fertile source of personal growth. Many employees acquire meeting and leadership skills by taking on roles as school governors or youth leaders, for example. Share, a charity recently launched to support social inclusion of mentally disabled or socially disadvantaged young people, markets its befriending programmes on the basis that they provide a remarkable opportunity to develop influencing and motivational skills.

Disciplines from work can also have a powerful impact on the home. Few of us would perhaps wish to go as far as some of the pioneers in management, such as Frank and Lilian Gilbreth, who designed their home and their children's lives around their theories of time and motion. For example, one of their 12 children each year had the task of buying all the birthday presents, to save time. However, goal-setting, project management, budgeting and clear division of responsibilities can all have a place in managing what, for most people, are much more complex lives than our ancestors led. So can managing virtually – many young families already conduct their relationships in large part through texting on mobile phones.

The goal of integrating work and non-work is gathering increasing attention as an alternative to the traditional perception that these two parts of our lives are and should be separate. Why do we build the rest of our lives round a block of activities called work? Because work has in recent centuries become the core of how we define our lives. The fact that this tradition remains in a technological age, when the amount of work needed to provide food, shelter and health is steadily decreasing, suggests that work is in some way more important than any other part of our lives. If we question that assumption, we also have to question the way we relate work and non-work activities and how we allocate time and attention between them.

Those who work at home some or all of the time often report that they have regained the choice about when and how they allocate time to work and to pursue non-work interests. Taking time out in the middle of the day to visit the gym, to help out at your child's school, to visit the hairdresser, the dentist or simply go for a walk becomes a lot easier when you decide for yourself when to do things. Seeing the working week as made up of multiple small blocks of time out of which work is entitled to a certain number, creates a very different perspective.

Studies of senior managers indicate that they value greatly the flexibility that allows them to manage their time with this sort of interchangeability of lifestreams. Over three-quarters of senior managers surveyed by the CIPD felt they could benefit from adjusting their working arrangements to cram five days' work into fewer days, either by working longer hours on those days or by working smarter. Nearly four-fifths felt they could work better (from both an efficiency and personal satisfaction point if view) if they could be more flexible in where and when they did their work.

Integration of work and non-work activities requires a significant shift in attitude, one that recognises that both can and should be enjoyable, that they require managing as one set of problems and opportunities rather than as multiple separate sets, and that each should *support* the other. HR needs to accept this reality, both publicly and in private, if employees are to be convinced it is acceptable to think in this way. HR must also be much more open than is currently the norm to wide variations in work routine – to see the maximisation of flexibility as an opportunity rather than as a threat.

HOW TO GET WHAT YOU WANT OUT OF WORK AND LIFE

To achieve a reasonable level of integration between lifestreams, employees can employ a portfolio of relatively simple tools and approaches, all of which can be imparted through fairly basic in-company education programmes. The approaches focus on:

- understanding the various demands on your time, mental energy and emotional energy
- being clear about your priorities
- spending reflective time to find ways to work smarter and to play smarter
- managing expectations and accepting the consequences of your choices
- building your resilience and your ability to stick to your choices.

Who has demands on your time and energy?

Because time and energy are both finite, it is important to be aware of just how much you have available. Even people who work 70-hour weeks still have some 'spare' (ie non-work, non-sleep) time. Allowing an average daily eight hours for sleep, they have 42 hours to allocate to other activities each week. What people do with their spare hours may be more important than how many they have. If the spare hours are eaten up by commuting, household chores, caring for dependants, and so on, leaving little or no 'me-time', they are more likely to feel stressed and have a sense that their lives are lacking. Genuine free time (and genuine free energy) occurs when the individual is able to make up his or her own mind about how to spend it. They may then decide to allocate it to close others, distant others, or even to a work-related project, such as reading around their job. But their choice is one they make freely, without obligation to others. Committed time, by contrast, is time already allocated.

Unfortunately, it's very easy to allow our free time to dissipate in a welter of activities which have little or no value to us. When that happens, we feel increased stress because we feel less in control.

Simply identifying the amount of time we have available and how we use it now can provide a pragmatic starting point for re-establishing control over our lives. A simple technique, which has proven effective for many people, is *responsibility mapping*. At base, this technique is about answering four key questions:

- Who are the people to whom you have significant obligations in terms of time, mental energy, and other resources?
- How much of each factor does that leave for you personally?
- If there is an excess of demand on you, what can you do to establish a better balance?
- If you have to stop doing some things, what are they, and how will you make sure it happens?

The easiest way to carry out responsibility mapping is to draw a matrix, with three columns (time, mental energy and emotional energy) and, say, 20 rows. In each column, list all the people or entities who have demands upon you at work, at home and elsewhere. Now work out how much time, mental energy and emotional energy you have available in a week. In terms of time, the figure will normally be minus time for sleep and eating. In terms of mental and emotional energy, assume that you have a hundred units of each to share out over the week. Now allocate how many hours and energy units each of the people or entities you have listed expects you to give them during that period. Add the columns and compare availability against demand. Now you have some data upon which you can make choices. For many people, especially parents of young children, the demand will exceed availability.

Now is the stage to add in the 'me' requirements. Everyone needs to spend quality time and energy on himself or herself. Stress is typically much more of a problem for people who lack me-time. Even if it is only a few hours a week, me-time must be found to keep the individual sane, healthy and effective in his or her various roles, both work and non-work.

Gaining a better balance between demand and availability boils down in large part to managing expectations – our own and those of other people. Seeing the issues starkly on a responsibility map forces people to confront them. Recognising that we cannot do the impossible, and that trying to meet too many demands is a recipe for doing everything badly, opens the way to practical reflection and discussion on what we can do to change things for the better.

Another useful question is 'Who evaluates you as an employee, as a community member, mother, etc?' We tend to respond more readily and invest more time and energy into those stakeholders whose good opinion is important to us.

From an HR perspective, helping people to reach this level of insight must have positive effects on working efficiency. In the project-based economy that most knowledge employees now work in, over-commitment is a substantial and growing problem. Employees typically only make a stand – 'I can't take on any more' – when their workload and stress levels have reached the upper reaches of the red. Any more and collapse will occur. But the point of inefficiency is reached well before that. Multitasking rapidly turns into lack of focus. Jobs get put down and picked up again on the basis of urgency rather than importance. Time and energy for reflection vanishes. While more time and energy may be expended, the beneficial results often fall – but the problem goes unnoticed because no one has time to measure. Similarly, stressed managers may be intellectually aware that their direct reports are overloaded but choose not to notice until they squeal.

If performance is measured on outcomes rather than on inputs, then the time to address demand/availability problems is when they have just entered the yellow. It may well be that the employee can take on more, but it should be in the conscious knowledge on both sides that this is a requirement above the optimum for efficient operation.

Having identified the scope of any capacity problems, the individual can now begin to make choices about what he or she can and should do less of, or stop doing at all. A remarkably effective exercise I sometimes undertake with managers is to get them to imagine they have been appointed to a task-force that will take 80 per cent of their time. They still have all their normal duties to perform, but they are not allowed to work any more hours to fulfil both requirements. How are they going to organise their time to achieve these apparently conflicting goals?

Relatively few managers ever succeed in planning how to let go of so much of what they do. But the vast majority achieve at least a 40 per cent reduction in the time they spend on the current job, by delegating more, instituting more efficient systems of simply not doing things that don't contribute to the core tasks they have been assigned. (A lot of meetings are dumped in this process!) Balance, it might be argued, is about what and where you let go.

Being clear about priorities

One of the most detailed studies of 'new man', by Katherine Gerson,[21] found that 'involved' men – those who managed to be both committed fathers as well as successful career men – had a much clearer idea of the choices (including work-life choices) they had made and why they made them. Knowing what you want is critical to achieving it. These managers were also typically the most productive managers and the best team players. An often quoted example of such a manager is a senior civil servant who took up his post only on the understanding that he worked his contracted 40 hours a week, so that he was able to have breakfast with his six-year-old daughter every day, and read her a bedtime story. All too often, when people are dissatisfied with their work-life balance, a contributory cause is that they do not have anywhere near the level of clarity about what is important to them and where the priorities lie that this individual has.

Simply talking to family and close friends is often the simplest way of working out priorities amongst the demands on one's time. But there are more disciplined approaches too. One I find often helpful is based on co-joint analysis. Write all the things that are important to you down the left-hand side of a page, leaving a line blank at the end. Write the same list across the page to make a matrix. Decide in each box which is more important out of the pair. Add up the number of times each is selected. The results should give a reasonable indication of the hierarchy of what you value.

Priorities, of course, operate at numerous levels. Within the work environment itself most people will be looking for a mixture of elements that range from the basic reward structure to enjoyment of the job. Job enjoyment stems from two main components – fizz and buzz. Fizz is the enjoyment that comes from the work itself – in particular, the intellectual challenge. Buzz comes from the social interchange – being with a bunch of people whose company you enjoy and find stimulating. In the work-life balance equation there are numerous factors to which each individual will attach different values.

Key questions that help people establish priorities include:

- How many of the tasks that seem so important now will have any meaning or value (for the company or for me) in three years' time?
- What could I stop doing and no one would notice?
- Whose job am I doing in addition to my own? What could I delegate?
- If I were guiding someone else in this situation, what would I tell them to do?

From an HR point of view, encouraging people to sort out their priorities, and perhaps educating them in how to do so, means that employees can provide line managers with a much clearer picture of what they want. It also helps line managers respond to requests for flexibility with alternatives that take into account the employee's hierarchy of values. In some cases, the ability to do so has directly resulted in the retention of key employees. While the manager may not be able to meet all of their needs, by addressing the most important, he or she builds loyalty and makes it less likely that the employee will find another job elsewhere, which is closer to his or her ideal integration of work and non-work.

Working (and playing) smarter

One of the most useful studies in recent years of personal effectiveness at work is by Heike Bruch and Sumantra Goshal,[22] who conclude that 90 per cent of managers squander a high proportion of their time in ineffective activities. They assessed managers against a matrix of focus versus energy. Nearly a third of managers fell into the low-energy low-focus category, described as 'procrastinators'. They did the routine of their task but took little initiative and did little to raise performance. One in five was 'disengaged' – showing high focus but little energy. They spend much of their time trying to convince themselves that problems don't exist, to avoid having to tackle them. High-energy low-focus managers (described as 'distracted') constituted the largest group, at 40 per cent. They 'confuse whirlwind energy for constructive action'. Only 10 per cent had high focus and high energy. They:

> *husband their energy. Aware of the value of time, they manage it carefully and consciously. Some refuse to respond to e-mails, phone calls or visitors outside certain times of the day. Others build 'think time' into their schedules.*

Instead of feeling constrained by external forces, such as their bosses, their job descriptions, or the volume of e-mails to answer every day, they 'work to manage the external environment so that . . . they can achieve their goals'.

The nub of Bruch's and Goshal's analysis is that personal effectiveness comes from exerting control firstly over oneself, then over one's environment.

If working smarter frees up time for other activities, then applying similar principles to non-work activities may also make sense for the time-pressed individual. Just as reflective space is essential for excellent performance at work, it also helps us achieve what we desire in sport, marriage, parenting, gardening or any other activity that is important to us. They all demand thinking time as well as doing time. And just as in the work environment, thinking time can often only occur when it is planned in, so it makes sense to allocate specific times to thinking about non-work issues. One technique I have found invaluable is to divide out the reflective space I have when I am driving home from work. Depending which direction I am coming from, I have a motorway roundabout that is my signal to change mental gear. Instead of thinking about work issues, from that point I start to think of issues related to home. As a result I am (more or less) on the same wavelength as my wife when I come through the front door.

Manage expectations and accept the consequences of your choices

Like a business, each of us has numerous stakeholders who have a claim on our time and attention. The responsibility mapping exercise is one way to register these stakeholders and recognise what they demand of you. From our interviews with managers and employees at all levels it seems that many (perhaps most) of the problems people experience in managing work-life balance stem at least in part from the expectation by stakeholders that they can have more of you than you are prepared to give. Such expectations almost always arise from lack of clarity about what is feasible and what you want to allocate to them.

Scholar Fernando Bartolomé, writing in *Harvard Business Review*,[23] maintains that the most important factors for a married couple are the ability to maintain an ongoing dialogue about their feelings, to ask openly for what they need from each other, and to have fun together. Candidly discussing mutual expectations over work-life balance is essential. Burying such issues simply allows the concerns of a spouse to fester and is a contributory factor to the rising divorce rate. Bartolomé recommends that managers recognise that being a good spouse, or a good parent, is not a natural skill that requires no attention to learning; and that partners should from time to time list the issues they avoid talking to their spouses about, as these are almost always sources of hidden friction. (The latter is quite a useful exercise to do within a team, too!)

It is not HR's role to help people manage the expectations of stakeholders outside the work arena. But it can and should help people to clarify what is expected of them in their job and to provide forums for the discussion of problems that arise from overexpectation. All too often the only guidance people are given is that they must 'do what's necessary to get the job done'. It is not surprising, then, that they are unclear about defining the boundaries of what is reasonable. Managers who typically demand too much of their people must be identified, counselled and, if necessary, disciplined. In our research we encountered one country manager in a multinational who had 15 direct reports, four of whom had suffered heart attacks in the previous 18 months. The fact that the team had met all the targets set for it had made the European board reluctant to take any notice of the cost of this performance achievement.

Under the new legislation on flexible working, it also makes sense for HR to help employees prepare and make the case for the alternative working arrangements they desire. Experience suggests that people who are helped to put their case together are typically more prepared to accept compromise and alternative solutions, because they have already thought through the issues from a dual personal/business perspective.

Although ideally colleagues and employers would be enthusiastic about the employee who works more flexibly, the practical reality is that they are sometimes suspicious or even resentful. The choice to work fewer or different hours, or to work from home, does have consequences, and it is important to be realistic about them. HR has a responsibility to ensure that employees who consider flexible working options are fully aware of those consequences. Those working at home, for example, must understand the nature of isolation stress and accept that 'out of sight, out of mind' may mean that they miss out on the most exciting projects. They should also understand that it may be more difficult for them to achieve promotion in cases where it would be difficult to manage a team virtually. There is far greater potential for litigation under equal opportunities legislation where these realities have been fudged than where they have been properly explained. HR will also need to keep an eye on changing circumstances so that, for example, remote workers are informed if it does become possible for them to take on larger responsibilities.

Building resilience

Resilience, in terms of work-life balance, is primarily about three things:

- remaining in touch with your values and priorities
- building an appropriate support network and being constantly on guard for signs of creeping overload in any one part of your life
- managing the crises in a focused manner.

Remaining in touch with your values and priorities requires frequent review and discussion about what you want and what you expect. This applies equally well in work and non-work situations. Building a support network comes down to the question: Who else can you get to help? At work, establishing relationships with colleagues that allow both of you to ease each other's workload from time to time is a sensible insurance. Managers can also build the capability of their direct reports so they can delegate more whenever they need to. The link between resilience and support networks occurs remarkably early in life – studies show that those children who survive and thrive unpromising environments typically have an uncanny knack to get adults to help them out.[24]

It is also important to consider how you will sustain flexible work solutions. Part-time employees often complain that they end up working more extra hours than their full-time colleagues. A *Dilbert* cartoon has Alice asking to work part-time. Her boss tells her it's OK as long as she makes sure all her work is done. Her triumph dissipates when her colleagues point out that all she has achieved is to halve her salary! Part-timers need to ensure that they keep to the hours agreed, and from time to time to review how their new working pattern is affecting each stakeholder and how extra demand can best be managed without undermining the original intention.

Managing the crises without trauma or without falling back into old working routines is a lot easier if there is a clearly defined process to deal with them. In many cases the solution is not one the individual can create and implement on his or her own: it requires the involvement of the manager and/or other team members. Some practical approaches for these situations are outlined in Chapters 5 and 6.

Once again, there are good reasons for HR to take an interest in this aspect of work-life balance. Daryl Connor,[25] in his book *Managing the Speed of Change*, argues eloquently for the link between an organisation's ability to bring about change and the resilience of its employees. Resilience, he explains, is built up through a mixture of positive attitude, personal effectiveness and gradual exposure to more and more change situations. Resilience also turns out to be a key characteristic of managers who have fewest problems coping with the dual demands of work and family. As long ago as in 1980 Fernando Bartolomé and Paul Evans carried out a study of 2,000 executives and many of their wives, and concluded:

> *The executives who successfully cross the line from job to private life are able to do three things better than others. They adapt well to change in jobs, they find the right jobs for them, and they handle career disappointments well.*[26]

By contrast,

The executives whose private lives deteriorate are subject to the negative effects of emotional spillover; work consistently produces negative feelings that overflow into private life.

Given the truism of incessant change, it makes sense to enhance employees' resilience overall. If this also helps people to manage their work-life balance, so much the better.

THE ROLE OF HR

The role of the organisation, therefore, is to provide resources that enable people to think work-life balance issues through, and to help them achieve solutions that are beneficial to all their stakeholders – work, home and community. Those resources are likely to include:

- pragmatic education programmes that make people aware of choices

- easily accessible processes to help people think through what they want in both the work and non-work lifestreams, and how they might achieve it (the self-diagnostic *Work-life balance: How do you score?* can be sampled online at www.worklifequality.co.uk)

- the education of managers to be a coach and sounding-board as people attempt to think through these issues and test out what the implications of alternative emphases might be on their work and career

- as a last resort, professional counselling for those who struggle to see their way forward.

REFERENCES AND READING

1 BRANNEN J., MOSS P., OWEN C. *and* WALE C. (1997) 'Working fathers'. *Labour Market Trends*. Vol. 105, 7. pp259–267.

2 TAUSIG M. *and* FENWICK R. (2001) 'Unbinding time: alternate work schedules and work-life balance'. *Journal of Family and Economic Issues*. Vol. 22, 2. pp101–119.

3 SCHEIN E. (1978) 'Career dynamics: matching individual and organisational needs'. Addison Wesley.

4 WORKLIFEBALANCE.COM (2003) *Success Survey Conducted by WorkLifeBalance.com.* Atlanta, GA, WorkLifeBalance.com. Available at: http://www.worklifebalance.com [Accessed 10 July 2003].

5 LALIBERTE R. (2002) 'The daddy bind'. Harlan, IA, Gruner and Jahr Publishing. Available at: http://www.parents.com/articles/family_time/4280.jsp?page=1 [Accessed 11 July 2003].

6 See reference no. 4 above

7 YOST P. R. *and* PLUNKETT M. M. (2002) 'Turn business strategy into leadership development'. *Training and Development*. Vol. 56, 3. pp49–51.

8 APGAR M. (1998) 'The alternative workplace: changing where and how people work'. *Harvard Business Review*. Vol. 76, 3. pp121–136

9 FLEXECUTIVE (2002) *Work-Life Balance or Career Death? Issues and Paradoxes Facing Marketing and Human Resource Professionals.* London, Flexecutive. Available at: http://www.flexecutiveclient.co.uk/client/cli_02ij.asp [Accessed 11 July 2003].

10 AMUNDSON N. (2001) 'Three-dimensional living'. *Journal of Employment Counseling*. Vol. 38, 3. pp114–127.

11 JOLLY R. (No date) 'Roam alone – the new boundaries of e-mobility'. Available at: http://www.stokesjolly.com/our_thinking.htm [Accessed 11 July 2003].

12 HOCHSCHILD A. R. (2001) *The Time Bind: When Work Becomes Home and Home Becomes Work*. Allston, MA, Owl Books.

13 DEMETRIOU D. (2002) 'Tired and overworked'. *London Evening Standard*. 7 October. p.17. Online version available at: http://www.thisislondon.com [Accessed 11 July 2003].

14 WORRALL L. *and* COOPER C. L. (2001) *The Quality of Working Life: 2000 Survey of Managers' Changing Experiences*. London, Institute of Management.

15 DOYLE J. *and* REEVES R. *Time Out: The Case for Time Sovereignty*. London, Industrial Society.

16 BAILYN L. (1997) 'The impact of corporate culture on work-family integration', in S. Parasuraman and J. Greenhaus (eds.), *Integrating Work and Family*. Westport, CT, Quorum Books, pp209–19.

17 RICE M. (2002) 'Balancing acts'. *Management Today*. September. pp52–59.

18 COVEY S. (1992) *The Seven Habits of Highly Effective People*. London, Simon and Schuster.

19 BARTOLOME F. (1983) 'The work alibi: when it's harder to go home'. *Harvard Business Review*. Vol. 61, 2. pp67–74.

20 GERSON K. (1993) *No Man's Land: Men's Changing Commitments to Family and Work*. New York, Basic Books.

21 See reference no. 20 above.

22 BRUCH H. *and* GOSHAL S. (2002) *Beware the Busy Manager*. Harvard Business Review. February.

23 BARTOLOME F. *and* EVANS P. A. L. 'Must success cost so much?' *Harvard Business Review*. Vol. 58, 2. pp137–149.

24 COUTU D. L. (2002) 'How resilience works'. *Harvard Business Review*. Vol. 80, 5. pp46–55.

25 CONNER D. R. (1993) *Managing at the Speed of Change: How Resilient Managers Succeed and Prosper Where Others Fail*. New York, Villard Books.

26 BARTOLOME F. *and* EVANS P. A. L. 'Must success cost so much?' *Harvard Business Review*. Vol. 58, 2. pp137–149.

4

Policies and processes

In this chapter, we attempt to scope out the policies that underpin an effective approach to promoting work-life balance. We also explore some of the practical processes which contribute to making the policies work.

As part of the research for this book, we conducted a short survey of UK companies to explore their policies towards work-life balance. A total of 74 organisations responded, ranging in size from a few dozen employees to many thousands. The first question concerned whether they had an overall policy on work-life balance – only one in three did so. Of these, 48 per cent felt that the policy had had a high or very high impact in changing people's lives.

Having a policy provides – at least in theory – a benchmark against which employees and their managers can assess decisions and behaviours. It also helps to place the issues more firmly on the top management agenda. Having a policy does not necessarily mean that it will be implemented, however. As we have seen already in earlier chapters, people feel inhibited from taking advantage of opportunities, for a whole variety of reasons. Among these, says the Institute for Employment Studies (IES),[1] are:

- impact on earnings – a change in working pattern may mean a reduction in standard of living
- heavy workloads – 'There's no one else to do the work if I'm not there'
- employers' relying on people to find their own solutions – ignoring the fact that the best solutions usually require an accommodation between the organisation and the individual
- damage to career prospects – the most important high-profile projects and the majority of promotion opportunities tend to go to those who work a 'normal' profile
- entrenched long-hours cultures, where those who might opt for flexible working do not do so because they feel they will be perceived as letting the side down.

A policy alone simply cannot resolve all these issues. It has to go hand in hand with an implementation programme aimed at creating the kind of culture where work and non-work are no longer in competition for employees' attention and commitment. Indeed, some companies, such as Marriott Hotels, make a point of *not* having a policy at all.

It is probably true that a culture which is truly supportive of work-life balance can operate without an overarching policy. If everyone knows what they should be doing, why keep telling them? Nonetheless, for most organisations, achieving such a culture change will require a great deal of education, example, persuasion and, in some cases, coercion. Although it may be a blunt instrument, a broad work-life balance policy provides the foundation on which a supportive culture can be built.

The problem with many of the work-life policies we have encountered is that they are so far from the reality employees experience that they have no credibility. Making a policy real, therefore, requires that the company:

- is open and accurate about the situation now – warts and all
- engages employees in defining what the policy should be
- paints a clear picture of the situation it wants to bring about
- commits to specific actions that will reinforce the implementation of the policy and/or make it easier for people to put it into practice
- monitors how the policy is being translated into action and provides feedback on progress for the employees
- provides role models at all levels of the organisation in both working flexibly and enabling others to do so.

Some examples of broad work-life balance policies are included in Appendix 1. A simple approach, which is basically a short set of values statements, comes from Perry Christensen, director of human resource strategy and planning at Merck & Co. His core principles are that:

- People like to be successful in *all* areas of their lives that are important to them.
- Everyone is unique.
- People thrive on independence and choice.
- People excel at things they enjoy doing.
- If the organisation is successful in matching people's unique talents to its needs, then it should also be able to trust them to manage how they make their contribution.[2]

Putting life into the overall policy will also normally mean supporting it with a portfolio of other policies on specific issues. Our survey also explored what issues relating to work-life balance the organisations had individual policies on. These included stress, long hours, conflict with home demands, recruitment, retention of talent, and return after maternity leave. Across all of these issues a pattern emerged. A majority considered that the issue was important and had a policy to address it. Yet only a relatively small minority measured whether the policy was being implemented. Particular issues that stood out included stress, which although rated as important by the highest proportion of respondents was one of the issues that only relatively rarely had an attached policy (just over 50 per cent). Just one company in 12 measured whether its employees encountered conflict between the demands of home and work.

For smaller organisations, the policy portfolio may be subsumed into a general policy that says, 'We will attempt to accommodate any reasonable pattern of working time and location which enhances the quality of life of our employees without compromising customer service.'

For most organisations, however, a more substantive set of guidelines is needed as a benchmark for managers' decisions. The rest of this chapter examines some of the key areas such a policy portfolio should cover. It also looks at some of the implications, in terms of how the policies are applied in practice.

A practical approach to managing the policy issue is to break it into manageable chunks. All the key policies we have observed in companies appear to fall into one of three categories:

- those relating to flexibility of time
- those relating to flexibility of location
- those which are generally supportive of a flexible and fulfilling working environment.

Let's look at each of these categories in turn.

FLEXIBILITY OF TIME

Our survey asked organisations about six different forms of flexible working times and two of flexible working location. Most of the organisations were known to have initiated some form of work-life balance initiative, so the sample was to some extent biased towards the positive – a more random sample, using a different survey method, would be expected to come up with lower usages of all the flexible working approaches covered. The overall response with regard to working times is shown in Table 2. One immediate inference from these figures is that many companies are still reluctant to open flexible options to *all* staff. Another is that although flexible working hours, job-sharing and part-time work have gained a relatively high level of acceptance, term-time working and the nine-day fortnight have not. A surprise was the high proportion of organisations that offer sabbaticals (47 per cent).

Table 2 Policies for flexible working times

Type of option	Option offered	To all?
Flexible working hours	84%	57%
Job-sharing	66%	31%
Part-time work	86%	46%
Nine-day fortnight	19%	14%
Term-time working	24%	9%
Sabbaticals	47%	27%

Flexible working hours

The basic principles of flexible working hours are well known. In most systems, employees have a core period when they must normally be at work, and non-core times when they are able to decide for themselves when to arrive and leave. Adaptations include variable lengths of lunch hours and a simple policy of allowing employees to decide when they want to do their work.

The problems with flexible working hours arise mainly from co-ordination, either with customers or with working colleagues. Says a frustrated manager in a consultancy company which has a team of work-life balance consultants among its portfolio: 'When they are in, they always respond promptly. But whenever I need to talk with them most urgently, they aren't contactable!' Companies operating flexible hours have often found it necessary to moderate the degree of choice people can make about when they will or will not be available, to ensure that there is always at least minimum cover for customers. (The nightmare scenario is to have a reduced workforce run off their feet in the early morning and early evening, and overstaffing in the middle of the day!)

Flexible working hours work best where individuals can get on with their tasks largely independently of their colleagues and without constant customer interaction. Where work is more interdependent, flexible working hours are still feasible, but only where the work team is able to manage the process efficiently together. We will cover this issue more fully in Chapter 7.

Annualised hours

Annualised hours originated in Germany and were first experimented with by a large retailer, Kaufhaus Beck in Munich. In general, they offer a more flexible method of matching employee and employer needs than traditional flexible working hours because employees are not constrained by the need to work the same core hours every week. The original scheme was driven by the need to raise the calibre of recruits and to retain talent. Among the features of the scheme was the potential for department managers to 'trade' surpluses or deficits of people's time when one area had a surge in demand and another was quiet. Instead of more senior managers having to arrange temporary transfers, the employees and their managers made arrangements at their own level. HR acted as a banker, receiving deposits of hours and paying them out.

The main benefit of annualised hours is that it starts from the perspective of identifying the peaks and troughs of demand and then seeks the best possible accommodation between the needs of the company and the needs of the individual employee. Being able to plan closely against actual workloads also helps to keep the team lean and boost productivity. The potential disadvantages include the need for relatively bureaucratic systems of record-keeping, frequent discussions and negotiations about who is going to work when, and the fact that there may be so little slack left in the system that a sudden and unexpected absence through illness of one or two individuals can have a disproportionate effect on the team's ability to perform.

Glenmorangie

Glenmorangie, the Scottish whisky distiller based in Edinburgh, operates an efficient system of annualised hours. Employees are contracted to work a set number of hours in a year, and the company then has the flexibility to tell employees how many hours they are to work in the coming week. They are informed of their shift pattern at least seven days in advance of the start of the working week it applies to, and must work a minimum of 24 hours in a week, with a limit of 48 hours set during peak times. Employees are paid the same amount each month, regardless of how many hours they have worked.

Glenmorangie has adopted the annualised hours system due to the seasonal nature of its work, as Ian Drysdale, UK HR Director, explains:

> *Employees may work only two or three days a week during our quiet time at the beginning of the year, but this will increase to five or six days a week during our peak time from September to December.*

The company actively seeks flexible workers when recruiting, and makes the working pattern clear in its recruitment literature. Time attendance is monitored by a computerised system which eliminates the possible costs associated with timely administration duties.

Dutton Engineering

Annualised hours have also worked very well for Dutton Engineering, a small engineering firm with 50 employees in south-east England. Workers are contracted to do a standard total of 1,770 hours per year, plus 160 hours overtime (calculated as the average yearly overtime worked in the three years before implementation of the scheme). Teams are expected to deliver quality products on time to customers, so hours are determined by customer demand. Employees can therefore go home if they need to during quiet periods, as the team will cover for their absence. If a team member is off ill, people will work harder to cover for them, and anyone who is away sick is expected to work extra hard on his or her return to make up for the efforts of colleagues during the absence.

Employees are paid the same salary on the 20th of each month, regardless of how few or how many hours they have worked. This very often works in their favour, as Dean Meeks, business manager, highlights:

> *Most people don't achieve the 1,930 hours that they are paid for in a year, so they are effectively paid for overtime that they haven't worked.*

But employees never lose out if they happen to work more than their total allocated hours, as their contracts are renegotiated so that they are compensated for these extra hours. However, employees do not always immediately see the benefits of such a system:

CASE STUDY continued

Some people are driven by overtime – to begin with they might see themselves losing money in a busy month when they have worked a lot of overtime . . . but they always see it paying off eventually, as we enter a quiet month where they get paid for hours they don't do.

The success of the annualised hours scheme at Dutton has been huge. Not only has it benefited employees in terms of job satisfaction, it has vastly increased company performance, as founder Ken Lewis highlights:

Efficiency leapt up beyond all our expectations. Our teams are now not only facing the same direction; they are focused correctly and all pulling together . . . We can now compete with anyone worldwide.[3]

CASE STUDY

MD Foods

MD Foods (now part of Arla foods) introduced an annualised roster for each of nearly 200 teams of employees in the late 1990s. The process was complex – it required a computer to manage it – but the basic concepts were simple. Each team member had a 'bank' of hours. If he or she worked shorter hours than normal, the difference was added to the bank; if he or she worked longer hours, the difference was deducted. The number of hours in the bank was constantly monitored so that the company could move people around, or hire additional employees if the bank balance was depleted. Although this system has been recently modified due to the takeover by Arla foods, it presents a good example of an annualised hours system in practice.

Compressed workweeks

The principle behind both nine-day fortnights and four-day weeks is that many employees greatly value a longer weekend than the norm. By working an extra period each day, they accumulate the equivalent of a full day to be traded off for an additional day off. The exchange of longer hours per day for more days off has proved popular with both employers and employees. Several studies indicate that employees have more fulfilling and stable family lives, less stress and greater job satisfaction than when working on traditional shift schedules or standard weeks. One of these, James River Paper Co.,[4] monitored its workforce for two years after it introduced a working week of four 12-hour days, followed by four days off.

Given that most people complain their weekends are too short, having a consistent double-size weekend has its attractions.

Experience generally suggests that a nine-day fortnight is more mutually beneficial than a four-day week because the latter extends the working day to the point where people may begin to lose efficiency. Moreover, in environments where working an extra hour or more each day is the norm, the problem is compounded. The nine-day fortnight, by contrast, requires a much shorter additional daily time-load which is more easily absorbed. Some companies allow employees to decide which day of the week they wish to take off.

The danger with both of these approaches is that employees end up working their assigned hours and *still* have to work, albeit at home, on their additional free day or at weekends. That defeats the whole object, so HR must monitor very carefully what is happening in practice. Other potential problems are that long hours do not necessarily work so well in a knowledge environment, where creativity may suffer. Moreover, employees who use their days off to engage in another job lose the beneficial effects of the extended recovery period.

Bon Marché in the United States operates a hybrid of compressed workweeks and annualised hours. From February to October it offers compressed workweeks to all staff. From November to January, its busiest period, the option is much more limited. In its employee surveys the company has found that the flexibility staff have for most of the year is seen as compensation for having to work harder and for having sometimes to do overtime during the peak months. In all, 80 per cent of Bon Marché's headquarters staff work flexibly, and 50 per cent of senior employees.

Four-day weeks are another example of a compressed hours system. At Precor, a US exercise equipment manufacturer, the move to a four-day week for manufacturing staff has yielded huge benefits. Production levels increased by an estimated 5–10 per cent after the switch to a compressed working week, as more treadmills were produced in four 10-hour days than the previous five 8-hour days pattern. Part of the productivity increase was down to the reduced start-up and shut-down costs under the new system, as employees were seen to take 30 minutes to reach full speed after the start of each shift and after each break. The longer working day ensured greater momentum and therefore higher productivity. Precor introduced two manufacturing shifts for employees working four-day weeks, allowing the company to be in production $22\frac{1}{2}$ hours a day, Monday to Thursday – Fridays and Saturdays were therefore free to schedule overtime. Other benefits seen following the introduction of this scheme include a wider geographic recruiting area and a higher proportion of women workers as a result of the perceived extra free family time allowed by shift patterns. The company also reports less absenteeism and more overtime potential.[5]

At First Direct in the UK, employees on four-day weeks can also earn overtime if they want to make up their hours at particular periods. The four-day week is one of a broad variety of shift patterns operated by First Direct staff in order to successfully operate a 24-hour business. Hours worked may be a mixture of evenings and weekends, and staff have some choice as to which shift they can work in a particular week. However, this choice is somewhat limited, as the four-day week pattern is driven by business need rather than a focus on work-life balance needs.

Part-time work

According to a study by IES, employees commonly felt that jobs available to part-timers tended to be of lower status and lower quality, and this was a major reason for avoiding them. Such perceptions are not without foundation – more women than men are in low-paid jobs and more women than men are in part-time work. Definitions of part-time work, both official and common-language, differ, but generally seem to centre on the number of hours worked versus a standard 35-hour week.

One of the problems with such an approach is that contractual full-time hours and actual working hours often bear little resemblance to each other, even in countries which have been more rigorous than the UK in applying the Working Time Regulations. To a junior doctor working 70 hours a week, anyone working just 35 hours might seem very part-time! In reality, the concept of part-time work is no more than a convenient legal fiction that allows employers to limit their obligations towards certain categories of employees.

Some sectors, such as hotel and leisure, or retail, rely heavily on part-timers to fit around patterns of customer demand that fluctuate over the day or the week. These are also the sectors which have some of the highest rates of turnover of staff. Those companies which succeed in retaining staff better than their competitors seem typically to have adopted a policy perspective that effectively ignores artificial boundaries between full- and part-time staff. From the senior executive to the shelf-stacker, each employee is a resource in which the company has invested. From such a perspective it becomes relatively easy to move to an approach towards working hours that aims to find the right package for each individual, no matter how lowly or how many hours he or she wants to work each week.

Term-time working

Term-time working has obvious attractions to young parents and particularly to single parents. It is remarkably simple to operate but carries some basic disadvantages in that few businesses have peaks and troughs of demand that coincide with the school calendar. Wakefield Metropolitan District Council (MDC) is an example of an organisation that offers its employees the option of term-time working. This option is only available where the job allows it to be feasible, and the decision is made by the employee's manager, with advice from the department personnel officer. For those who are able to work under this scheme, both salaries and holiday entitlements are calculated on a full-time pro-rata basis. Term-time working is seen by the council initially as only a temporary arrangement, and employees are limited to a 12-month period working in this manner – an extension is subject to the approval of the employee's manager.[6]

Job-sharing

The term 'job-sharing' has often been confused with 'job-splitting'. The distinction is relatively straightforward. In job-splitting a number of tasks that might make up one or more jobs are divided between several people. Each takes accountability for a discrete role and there is little or no reason for them to liaise closely with each other. Job-sharing, by contrast, requires the people concerned to have joint responsibility for the same tasks. Although they may each have some specialisation and would leave subtasks to each other, they manage a joint outcome. The need for liaison – particularly at handover points – is great. The main characteristic that job-sharing and job-splitting share is that the participants of both work part-time in this role. (A job-sharing pair's contracted hours might add up to more than a normal week, but each would work substantially less than 35 hours.)

Job-sharing pairs have included a wide range of occupations, from headteacher to account manager. There are some jobs where accountability has to reside with one person (for example, being a judge), but these are relatively few. One of the most successful examples I have observed is a joint managing director role taken on by two women in addition to their normal director responsibilities. They liaise to ensure that there is almost always one of them there to deal with issues that arise. To operate at this level of interchangeability requires great skill and an excellent relationship of high mutual trust, however.

The pattern of distribution of job-sharing is very heavily biased towards the public sector, virtually all local government employers making some use of it, as compared to only a third of manufacturers and just over half of retailers. The numbers of people working in genuine job-sharing arrangements is still small, however.

The term 'job-share' first came into common use in the 1970s. One use at that time was to help companies tide over periods of bad trading. Rather than lay off employees, they offered the opportunity of job-share contracts, with the promise that everyone who took up the option would be able to resume full-time working when the work need arose. For many employees the opportunity to work reduced hours was well-timed. Some chose to take a year to study part-time; some enterprising job-sharers even negotiated terms that allowed them to work three months on and three months off, so they could fulfil their dreams of overseas travel. For the companies the arrangement saved costly redundancies and meant that they retained talented staff. When the business upturn eventually came, the company found that the high level of loyalty felt by these staff made them resistant to headhunters (for an example of an active job-share policy, see Appendix 2).

Adjustable shift patterns

Although the traditional production line demanded rigid shifts, where hundreds of workers clocked on and off at the same time, very few jobs require anywhere near that level of synchronicity. Indeed, if anything, the opposite trend is occurring – global operations increasingly need to stagger shifts so that there is always someone to respond to queries or tasks from other time-zones. The more asynchronous work becomes, the easier it may be to be creative and flexible in designing shift patterns that satisfy multiple needs.

Bradford, although not known as one of the UK's primary tourist towns, was suffering from a severe lack of hotel staff, in particular for chambermaids. At the same time, there was a pool of young, single mothers without work. Most of the hotels advertised job hours as 7 am to 3 pm. When they were made aware of the labour pool available, many were able to offer shifts from 9 to 3, giving the mothers time to take their children to and from school.

Sabbaticals and career breaks

Sabbaticals, which used to be a rare privilege restricted to academia and the John Lewis Partnership, are now increasingly widespread. Microsoft offers a four-month unpaid sabbatical after four years. Eli Lilly offers a sabbatical or a career break of up to two years after five years' service.

A number of employers offer generous benefits in terms of time off to take part in charitable or community work. SAP operates a 'matched time off' scheme in which the company will match any holiday taken by employees (up to a maximum of five days) in order to do work in the local community or for charity. Employees have the choice over where they do this work, whether it is helping to install a computer network in a local school or helping to collect money for a charitable cause. The scheme also allows up to six months off to work on voluntary projects overseas, and a six-month unpaid sabbatical for employees with a good performance record and a minimum three-year tenure with the company.

Variable annual holiday

Length of holidays is also an important factor in people's sense of a fair work-life exchange with their employer. One company we encountered in our research offers 20 days holiday a year, but insists that three of them are taken at Christmas. The employees felt that those three days had been 'stolen' from them because they had no choice or control over them.

CASE STUDY

A healthy market in holiday time

Employees at Nationwide Building Society can buy or sell back to the company up to five days of holiday every year. The scheme forms part of employees' flexible benefits package, and allows employees to pay for extra days' holidays, or sell from their initial holiday allowance direct from their salary. These types of scheme seem to be increasing in popularity, as several companies surveyed had just introduced, or were about to introduce, similar initiatives.

It's one thing to have an allocation of annual leave, but another for people to be able to take it. One of the surprises of the individual interviews in our research was how many people, at all levels, felt unable to take their entitlement of holidays.

Many companies also still insist that employees cannot carry holiday entitlement over from one year to the next. Some useful ideas in dealing with this issue include:

- allowing untaken holiday to accumulate in a sabbatical fund, exchangeable after an appropriate number of years for a funded or part-funded career break

- monitoring the level of untaken holiday and providing counselling for those people who persistently fail to take their entitlements

- penalising managers whose direct reports are unable to take their holidays because of workload

- encouraging people who don't want to take large blocks of time away to shift to alternative patterns, such as nine-day fortnights.

Parental leave

Time off for parenting varies widely amongst UK companies. Amongst the most generous for maternity leave is Unilever, which offers 40 weeks' pay after one year's service. Some companies also offer return-to-work bonuses. Churchill Insurance offers two weeks' additional pay to those who stay six months after returning from maternity leave. TGI Friday offers a remarkable nine weeks' pay three months after returning. These can be compared with Ernst & Young in the USA, who introduced a parental leave programme after actuaries predicted that 1,000 births would take place to employees in the year between October 2001 and September 2002. The company now offers 16 weeks' unpaid parental leave – more than the 12 mandatory weeks required by the US Family Medical Leave Act.

Generous paid paternity leave is also a common benefit among companies which have strong work-life values. At least one company (MBNA) offers a week of paid leave for new grandparents. However, the trend in general is that men tend to take paternity leave in small chunks and rarely use their entitlement. We have yet to find a company that asks its male new parents why they do not take advantage of this provision.

Fostering leave

Fostering leave recognises that adoptive parents may have as many and perhaps more issues to deal with than genetic parents. Generous towards adoptive parents are Morgan Stanley (up to 126 days' leave), Churchill Insurance (18 weeks' leave), Unilever (90 days') and Home Service (75 days').

Family care days/emergency leave

Knowing that people can drop all their work responsibilities to cope with a personal or family crisis is one of the factors that contributes towards a sense of trust between employer and employee. Many companies do not see the need for a specific policy on this issue, preferring to leave it to the common sense of the line managers. A few examples of compassionate responses are often enough to create an appropriate climate and embed such behaviours in the culture. However, others feel it necessary to spell out the rules. For example, credit card company Capital One has a formal policy that allows employees up to three family care days over and above their 25-day holiday entitlement. They can also take emergency time off at half an hour's notice, although this is deducted from annual leave.

CASE STUDY

Heery

Construction firm Heery has 160 employees. Recognising that the long-hours culture of the industry was damaging to retention and to effective working, the company has embarked on a number of counterbalancing initiatives. To legitimise taking time off at short notice for domestic reasons, every employee receives three cards, which they can exchange whenever they need to, without explanation, for three hours off work. To compensate employees for cancellation of holidays – something that happens when there is a sudden and urgent client requirement – Heery doubles the number of lost days they can take in lieu. Alongside a holiday allowance of up to 28 days per year, this initiative forms part of a people-oriented and flexible working culture at the company.

Flexible retirement

There are two main strands of flexible retirement: retirement date flexibility and retirement method flexibility. The first strand offers employees the choice of when they retire from an age band (for example 50 – 75 in the case of Tesco).[7] The second strand, sometimes called phased retirement, incorporates the basic idea of allowing people approaching retirement to work gradually fewer hours per week. Originally introduced as a formal, highly planned activity, often alongside retirement planning assistance, it has now become a much more informal ad-hoc arrangement, especially in smaller businesses. However, there are good arguments for making rather more of this flexible option than companies normally do. Among them:

- It provides an excellent opportunity to phase in a younger person to the retiree's job, particularly in management roles or jobs involving specialised craft skills.

- It allows the employee to get used to extended leisure time bit by bit, rather than receiving his or her engraved watch one day and wondering what to do with all the free time the next.

- It provides time for the capture and recording of the employee's knowledge.

According to a CIPD survey, *Age, Pensions and Retirement* (2003), 31 per cent of employees in their fifties want to work beyond the age of 60 and eight per cent do not want to retire formally. Further, a number of studies show that going from full-time work to total retirement is bad for people's health, as they are so unprepared for the radical lifestyle change.[8] Such evidence presents a case for the introduction of flexible retirement policies, although these are yet to be introduced in many organisations.

Time off for community duties

Lean companies often prefer to donate money rather than time to good causes – time is a much more valuable commodity. Even companies which have a policy of matching employees' cash donations to charity are sometimes reluctant to endorse their taking a few hours here and there for civic duties, being a school governor or mentoring a small business owner, for example. However, they may be more positive about activities which can be demonstrated to have a payback in terms of team-building (like doing the Three Peaks Challenge for a charity) or leadership development. In the same way that the company expects the employee to make a business case for working a different pattern of hours or location, it is probably not unreasonable to expect the same for allowing time for community involvement.

A recent booklet from Business in the Community provides guidelines on how to set up 'time-off policies' which allow employees paid time off to volunteer in community duties during working hours. In a recent survey carried out by the National Centre for Volunteering, 69 per cent of respondents said they would be encouraged to volunteer if they were able to do so in working hours. Further research published by Business in the Community shows that a third of US companies have a formal policy giving workers time off for volunteer work.[9]

Barclays introduced its Volunteer 2day Scheme in June 2002. Each employee is given a minimum of two business days per calendar year to work in community activities, which includes work with almost any charity. The decision on whether the employee can participate in this work rests with the line manager, and time taken in such activities is monitored by a specialist computer programme. Participation in the scheme has been impressive, more than 18,000 employees taking part in Barclay's supported community activities in 2002.[10]

Go-home-on-time days

Although not strictly a policy for most of the organisations that have experimented with it, Go-home-on-time days are a useful method of raising awareness. They are also an opportunity to identify those people who cannot or do not want to work normal hours.

Some wider issues of time flexibility

Part of the business case for flexibility in employment is that it allows the organisation to adjust staffing levels according to need. This is particularly useful in project-based environments, such as television and large-scale civil engineering. For some employees, such as the growing army of interim executives, this is an ideal form of working. Being able to hop from one working environment to the next can be very attractive. Some interims have designed unique lifestyles – for example, working alternate three-month periods, or simply working a contract, then taking a long holiday before seeking the next.

However, for many employees a short-term contract culture creates insecurity and stress. For those people who seek permanent employment, whether full- or part-time, but have been obliged to settle for a succession of short-term contracts, the psychological contract is one where lack of commitment by the company can easily become lack of commitment by the individual. Some of the UK's otherwise exemplary employers have made the achievement of permanent status a reward for staying the course of short-term contracts for sufficient years. Legislation to ban such practices would probably misfire, but it is difficult for any company to achieve a culture change supportive of work-life balance if the basic contractual terms on working time are perceived to be inequitable.

A more positive view of short-term contracts comes from research by the Work Foundation. It concludes that despite the potentially negative aspects associated with contract working, such forms of work can be beneficial to both the employee and employer. Firstly, a short-term contract is a useful way of entering into the labour market and permanent jobs in particular. Secondly, short-term contracts can help increase labour market flexibility, which can be beneficial to both business and employees. Lastly, contract workers have greater choice under a short-term contract than a permanent one if they want to control or vary their patterns of work.[11] The key appears to be whether the arrangement is intended to be one-sided (ie simply to meet the company's needs) or an equitable match between the needs of employer and employee.

A genuine employee-focused approach to time flexibility seeks to create a win/win environment for both the individual and the organisation. The goal, says an executive from retailers Bon Marché, is that:

When you have people with skills that are sought after, you need to figure out how you can help them work their job around their life. That's what it's all about – getting people to decide, 'No, I don't want to consider going to a competitor because I have a schedule here that works for me and my life.'

Policies on working time flexibility must therefore cover:

- the rationale for each flexible option, from both the employee and employer perspective

- who it applies to (and doesn't apply to) and why (eg types of job, types of personal circumstances)

- opportunities, if any, to sample an option to see if it works out for both parties

- whether taking each option might have any positive or negative impacts upon career progression.

The policy should also be accompanied by more detailed information, including:

- the pluses and minuses of each option

- some examples of people who have worked using this option

- any sources of further advice.

FLEXIBILITY OF LOCATION

Recent research estimates that over 9 million people in Europe are now 'eWorkers', with this figure estimated to rise to 27 million by 2010.[12] Our survey explored two options of location flexibility: working from home and working from a neighbourhood centre. By far the majority offered the option to work from home, but only 26 per cent offered it to all staff. Only a handful of companies offered the chance to work from a neighbourhood centre, and again, in most cases this only applied to certain employees.

Like part-time work, working from home is not easy to define. At one extreme are the many people who work entirely from home, with perhaps occasional trips to meet their office-based colleagues. At the other is the much greater volume of employees who work from home occasionally, either to meet domestic circumstances (like letting in the gas man) or to gain some concentrated and uninterrupted creative space. Also in the equation are the many people who simply take work home at night and weekends because they cannot finish it during their normal working hours. Some people work in neighbourhood centres (though far fewer than were predicted a decade and more ago); others spend most of their time on customer premises. A variation on the theme is the idea of:

Table 3 Policies for flexible location

Type of option	Option offered	To all?
Working from home	73%	26%
Working from a neighbourhood centre	8%	5%

touchdown sites [which] enable location-flexible employees to drop in and have access to corporate systems or specialist facilities, meeting rooms, secretarial services and so on.[13]

These do not have to be at the company's own sites; several companies may combine to operate a touchdown site and share the costs.

All these are different issues, and any policy on working location must be flexible enough to recognise and manage each circumstance.

By far the greatest proportion of partial home-workers consists of senior managers. Those who spend around one third of their time working at home also seem to be the most satisfied with their work-life balance.[14] This may have something to do with being more able to control when and where they work, without asking permission. A recent study concludes that people who have the *option* of working from home are most likely to be well-educated, male professionals under 30. Those who do most of their work at home, by contrast, are most likely to come from the lower levels of organisations and to be female. The authors of the study conclude that working from home is often just another perk for those who already have a relatively high level of control over when and how they work.

CASE STUDY

Sun Microsystems

Sun Microsystems promotes teleworking by offering courses in how to manage 100 per cent flexible working: people can work from any flat surface, from the kitchen to a Java cafe in the office or the drop-in centre in London.[15] At the time of writing the company is about to implement a formal scheme at their headquarters in Hampshire, whereby the majority of employees who work on a hot desk basis will be able to work from home for a set number of days over a designated time period. According to an HR worker at the company's UK headquarters:

A formal system of teleworking will help people to feel more empowered, so they will work harder and more efficiently, as well as having the convenience of working at home.

The benefits to the employee of working from home are considerable. Time which would otherwise have been wholly or partly wasted commuting can be put to productive use – or you can simply get up later! It is easier to concentrate when you are alone and have no one to interrupt you (apart from the telephone and e-mail). Most telecommuters claim to be more productive at home than at an office. And it can be easier to get out to the dentist, chemist or optician when you need to. Teleworking – working from home via a computer and modem – has a strong appeal to many employees and particularly those who have caring responsibilities or suffer from a disability that makes travel to work difficult or impossible.

According to a survey for BT,[16] 73 per cent of teleworkers felt they had a good or very good work-life balance. Ten per cent of teleworkers – primarily people with children, or carers, or people with special needs – would not be able to do the same job if it were not home-based.

However, there are downsides as well. Other people may assume that because you are at home you are not really working and can be called upon for all sorts of other activities – family, social or community. It can be very lonely working on one's own much of the time. (Some telecommuters in a local area club together to have their lunch break at one another's houses, just so they have someone to talk to face to face.) Social interaction is a key part of a positive working experience for most people. One of the main reasons people continue to work, even when they are financially independent, is that they value the socialisation of meeting and working alongside other people. Parents may find that they are frequently distracted by the demands of children – it is not so easy to take a day off to look after a sick child if you are based at home. And having to give up a room to be a permanent or make-shift office can be difficult.

Telecommuters also report that they experience prejudice from other working colleagues, who don't believe that they are really working all the time they are supposed to. They are more likely to be overlooked when it comes to promotion opportunities. And, as a recent *item* study[17] showed, they often feel left out in terms of being kept informed and having a chance to influence thinking in the team and in the company as a whole. Finally, some studies indicate an association between working at home and burnout.[18]

For the organisation, the positive side of telecommuting is that it reduces the need for office space, that it helps to ensure that employees are fresh when they start work (one HR director in the City estimates that it takes employees who have struggled to work on crowded tubes 40 minutes on average to wind down sufficiently to concentrate fully on their work!), and that people do appear to be more productive. Retention rates are generally higher among telecommuters. However, not everyone is effective as a telecommuter, many managers struggle to manage a virtual workforce, and there are extra investments needed in equipment, time to explain and oversee projects, and liaison between members of the virtual team.

Only 14 per cent of UK employers make use of full-time teleworkers, compared with a European average of 18 per cent. Although the proportion is growing (a very modest 10 per cent growth between 1995 and 2000), it is surprising that it has not found greater favour, especially as so many employees now have experience of working occasional days at home in the same way. It is clear, however, that being a full-time teleworker is a very different situation, both for the employee, his or her manager and his or her office-bound co-workers. Formal teleworkers need not live within travel distance of the office; they can be anywhere in the world. (One of our most effective teleworkers lives on an island an hour's ferry ride from Vancouver, Canada!) There are also potential problems with managing their time/output, data security, health and safety, and the contractual terms under which they are employed. (Increasing numbers of teleworkers subcontract to several organisations at the same time; the employer has to be sure that they are not, for example, misusing data from one source to the benefit of another.)

Two countries that make substantial use of teleworkers are Germany, where 29 per cent of employers use teleworkers, and Sweden, where 75 per cent do so and where the extent of usage in most of these organisations continues to grow. According to the Cranfield School of Management,[19] one of the stimuli to increased teleworking is a change in attitude both of the trade unions, which no longer equate it with low-paid, low-qualification and low-stability work, and of employees, who no longer see it as a risky option. This change is due at least in part to improved contractual terms offered by employers.

A policy for working at home needs to cover a wide range of expectations and circumstances, including:

- why the company supports this flexible working option
- health and safety issues (including the ergonomics of the home environment)
- how the quality and quantity of work will be assessed
- who is eligible
- the implications in terms of career progress and compensation.

The company should also provide detail on the practicalities of telecommuting and on what kind of employees will adapt most easily to this kind of working. In general, telecommuting requires people who are self-disciplined, are good time managers, and are able to work without an externally imposed structure.

At a practical level, HR needs to ensure that the selection of both participants and their supervisors is carried out with sufficient forethought. For organisations beginning to experiment with full-time telecommuting, experience suggests that it is better to prove the concept using new teams, designed for the purpose, than to change radically the working patterns of an existing team. The existing team may simply have too many habits and routines that rely on frequent face-to-face contact; and the supervisor may also find it hard to manage them in a radically different manner.

It is also essential for HR to ensure that people working virtually are supported as well as they would be if they were in a central office. They need efficient and prompt technical support, and perhaps access to back-up equipment in a serviced office – if equipment breaks down, for example. They need training in how to work remotely – not just in the technicalities but also in how to adapt their personal routines. They need to be kept in touch, so that their networks within the organisation do not atrophy. This can be quite difficult where access to centralised computer services is strictly controlled to avoid security breaches. If it is not possible to gain full access to the company intranet, what alternative routes can HR offer to ensure they are kept informed? The managers of remote workers also need to be trained to provide the day-to-day support they need and – frequently forgotten – so do co-workers, who need to be understanding about the remote employees' need for 'coffee-machine' chit chat and to be part of the grapevine. Also frequently forgotten is the need to educate customers and other stakeholders, with whom the remote worker has frequent contact.

A report by the US Office of Personnel Management[20] identifies three key elements of successful teleworking:

- managers with a willingness to experiment – Most of the managers interviewed in the study expressed reservations about teleworking, but were willing to take a chance. All reported their concerns had been unfounded
- motivated, self-starting employees – Where it was the employee who had proposed teleworking and had thought through how it would work, the outcome was always positive

- clearly defined expectations – Both parties agreed upfront on schedules, outputs and reporting procedures.

Experience of UK companies also suggests that it is important to set and keep to a trial period, and to have a clear and agreed set of criteria against which to assess how well the new way of working has delivered.

For partial or occasional telecommuting, it makes sense to be very clear about the circumstances in which the company wants to support people working in this way. Can people decide for themselves and tell their manager; or do they have to make a formal request? Is there a limit on how many days per month, or per week, someone can work from home? Is there to be 'one law for us and another for them'? (There seems to be something of a self-fulfilling prophecy here – the less people feel trusted, the more likely they may be to abuse the privilege.) If the policy simply requires agreement 'with your line manager', what are the procedures by which someone develops an agreement?

There are, however, other issues related to the increasing teleworking trend. Persistent working from home enabled by mobile Internet technology has the potential to blur the work/home divide, to the point where the two become indistinguishable. The ramifications of this for work-life balance are potentially disastrous. Teleworking offers the opportunity for workaholics to develop and thrive because they are able to exist in a constant working environment in which they define their self-identity predominantly through work achievements.

The aim of teleworking, as with all flexible working, is for the company to create the circumstances where employees can contribute most effectively. At its simplest, as long as telecommuting achieves that aim, HR should attempt to make it as widely available as practical.

POLICIES ON BENEFITS AND SUPPORT FOR WLB

Not everyone wants to work different hours or from home. Those employees who are happy to work normal hours in an office or workshop may need very different support from the organisation to enable them to work at their most effective. The range of benefits companies can provide is increasing all the time, from crèche facilities to concierge services. Most of these aim to reduce the real or potential conflict between work and non-work demands on the individual.

Childcare

Childcare has been described by some HR professionals as the bugbear of benefits. It is, by and large, expensive to provide, addresses the needs of only a small proportion of the workforce and, if run in-house, introduces a welter of red tape, from additional health and safety requirements to police checks on staff. It is not surprising, then, that only 23 per cent of the companies in our survey offered childcare facilities, and only 15 per cent did so to all employees. A high proportion of companies use childcare vouchers rather than provide their own facilities; in this way they avoid at least some of the administrative burden.

Nonetheless, many companies do see the provision of some form of childcare facility as an essential element in their work-life balance support package. Scotland Yard Commissioner John Stevens has recommended that police stations install crèches, to help attract more female recruits who would not otherwise be able to work full-time. At Innovative People Solution (IPS) Pty Ltd, a Sydney-based professional consulting firm, on-site childcare facilities have developed with the business within a strong people-based culture that heavily promotes work-life balance. The company now has a purpose-built crèche within its office building. Parents pay for care-givers, whom they select themselves.

In making childcare facilities work, says Families at Work, a consulting company specialising in this area, several important factors must be considered. These range from issues to do with cost-effectiveness of childcare schemes, potential present and future demand for the service, affordability of childcare provisions and possible financial aid from the company, to the infor-mation required to implement the project, cost and benefit analysis, employee recruitment and retention, and return rates from parental leave.[21]

Various studies suggest that childcare subsidies or more direct childcare support contribute substantially to employee retention, reduced absenteeism, reduced lateness, the ability to con-centrate on work and overall job performance. NationsBank reduced turnover among tellers by more than two-thirds by introducing a subsidy for childcare. Another major practical benefit, with the advent of employee rights to request non-standard working times, is that employees may be better able to accommodate the company's needs if they do not have to worry about when they collect their children.

Most HR professionals perceive childcare solely in terms of the provision of nursery or pre-school supervision. But a comprehensive approach to childcare establishes support and makes accommodation for children of all ages. It may also encompass practical help in parenting – for example, providing workshops for new parents, subsidising specialist counselling on child health or child behaviour. At a local level, employers can encourage staff to take on roles out-side work as youth leaders. Hillingdon Hospital not only has childcare facilities on-site; it also operates a play scheme to look after employees' school-age children during the summer holidays.

It all comes down to 'How can we help our employees focus on their work?'

Another growing benefit is a back-up day centre for kids, for use in emergencies, such as when the employee's normal childminder is ill. Chase Manhattan finds the cost of running its centre is well outweighed by the fact that people can come to work on such days.

Dependant care

Providing employees with insurance against having to support elderly or sick relatives for a long period is not a common benefit in the UK. But experience elsewhere[22] suggests that it doubles the chances of affected employees remaining in their jobs and removes a major cause of stress and reduced productivity. Given that five out of six people faced with the need to care for an elderly relative gave up their jobs, permanently or temporarily (the average time spent caring for an elderly relative is eight years, according to one study), this is a tremendous waste of resources. What's more, the peak age for caring is 45–64, when many employees are at their most experienced.

Moreover, population demographics mean that caring for elderly relatives or partners will become an increasing burden for employees. Baby-boomers are now entering their sixties, so the next decade is likely to see an explosion of need for dependant care. One in five people is expected to be caring for an elderly or disabled relative by 2010 (against one in eight employees now), and the dependant elderly will outnumber dependant children by 2020.

Employees caring for elderly or disabled relatives often have different patterns of need from people with young children. In particular, they need:

- greater flexibility, to cope with sudden, unpredictable crises (eg time off unpaid or part-paid at short notice; working different hours or from home)

- access to information about specialist help available (eg local carers' support schemes and national helplines)

- supportive line managers who are sufficiently clued up about the problems carers face and the organisation's policy towards carers – and with whom they can talk about the issues they face (sometimes the most important thing is to have someone who will listen sympathetically while they work out their own solutions)

- access to a telephone they can use with privacy at crisis times.

Fitness and wellness

Looking after one's health is one of the six key lifestreams discussed in Chapter 3. It is import-ant for the company that employees remain fit too. Sickness absenteeism costs UK companies £11 billion a year.[23] As stress in the workplace rises, it makes sense to help employees counter-act the effects of a demanding lifestyle.

Not every company can afford to provide an in-house gym or to subsidise membership of public facilities. But there are lots of other ways in which they can help. Providing healthy options in the staff restaurant is the minimum that should be expected. Benefits offered by organisations with a focus on employee well-being range from reflexology and stress counselling (Volkswagen) to chiropody. A surprising proportion of the Best Company list offer massages to their staff.

Construction company Mace holds health fairs that give advice on topics such as stress and on-the-spot health checks.

Companies in the USA, such as Xerox, which have invested heavily in wellness programmes report a 500 per cent return on investment. UK companies typically do not have the same costs of healthcare support, but they can benefit from reductions in injuries, absenteeism and stress.

Rand Corporation, which carried out a controlled study to compare what happened to employees suffering from depression, found that those who participated in wellness pro-grammes remained at work for longer than those that did not. (The effect was small, but significant.)

Goldman Sachs Wellness Centre

Like many companies in our research, Goldman Sachs is cautious about promoting work-life balance, on the grounds that people often attach a very narrow meaning to the term. It has, however, placed a great deal of emphasis on wellness, which it sees as a much more comprehensive concept that embraces a wider set of issues, and on achieving a positive lifestyle.

Neil Snowball, manager of the Wellness Centre in London, talks of the need to have corporate athletes:

> In the world of athletics, people train every day for a few occasions when they need peak performance. They take care of their diet, their overall fitness and their psychological well-being. In the corporate world of investment banking, people need no less to be able to work at their peak, when the occasion demands it. That means they also have to exercise, have quality leisure time, think about what they eat and so on.

While the company cannot nanny its employees, they are all sufficiently intelligent and self-motivated to see the sense of taking care of themselves. Snowball's role is to ensure that the company provides the resources that help them to do so. 'Our people are high achievers; they typically want to achieve excellence in their personal lives as well as their work lives,' he explains.

Snowball's remit extends throughout Europe, Africa, the Middle East and Asia-Pacific, although he cannot provide such dedicated resources in all locations as are available in London. There, employees can make use of a comprehensive fitness centre, an equally comprehensive medical centre, and a children's centre for back-up when an employee's childcare arrangements break down. Employees receive professional advice on diet from an external provider. In preparation for the 2003 London Marathon, in which 40 Goldman Sachs staff competed, there was a series of seminars on topics such as injury avoidance and training technique.

Employees were consulted in the setting up of the centre and its services, and they continue to advise on what they want. They also pay for the services they use – and use them they do. More than 80 per cent of staff in London have used the wellness programme in some way, and 68 per cent are members of the fitness centre.

The commercial reasoning behind the programme, which was introduced in 1999, is that it will help with four key business drivers:

- having a healthier, more productive workforce
- recruiting world-class people
- keeping them
- enhancing the reputation of the firm.

Demonstrating a direct link between the wellness programme and either individual or business performance is difficult. However, Goldman Sachs is participating in studies by the Institute for Health and Productivity Management, which aim to produce useful data.

The statement 'You are what you eat' is being supported by a constant flow of new evidence from research. Experiments in a British prison, for example, found that behaviour and learning ability improved significantly with a healthier diet. Many employers now offer 'healthy alternatives' on their staff restaurant menus. However, it could be argued that there is a good business case for more proactive dietary intervention on the part of employers. After all, it seems very clear that dietary behaviour affects creativity and productivity – the most obvious example being the deleterious impact of large, alcoholic lunches on afternoon work. This is not to say that organisations should start nannying their employees into dietary regimes. It may well be appropriate, however, to educate them on the relationship between what they ingest and how they perform at work, sleep at night, and so on. Providing a resource where individual employees can seek dietary advice is unlikely to cost much, but it could potentially have substantial returns in absenteeism, as well as quality and quantity of work. Some companies already incorporate this kind of assistance into more general medical advice benefits.

Concierge services

Concierge services are evolving from being a yuppy benefit (having someone to walk the dog) to a much more routine cost-effective provision that allows employees to concentrate on their jobs while someone else sorts out difficult problems, such as arranging for a plumber to fix an urgent leak. Primarily used by large companies, the main costs are born by the employees.

Ten UK is an example of a 'lifestyle management' company that provides concierge services for around 30 organisations in the UK, including SAP. Employees at SAP may choose to have access to this service as part of their flexible benefits package. According to Stuart Affleck, HR consultant and recruitment manager for SAP UK and Ireland, Ten UK provides all manner of services 'from looking after day-to-day chores to organising once-in-a-lifetime experiences, such as a trip around the world'. The cost of this service is incurred by the employee and is taken directly out of his or her annual basic salary – the amount depends on the level of service required, but a 50–60 per cent corporate discount is applied.

Flexible benefits

Of course, all of the provisions outlined here could be provided by employers if they wanted to. But containing the overall costs of benefits packages is critical for most companies, so it is just not practical. Moreover, people at different stages of their lives tend to have very different requirements. What is now emerging within some companies is an integration of work-life balance provision with an overall flexible benefits package, as the case study below illustrates.

CASE STUDY

Lloyds-TSB

Just as everyone has different tastes, says Tim Fevyer, Senior Manager, Compensation and Benefits, Lloyds-TSB 'the decreasing pool of increasingly talented people we are trying to attract and retain are very diverse, not only compared to each other but in the way their needs change from year to year, or even month to month.'

The Work Options package allows people to negotiate when they work, to suit their personal circumstances – be that to work compressed weeks, or to stagger their hours to avoid the peak traffic times. Such requests will always be accepted unless there is a good business reason against them. Other elements within a broader benefits policy include discounted retail vouchers, cheap insurance, tax- free computers, share options and an option to buy or sell up to five days holiday.

The flexible holiday policy caused extensive debate. There were strong arguments for retaining some central control over decisions about allowing employees to use the option, but in the end it was agreed that the spirit of the programme was one of decentralisation and enabling people to make their own choices as far as possible.

Says Favyer: 'We had found that, if people take the option to work compressed working weeks, the company lost nothing. They would still make sure the work got done. The same has proved true for people, who take the extra holidays – they work around any potential problems to make sure they do the same job.' In the first year of the holiday scheme option, 20% of employees opted to buy more holiday, 3% to sell some days. Those that sold opted usually either for more cash, or other specific benefits, which suited their lifestyle.

PROCESSES THAT SUPPORT WLB

Putting the work-life balance policy into practice requires a supportive culture (which we will explore in later chapters) and a supporting infrastructure. This typically consists of:

- processes to ensure more effective organisation and reorganisation of work, so that it accommodates both business and individual priorities
- technological support
- an overhaul of HR systems to ensure that they do not promote behaviours and practices that hinder work-life balance.

Work organisation

As we shall explore in more detail in Chapter 5, line managers have to be creative when they look at what is possible in how work could be arranged. It is all too easy to assume that the existing processes and approaches are the most effective. Peter Ambrose, the HR manager at P&O Ferries had to demonstrate to line managers that different working patterns were feasible by doing the analysis and calculation with them, step by step. But the reward for thinking creatively is the design of working practices that are often much more sustainable.

The scope for improvement appears to be huge. One survey suggests that 40 per cent of managers consider long working hours have more to do with inefficiency than workload.[24]

The starting points for work redesign that takes work-life balance into account are a clear understanding of what time employees are willing to make available and when (including an element of non-contracted extra hours, whether paid or not), and of what tasks need to be done to achieve the team's objectives. The major barrier to this process at Nationwide in the UK, according to ex-diversity manager Melanie Fyans, was that middle management was averse to change because the managers were used to carrying out policies and procedures that had been in place for years. Indeed, breaking these initial barriers is often one of the first challenges that companies face when attempting work redesign.

Although presented as an issue about working time, the description in the following extract is fundamentally about work organisation.[25]

> *For service employees, the time issue that made their lives difficult was its uncertainty. They never knew when they might be called upon to work unexpectedly or when they would be on a service call that required them to work well into what they had expected to be their free time ... The assumptions concerning time, deeply embedded in the work culture of each site, created difficulties for employees' private lives.*

One of the work organisation factors that may have been lacking in this example was good practice in hand-over management. Jobsharers have this issue all the time and learn how to ensure that the incoming partner is fully briefed on the situation. An alternative solution might have been to stagger shifts so employees are expected to spend the final half an hour or more working on non-customer-facing tasks, such as completing reports. This time then also becomes a buffer zone in which the employee can deal with any unexpected requirement for longer time with the customer.

Among knowledge workers, significant improvements in both efficiency at work and work-life balance have been achieved simply by looking at the volume of meetings people attend. Reducing the number of meetings and training people to manage and contribute to meetings more effectively can create opportunities for radically different – and usually, much more satisfying – working patterns.

It is also important to seek opportunities for *work-work* balance. People can tolerate relatively long hours if the work is kept interesting, by being varied, and if they have opportunity for interaction with colleagues outside of the formality of meetings. For example, banning e-mails one day a week – an 'electronic day of rest' – has been adopted by a number of companies, including Camelot, Hogg Robinson, Thomson Travel and Nestlé. In each case the aim is to create a breathing space in the normal routine and encourage employees to spend more time talking to each other, developing ideas and exploring issues in more depth. According to a Nestlé spokesman, 'People are starting to think about how and what they are communicating, and are re-finding their voices.'

Some of the signs that indicate work could be better organised to improve both effectiveness and work-life balance include:

- multiple reporting lines, unless there is very clear contracting about how much time is available for each
- uneven spread of workload between team members
- travel time taking up a substantial proportion of the whole
- more than 30 per cent of time spent in meetings

- tasks often taking longer than estimated
- an emphasis on cost-cutting that is greater than that on service delivery (workloads rapidly increasing to the point of inefficiency).

Several years ago ASDA made radical changes to its roster system for store managers. Among the reasons for the change was a desire to retain managers who were frequently working much more than their contracted hours, as the company gradually moved to extended trading hours. With working smarter as one of the planks of the initiative, ASDA engaged managers in developing a set of ten principles, which it called commitments. These included a maximum working week of 45 hours, working no more than one Sunday in three, having a long week free after each Sunday they did work, and having full cover on Fridays. To make the new system work, the company invested in developing supervisors so that managers could delegate more to them. The changes allowed ASDA to achieve its business objectives without imposing further on managers' non-work lives.

HR SYSTEMS

The impact that HR systems have upon work-life balance issues is largely hidden and often insidious, acting to create a glass ceiling on those who opt to take on flexible working patterns. If HR is to take the lead in establishing a culture supportive of work-life balance, it must carry out a rigorous audit of all the systems and procedures it controls or initiates. Below we examine some of those systems and suggest some of the questions such an audit might cover.

Reward and recognition

Reward and recognition systems aim to stimulate and reinforce specific behaviours. Unfortunately, they often have unexpected and negative side-effects. For example, too much emphasis on individual targets for salespeople can lead to a breakdown in co-operation and teamwork. HR must assess recognition and reward systems regularly against such criteria as:

- Are people praised for working long hours or for great results?
- Is there any unintentional discrimination against part-timers and/or remote workers? (Do they perceive the systems to be discriminatory?)
- Do line managers understand and act upon the need to praise remote workers as frequently as 'line of sight' employees? (It's easy to give positive feedback to someone you meet in the corridor, but it may take more effort to do the same for someone you rarely meet in person.)
- Is it easier for full-timers and centrally-working employees to earn good performance bonuses than part-timers and telecommuters?
- Do part-timers lose out on subsidiary benefits, such as share option schemes?

A critical issue here is defining accurately what the desired behaviour is. Many organisations look for 'commitment'. Few, however, define what they mean by the term. As a result, managers provide their own meaning, which can all too easily become 'putting the extra hours in'. (Two thirds of respondents to one survey thought that working long hours was often confused with commitment.[26]) Even a definition such as 'going the extra mile for customers' can discriminate against employees who have non-work responsibilities, such as childcare, because they may not be able to stay beyond time to manage a customer's issue. Conversely, there are cases of part-time employees who have put in extra hours but whose efforts have gone unrecognised because they are not noticeably staying after normal working hours. Genuine commitment includes factors such as caring enough to identify the elements of a task that are really important and making sure that those are done whatever.

Trawling for good ideas in changing reward processes to be more supportive of work-life balance, we discovered the following:

- tying employees' bonuses to fulfilment of personal objectives as well as work ones
- making performance in supporting work-life balance for the team part of managers' bonus calculation
- linking efforts to reduce working hours (by working smarter) to community targets: employees would be encouraged to pledge a proportion of the hours they won back from work to non-work participating in a community activity.

Succession planning and promotion

Who gets promoted provides one of the strongest symbols of cultural values in an organisation. If there are few or no examples of flexible workers achieving promotions, especially high-profile ones, then people will draw their own conclusions.

People with career ambitions, especially if they are in management positions, find it hard to accept that requesting flexible working will not harm their careers. The Work Foundation study in 2001[27] has helped to provide rational arguments to employers that, far from showing evidence of reduced commitment, those executives who work flexibly have higher levels of commitment and positive leadership behaviours than average.

According to a Families and Work Institute study, the quantity and quality of flexible working opportunities offered by companies is strongly influenced by the proportion of women in senior positions. Where half or more of the top executives were women, 82 per cent offered flexible working, compared with 56 per cent where there were fewer women executives; six times as many offered childcare assistance locally.

Key questions for HR to ask of itself include:

- What criteria are used to identify potential successors?
- Are these purely talent-based?
- Are part-time and/or remote employees excluded?
- Could potential vacancies that arise be suitable for flexible working or home-working?
- Does the organisation assume automatically that managers have to be based on site? Or that they have to work a 'normal' full-time week?

Training provision

We will deal with training issues in more detail in Chapter 5. In the meantime, here are some useful questions for HR to ask of itself in this context:

- Do part-time workers have to give up days of their own time to attend courses?
- Are times/locations appropriate for carers? Does the company help with the cost of surrogate care or help the employee find surrogate care?
- Are there alternative sources of training (for example, e-learning) that support flexible working?

Recruitment

One of the main reasons organisations fail to achieve diversity, especially at senior levels, is that the pool of available recruits is artificially reduced by the inflexibility of working arrangements. Even when flexible working is available, the company must ensure that it reaches a wide spectrum of groups, from single parents to ethnic minorities. An active listening campaign to understand what kind of working arrangements would suit different target groups is a good starting point. Attention may also be needed to the style and wording of advertising – does it emphasise the potential for alternative working patterns?

- Does the company seek to hire people who are able to work flexibly?
- If so, is this reflected in recruitment literature?
- Do people seeking alternative working arrangements perceive it as a company to approach?
- Are you hitting your ethnic minority and gender recruitment targets?

Job descriptions, appraisals and performance management

Job descriptions can easily limit the potential for flexibility if they are rooted in 'line of sight' assumptions about the work process. Similarly, the assumptions that lie behind appraisal criteria should be examined to ensure that there are no hidden biases against flexible working or employees who choose to work in a non-standard manner.

There is also a case for including feedback to the manager on how he or she has supported work-life balance, from direct reports as part of their formal appraisal meetings.

Questions HR could ask itself about these areas include:

- Do job descriptions focus on outputs or inputs?
- Could they be interpreted as restricting flexible working?
- Are appraisals based on performance, or presenteeism
- Do part-timers and remote workers receive as much coaching as full-time, centrally-located employees?

Overtime

The relationship between extra hours worked, the reward for doing so, and the impact on stress levels, motivation and productivity is complex, to say the least. However, a study by the University of Nijmegen[28] sheds some light on the interactions. It seems that people are more tolerant of working extra hours if they:

- choose to do so, rather than feel required or pressured to

- have a positive view of the effort/reward equation (reward need not be money, of course; it could be increased chance of promotion, opportunities to learn, or a challenge they enjoy).

The killer combination is a feeling of being pressured to do the extra work and a negative view of the personal reward for complying. This is associated with cynicism, emotional exhaustion, stress and resentment at the intrusion into home life.

Key questions to ask with regard to overtime practice include:

- Is working over and above contracted hours (whether paid or unpaid) the only way the job can be done as it is presently structured?

- Do employees feel positive or negative about overtime (ie do they see it as an opportunity or a burden)?

- Do all employees in the same team have to work the overtime hours?

- How much freedom do employees have to decide when they work the overtime (ie can they fit it around their own circumstances)?

- Does the overtime requirement effectively rule out this job for people with family or other caring responsibilities?

Anecdotal evidence suggests that re-evaluating overtime practice in the light of work-life balance requirements leads to a reduction in the need for overtime. In part, this may be because people who have become used to the extra income from overtime have a tendency to make sure that a certain quantity of tasks get left over each day or week; in part, it may also be that tasks are examined more closely to see if they need to be done at all.

Health and safety

- Is your health and safety policy about preventing accidents/harm or about promoting well-being?

- Does it include guidance on working at home? Are employees generally aware of it?

A work-life-balance-oriented HR systems audit does more than identify barriers to the implementation of work-life policies. If conducted openly, with input from employees at all levels, it sends a powerful message to them that the organisation is serious about changing the working culture.

TECHNOLOGY

In many ways, the technology is the easy bit. It doesn't cost a great deal to enable an employee to hook up at home, or wherever he or she happens to be. Laptop computers, docking stations and 'follow me' telephony – in theory at least – make location almost irrelevant in terms of getting work done.

A US study[29] of 250 companies with strong work-family policies found that nearly two-thirds believed the impact of technology to have had a mostly positive effect on employees' work-family life concerns. In particular, they are able to work from home when convenient and still access most of the information they need. However, the downside is that they can never 'log off' – in some cases not even on holiday. One in six companies expected employees to check e-mails after hours.

It may be equally important to consider how technology can support the work-life balance of employees who work all or most of their time on company premises. Small investments in extra equipment, for example, can have a major impact on a workgroup's ability to take temporary excess workload off a colleague. Investment in project management software enabled one team to prioritise work so much more effectively that they were able to reduce the number of times they needed to work more than an hour over contracted hours from an average of three to four times a week to once every two weeks. Route planning software, accessible at home, enabled another company's service engineers to start and end each day's work from home, rather than from a central location where work was doled out. The employees saved on commuting time and the company gained an extra four customer-facing hours a week per person.

THE LEGAL DIMENSION

All of the work-life balance policies and practices described so far are affected in some manner by legislation and HR will need to obtain professional legal advice. The legislation is changing constantly, with greater and greater emphasis being placed on statutory requirement rather than business benefit. Chapter 2, contributed by employment law specialists Peninsula, provides an overview of both the current situation and the likely legislative environment in the next few years.

It is noticeable that from a legislative point of view, women currently appear to have stronger rights than men in terms of flexible working – for example, an employer may in some circumstances be held to have discriminated unlawfully if he or she refuses to allow reduced hours to a woman returning from maternity leave. Parents of young children also seem to have stronger rights than non-parents or parents with teenagers (which some people would say is the age they are most demanding!). However, the broader pattern appears to be that legislation for specific groups is typically the thin end of the wedge.

A number of the HR directors we interviewed in our research had taken the view – and had convinced their top teams – that it was beneficial always to be at least a little ahead of the legislation. Not only does this avoid nasty surprises when laws come into effect, but it pays dividends in terms of goodwill with existing and potential employees.

A POLICY TO REINFORCE POLICY

As we've reflected several times in different ways already in this book, having policies does not mean that people will make use of them; people also need to believe that doing so will not have overt or hidden impacts upon them. Take the following cases:

> *I agonised all day about whether to keep a long-standing promise to my wife to attend her confirmation or to go to a sudden meeting demanded by a client across the country for the next*

evening. In the end I told my boss, who was also going to the meeting, that I had to give priority to my wife. From that day on I never worked on that account again, and I'm sure it's affected my career prospects with this company.

My boss had arranged a team-building event one weekend. That same Saturday my daughter was performing her first public concert. I said there was no way I'd miss that, so the team would have to do without me. Six weeks later there was a slice of redundancies. I can't prove that's why I was selected to go – but I'm pretty sure.

I was told on the first day I joined this company that people were judged on the basis of their 'commitment'. Essentially, this meant that you were never allowed to say no to an assignment on personal grounds. . .

When I went on holiday this year, my new boss asked me to take a laptop and mobile telephone. I refused and he made it clear I had a black mark against me.

No matter what the policy says, insidious hints by managers will constrain people's actual behaviour – unless there are effective sanctions and feedback systems. Processes to support the policies should take this into account. Among possible approaches are:

- including questions on work-life balance issues and managers' behaviour with regard to work-life balance in regular employee surveys or 180-degree feedback

- providing an appeals system to which employees can take perceived breaches of the policy – in many cases it may be possible to achieve this simply by expanding the appeals processes for flexible working

- ensuring that managers whose direct reports consistently demonstrate high stress levels are penalised: the more obvious the penalty – for example, being passed over for promotion – the more effective the stick

- having a senior management champion who not only promotes work-life balance but actively seeks out examples of good and bad supportive behaviour by managers

- taking a searching look at HR's own example and attitudes. The IES study found that nearly one in four HR professionals believed it was not the employers' responsibility to help people balance their work with other aspects of their lives. In sharing our research with groups of HR professionals, one of the most common comments they have made has been that senior people in HR often exemplify the worst practices in terms of both demonstrating balance in their own lives and in the demands they make of their HR direct reports. (We have also, to be fair, encountered a good many examples of HR managers and HR directors who are excellent examples of good practice!)

- being prepared to open up the difficult and controversial issues for open dialogue. We found that HR functions are often expected to 'keep the lid on' the most serious of work-life balance issues where the solutions are not obvious. For example, a large international financial services company has developed over decades a culture of very long working hours. It accepts that there will be constant turnover of talented people who want to place other aspects of their lives first after several years of working in this intensive mode. What it is finding difficult to manage is a rising proportion of employees who say they want to stay with the firm but do not want to work excessive hours. Because it does not know how to deal with this issue, it is fighting a constant rearguard action to keep it off the agenda. A more positive approach might be to look for ways to create different career paths and reward packages for those who want to give their whole lives to the organisation and those who do not.

TACKLING THE TABOOS

Most organisations have some such taboos; some have a lot. Three of the subjects most commonly avoided are the issues of career-life balance, stress and thinking time.

Career-life balance: when does your company demand most from its employees?

The first of these taboo topics relating to work-life balance concerns how the organisation matches its pattern of demand from employees to the pattern of demand in the rest of an employee's life. The trend to have children later – typically in a couple's late twenties and early thirties – has created an increasingly severe timing clash (see Figure 5 below). Just at the time when people should be spending more time with their spouse and young children, organisations typically look to them to show high commitment and dedication to work. This is the career cusp, where the high flyers are sorted from the also-rans, so pressure to perform is high.

Stress

Workplace stress is another of those topics which people – including HR professionals – prefer to avoid. Yet the impact of stress on individuals, their colleagues and the organisation may be very damaging – and costly to the organisation, if employees crack up and sue for compensation. Time and again, in the research for this book, we have found that the trigger for top management commitment to work-life balance has been the shock of a colleague suffering a mental breakdown or fatal heart attack.

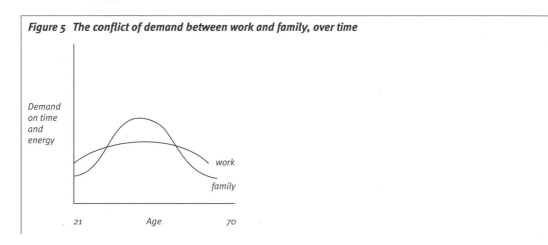

Figure 5 The conflict of demand between work and family, over time

Having clear, unequivocal guidelines and expectations about unacceptable stress at work – how to recognise it, how to raise the issue formally, and how to deal with it – is essential in managing work-life balance, and a very sensible precaution for the organisation generally. An effective stress policy includes resources for people to obtain professional advice, a process for monitoring stress levels and a means of distinguishing the short-term stress that accompanies occasional crises from the grinding long-term stress that causes the most damage. Our survey of UK companies, however, found that although 85 per cent consider stress an important issue, only 31 per cent had policies about it, and 20 per cent measured whether those policies had any impact.

CASE STUDY

How NASA helps employees manage stress

NASA began to take issues of workplace stress more seriously in 1998, when it conducted a swathe of focus groups among employees up to middle management across all its sites and functions. Over 200 recommendations on 30 main areas of concern were made, and NASA has since been working its way through them.

A key element in NASA's stress management strategy is its Employee Assistance Program, which is open both to employees and to their families. It has invested heavily in providing continuous training for EAP personnel; its investment in providing critical-incident stress management training for counsellors helped many employees cope with the loss of space shuttle *Columbia*. Its intranet includes online training programmes for supervisors in how to recognise the symptoms of stress, and for employees in general on how to alleviate stress in their own lives. Over the first month, this site received more than 40,000 hits.

For employees who are reticent to approach the EAP staff directly, NASA provides an anonymous self-assessment questionnaire. Stress management, says its chief health and medical officer Richard Williams, is 'an integral part of achieving a work-life balance essential to health and safety'.

HR has at least a moral responsibility to ensure that employees are not trapped in jobs which generate unreasonable, continuing levels of stress. Although there is also a responsibility on individuals to extract themselves from such situations, people are often unable to do so without help. Gaining clarity about stress levels should be an automatic function of regular appraisals and/or of routine team meetings. HR should educate managers on the importance of avoiding excessive, sustained stress on their teams, provide them with the tools and techniques to help them do so, and ensure that managers who do create excessive stress are punished rather than rewarded.

HR's responsibility extends to ensuring that people are in the right jobs. A leader by Graham Searjeant, financial editor of the *Times*, puts the point passionately:

A job where you cannot win, cannot achieve and therefore cannot be satisfied, is doubly stressful. Designing jobs wrongly, leaving the wrong people in them and giving no achievable targets, are all signs of bad management. If anyone has to work long hours routinely, then either the job, or less often, the person, is wrong. An employee should not need to crack up before this is realised.[30]

A regular survey by the HR Professionals Panel,[31] run by market research organisation ORC International, suggests that one in three large employers provides some form of stress-awareness training and about the same proportion carries out surveys to assess the level of stress employees are feeling. About half offer some form of stress counselling. Some companies also offer back and shoulder massages at workstations, while others provide such facilities in designated areas of the building. US computer games developer Electronic Arts brings in a masseuse once a week, and employees are informed of her arrival and availability via e-mail. A half-hour session can be booked via e-mail or by phoning in advance of her arrival.

Recognising the impact that stress and stress related illness has on UK companies, a team of academics from the University of Manchester established Robertson Cooper Ltd (RCL) with the ultimate aim of teaching organisations and employees how to limit and manage stress through stress awareness training and stress audits. A major project undertaken by the company has been a stress audit of the UK Treasury, where stress levels among top-ranking employees are traditionally high. After hearing employees' main concerns through a confidential telephone helpline, RCL identified a number of changes that would reduce stress levels. The changes concentrated on a reduction in working hours and a move towards a more rewarding and praising management culture.[32]

THE WACKY SIDE OF STRESS MANAGEMENT

Approaches taken by US companies[33] include:

- aromatherapy candles in conference rooms
- hug therapy
- replacing Muzak with more soothing music
- white flags to wave during frustrating sales calls
- delivering fresh flowers to employees' desks
- having an office dog to romp with (one, called Merlin, has his own business card with the title 'director of stress management')
- meditation rooms.

Although an initial reaction to such activities might be to dismiss them as mere gimmickry, there is a serious point to be made. Why do we design offices to be so different from homes? Do we want employees to feel more at home in the office? There is at least anecdotal evidence that importing a little bit of home into the office helps to relax people. (Importing a bit of the office into the home is already a reality for all those who do some work from home.)

The discussion about the relationship between work and play (see Chapter 5) is also relevant here.

Thinking time

Over the past five years, I have conducted a simple experiment with managers and other employees from thousands of companies. The topic is: *Where do you find time for deep thinking?* With very few exceptions, people do almost no real thinking at work; they are in reaction mode most of the time. Their real thinking time – when they are at their most creative – occurs when they are away from their workplace. Typically this is on the train, in the bath, out jogging or walking the dog, doing the ironing, driving, or when they finally lie down to sleep. The one common exception to this role is when they are engaged in a mentoring or coaching session, where they are able to focus fully and creatively on one issue.

The working culture in most knowledge-based businesses has been likened to the spine. What makes the spine – a marvellous piece of natural engineering – able to fulfil its function is firstly, the fact that it is made up of lots of small pieces, so it can move in many directions; and secondly, that these pieces are cushioned with cartilage (otherwise they would grind against each other and seize up). The typical business culture is like a spine without cartilage. People rush from one meeting to another, with half-finished agendas and minimum time to think about what has been concluded in the meeting just gone, or what they want to achieve in the meeting they are just entering. Then they sort out all this jumble at the end of the day, or the next morning. Radical change can be achieved by teaching people to build in thinking time between meetings and persuading senior managers to both demonstrate good practice and insist that their direct reports follow suit.

The benefits of such an approach are:

- People are less likely to take all their problems home with them.
- Meetings tend to be shorter, more efficient and have clearer outcomes and accountabilities.
- Employees feel less stressed.
- People actually start to enjoy the meetings they go to.
- You will hear fewer complaints about 'having to attend all these bloody meetings'!

MEASURING THE IMPACT OF WORK-LIFE POLICIES AND PROCESSES

Less than half of companies with flexible working programmes and policies measure their impact.[34] Our research suggests that measurement needs to take place at three levels:

- impact on employees
- impact on the organisation
- impact on the community.

Key issues to explore under impact on employees include:

- What proportion of employees have taken up flexible options?
- What proportion would have liked to but felt inhibited from doing so?

- What proportion of employees feel reasonably satisfied about their work-life balance?
- What proportion feel the company is doing all it can to help them resolve work/non-work conflict?
- What specifically has changed for them (eg stress levels, ability to do things they otherwise would not have been able to, less guilt)?
- How has their overall attitude to the company changed?

Key issues for the company might include:

- What is the retention level among employees working flexibly versus others?
- Does flexible working contribute to greater productivity? Employee motivation and commitment? Product or service quality?
- Has our reputation as an employer of choice been improved (or maintained, if it is already strong)?
- Can we see evidence of greater creativity and innovation as a result of work-life balance policies and practices?
- How do line managers feel about supervising employees working flexibly?
- Has the company been able to save money on premises?
- Has the company made progress against diversity targets through having a wider pool of people working different patterns to call upon?

Key issues with regard to the community include:

- Do our employees feel more able to contribute time to community activities?
- Is the company well regarded within the local community?
- Has the company been able to give employment to people who would otherwise have been marginalised because they cannot work 'normal' hours?

As with any other kind of change process, it is important to design the measurement process and the questions to be asked before implementing any work-life balance initiatives. That way it is easier to monitor progress and to present a more convincing case to the various sceptical audiences HR may be obliged to address.

THE PUBLIC/PRIVATE SECTOR SPLIT

In this very broad-ranging review of work-life policy and implementation processes we have drawn from a wide spectrum of organisations, both public and private. It is clear, however, that the public sector in the UK is much more advanced in terms of both policy and practice than the private, as Table 4 indicates. Moreover, benchmarking between organisations, where it occurs, tends mostly to stick within sectoral boundaries. There is, I believe, a strong case for far more good practice exchange not just amongst the HR professionals but at all levels of organisations. (There is a lot more credibility for junior managers in the experiences of someone like themselves than in the exhortations of HR professionals.)

Table 4 Work-life balance comparisons between public and private organisations

Actions/ policies/achievements	Public sector	Private sector
Work-life balance recognised and formal policies in place	71%	22%
HR managers and staff given work-life balance education	87%	39%
Success of work-life balance policies formally measured	95%	50%
Job-sharing offered	92%	27%
On-site crèche or childcare service available	27%	3%
Support for employees caring for elderly relatives or children with special needs	76%	33%
More than three-quarters of mothers returning after maternity leave	75%	50%

Source: CCH Flexible working briefing Issue No 93
Reproduced with kind permission of the Human Resources Centre at Croner Publishing

For the private sector, in particular, the achievements of the public sector should provide an excellent steer on what can be achieved. What would be the cost benefit to private sector employers if they were, for example, to match the public sector figures on mothers returning after maternity leave? Of course, policies and procedures need to be adapted, but there is more than enough good practice to beg, borrow or steal to make the task of introducing a comprehensive portfolio of work-life balance policies a relatively straightforward task.

REFERENCES AND READING

1 KODZ J. (2002) 'Bridging the work-life balance take-up gap'. *In Brief : the Institute for Employment Studies Newsletter.* Available at: http://www.employment-studies.co.uk [Accessed 10 July 2003]

2 CHRISTENSEN P. M. (1997) 'Toward a comprehensive work-life strategy', in S. Parasuraman and Greenhaus, J. H. (eds.), *Integrating Work and Family: Challenges and Choices for Changing World.* Westport, CT, Quorum.

3 DEPARTMENT OF TRADE AND INDUSTRY (2003) *Flexible Working: The Business Case – 50 Success Stories.* London, Department of Trade and Industry. Available at: http://www.dti.gov.uk/work-lifebalance/publications.html [Accessed 10 July 2003]

4 See reference no. 35 below.

5 *Precor Case Sudy,* (1999), [Pullman, WA], Washington State University Cooperative Extension Energy Program. Available at: http://www.commuterchallenge.org [Accessed 10 July 2003]

6 WAKEFIELD METROPOLITAN DISTRICT COUNCIL (No date) *Term-time Working.* Wakefield, Wakefield Metropolitan District Council. Available at: http://wakefield.gov.uk [Accessed 10 July 2003]

7 WINN S. (2003) 'Winding down'. *Human Resources.* June. pp42–45.

8 BALL S. (2003) 'Into extra time'. *People Management*. Vol. 9, 11. pp36–37,39.

9 BUSINESS IN THE COMMUNITY *and* NATIONAL CENTRE FOR VOLUNTEERING (2003) *Time-off Policies: Manager' Briefing*. London, Business in the Community. Available at: http://www2.bitc.org.uk [Accessed 10 July 2003]

10 BUSINESS IN THE COMMUNITY *and* NATIONAL CENTRE FOR VOLUNTEERING (2003) *Time-off Policies: Manager' Briefing*. London, Business in the Community. Available at: http://www2.bitc.org.uk [Accessed 10 July 2003]

11 WORK FOUNDATION (2002) *Response to the consultation on the European Commission Proposal for a Directive on the Working Conditions of Temporary (Agency) Workers*. London, Work Foundation. Available at: http://www.workfoundation.com [Accessed 10 July 2003]

12 BATES P. *and* HUWS U. (2002) *Modelling E-work in Europe: Estimates, Models and Forecasts from the Emergence Project'*. IES Report, No 388. Brighton, Institute for Employment Studies.

12a JOLLY, R (No date) *Roam Alone: The New Boundaries of E-mobility*. Available at: http;//www.stokesjolly.com/RoamAlone.doc [Accessed 10 July 2003]

13 TOSHIBA *and* [HOP ASSOCIATES] (2002) *The Complete Guide to Flexible Working*. Cambridge, Hop Associates.

14 McCALL A. (ed.) (2003) '100 best companies to work for 2003'. *Sunday Times Supplement*. 2 March. Online version available at: http://www.timesonline.co.uk/section/0,,2096,00.html

15 BOZTAS S. (2003) 'The flexible firm wins on all fronts' in A. McCALL (ed.), '100 best companies to work for 2003'. *Sunday Times Supplement*. 2 March. Available at: http://www.timesonline.co.uk/article/0,,2096-587260,00.html

16 HOPKINSON, P., JAMES, P *and* MARUYAMA, T. (2002) *Teleworking at BT; The Economic, Environmental and Social Impacts of its Workabout Scheme. Report on Survey Results*. Bradford, University of Bradford in association with SustainIT.

17 CLUTTERBUCK D. *and* PAGE S. (2002) *Building a strategy for remote communications*. London, Melcrum.

18 STROH L. K., BRETT J *and* REILLY A. H. (1992) 'All the right stuff: a comparison of female and male managers' career progression' . *Journal of Applied Psychology*. Vol. 77, 3. pp251–260.

19 CRANET (2000) *Survey on International Strategic Human Resource Management*. Bedfordshire, Cranfield School of Management.

20 UNITED STATES OFFICE OF PERSONNEL MANAGEMENT (2001) *Telework Works: A Compendium of Success Stories. Report of a Special Study*. Washington, United States Office of Personnel Management. Available at: http://www.opm.gov/studies/FINAL-TELEWRK.htm

21 'Innovative people solutions – proving work-life balance can work', *Mt Eliza Business Review*, Winter/Spring 2000.

22 METROPOLITAN LIFE INSURANCE COMPANY (2001) *Care Giving Employees Stay in Workforce Twice As Long When Long-term Care Insurance is in Place for Care Recipient*. Westport, CT, Metlife. Available at: http://www.metlife.com/Applications/Corporate/WPS/CDA/PageGenerator/0,1674,P249,00.html

23 COOPER C. Professor, University of Manchester Institute of Science and Technology.

24 OLIVER J. (1998) 'Losing control: our great work/life debate shows how unhappy UK managers really are' . *Management Today*. June. pp 32–36,38.

25 BAILYN L. 'The impact of corporate culture on work-family integration', in Parasuraman and Greenhaus, J. H. (eds.), *Integrating Work and Family: Challenges and Choices for Changing World*. Westport, CT, Quorum.

26 OLIVER J. (1998) ' Losing control: our great work/life debate shows how unhappy UK mangers really are'. *Management Today*. June. pp 32–36, 38

27 DOYLE J. *and REEVES* R. (2001) *The Case for Time Sovereignty*. London, Work Foundation.

28 HULST M. v d *and* GEURTS S. (2001) 'Associations between overtime and psychological health in high and low reward jobs'. *Work and Stress*. Vol. 15, 3. pp227–240.

29 THE CONFERENCE BOARD (1998) *Technology's Effect on Work-life Balance*. Work-Family Round Table, Vol.8 (2).

30 SERGEANT G. (2002) 'Stress is a sure sign of bad management'. *Times*. 13 December. p35.

31 OPINION RESEARCH CORPORATION. (2002) *Wave One: February – March*. London, Opinion Research Corporation. 2002.

32 HAILE D. *Stress Busters Help Ministry Mandarins*. Press release. Available at: http://www.robertsoncooper.com [Accessed 11 July 2003]

33 WORK AND FAMILY NEWSBRIEF (2001). March p2. Available at: www.workfamily.com

34 FLEXECUTIVE (2002) *Work-Life Balance or Career Death? Issues and Paradoxes Facing Marketing and Human Resource Professionals*. London, Flexecutive. Available at: www.flexecutiveclient.co.uk/client/cli_02ij.asp›.

5

The people dimension

Changing the culture is not about systems or technology, although these can be powerful supports for the change process. It is about achieving sustainable changes in attitude and behaviour. From the organisation's perspective, focusing on the people issues in work-life balance is aimed at:

- ensuring that people understand what opportunities for working differently exist

- enabling individuals to take advantage of those opportunities

- ensuring that the provision of work-life balance opportunities contributes to the motivation, commitment and performance of employees

- ensuring that managers support and do not hinder the implementation of work-life policies.

For these to happen across the organisation, three key elements are required:

- credible role models/convincing demonstrations that the new work patterns are viable and beneficial

- information, education to provide people with an understanding of how to go about changing the way things are done, and involvement/participation in designing and implementing the solutions

- training, to give people the competence and confidence to live and work effectively in the new ways.

ROLE MODELS FOR WORK-LIFE BALANCE

For the most part this is a topic for Chapter 6, where we examine how the line manager can contribute to developing and sustaining a culture supportive of work-life balance. However, role models can often be found at any level in organisations. Where the company has a small number of people working flexibly and regards them as an aberration from the norm, relatively little role modelling occurs. The individuals concerned do not publicise what they are doing, for fear that it might jeopardise their status and freedoms. Managers do not refer to them as good examples, for fear they will start a flood of applications for similar working arrangements, and because, as one line manager expressed it, 'We don't want to make them feel special.'

Yet at the practical level, the flexible-working pioneers may be the most powerful ambassadors for work-life balance. Peers may give greater credence to what they say, especially if they are encouraged to give 'warts and all' reports of their experience. And being at the sharp end of the alternative working arrangements, they are able to provide much more practical detail and advice.

HR can help people engage with these experiences in a variety of ways – through video interviews, roadshows, and presenting at team briefings, for example. The more opportunities people have to interact with these exemplars in person, where they can ask questions and evaluate options through discussion and dialogue, the more effective the role modelling process will be.

COMMUNICATION

We asked in our short survey how organisations communicated their work-life balance policies to employees. The most common method by far was through employee handbooks, followed by team briefings. Surprisingly little use was made of employee periodicals or websites. In general, we gained a picture of very muted attempts in most companies to ensure that employees understood either the company's approach to these issues or how they could benefit from them. This is probably why the question *How aware do you think people are of these policies?* drew such a mixed response.

Listen before you tell

One of the strongest lessons learned by the HR professionals we interviewed was the importance of gaining a good, accurate picture of the status quo before launching a work-life balance initiative. A concerted campaign of listening, aimed at developing a deep understanding of the issues, is an essential precursor to action. Without this, it is highly likely that the initiative will be met with cynicism and/or that employees will not take up the options offered. In the latter case, the perceived failure of the programme may be taken by line managers as proof that 'this work-life balance thing doesn't work', and by employees to indicate that the organisation is not really serious about it.

It is important to recognise that people's receptivity – their willingness and ability to listen to and absorb messages – is determined in large part by their previous experience. If an organisation, which has largely ignored work-life balance issues in the past, suddenly starts telling

Table 5 How aware are employees of your work-life policies?

Very aware	3%
Quite aware	26%
Somewhat aware	31%
Not very aware	26%
Very unaware	13%

people how concerned top management is and actively adopts a bundle of work-life balance policies, it should not be surprised if the message falls on deaf ears. A financial services company made this mistake, then compounded it by repeating the message more and more stridently (on the principle that understanding can be achieved by raising the decibel level!). Eventually, several employees decided to take the company at its word and asked for work arrangements that would have been difficult to administer. The company prevaricated, the employees got cold feet about their requests, and the work-life balance initiative dropped dead in its tracks. The subject has now been mentally filed in the 'too difficult to tackle now' box by top management and discussion in formal forums has effectively been squashed.

The listening campaign should take place in a variety of ways, to obtain both qualitative and quantitative data. For quantitative data, the following questionnaire is a good starting point, although you may wish to add some questions specific to your organisation. It is best administered to all employees, but can be used unit by unit.

A QUESTIONNAIRE TO UNDERSTAND THE CURRENT STATE OF WORK-LIFE BALANCE

Each of the following statements should be responded to on a five-point scale, from 1 (strongly agree) to 5 (strongly disagree).

1 It's normal and expected for people here to work long hours.
2 I leave work on time more often than not.
3 My manager is supportive when I have domestic needs to take care of.
4 I often feel I can't cope with my workload.
5 I am often uncertain when I'll be able to finish work for the day.
6 I often have to take work home in the evenings.
7 I often work at the weekends.
8 I am often contacted about work issues out of hours.
9 This organisation is good at ensuring that workloads are appropriate.
10 I feel the organisation genuinely wants people to have a good balance between work and home.
11 When I get home I'm usually too tired to do anything active.
12 There's little time for thinking during working hours.
13 I feel my work is having a negative effect on my health.
14 I feel stressed at work at least twice a week.
15 Some of the stresses of work spill over into home life most weeks.
16 This company puts customer needs before those of employees.
17 Some of the stresses of home life spill into work most weeks.
18 During the past three months I have had to miss at least one event in my personal life to meet a work need.
19 During the past three months I have argued with my spouse or partner as a result of work pressures.
20 I feel guilty about leaving work on time.

---

21 The culture here makes it difficult to put non-work issues ahead of work.

22 You can't advance here without putting in the hours.

23 My manager sets a good example of work-life balance.

24 I think I have a pretty good work-life balance.

25 I could be more productive if I had more choice about where and when I work.

26 I often work more than 48 hours a week.

27 I think my career would suffer if I opted to reduce my standard hours or work from home.

28 I would be unlikely to find a job elsewhere that gave me such a good opportunity to balance work and life outside work.

29 This company puts employee needs above customer needs.

30 My job is too large for one person.

31 This organisation is family-friendly.

32 The company encourages and supports me to undertake community activities.

33 I feel under pressure to say yes when asked to take on additional tasks.

34 Most of the time I look forward to coming to work.

35 I can plan personal or family activities ahead of time without worry that work demands may force me to cancel them.

36 I think top management is committed to the business case for balance between work and home life.

© Clutterbuck Associates 2003

The advantages of the survey route are that it enables HR to assess the scope of problems and to explore the demographics of work-life balance in the organisation. For the latter reason, it is useful to ask also for personal data: gender, race, age, whether the respondent is a parent of young children, or a carer, what location he or she works in, and in what department or function. (It may come as no surprise that HR itself sometimes achieves the worst scores.) It is important that people are assured that the information they provide is confidential (using an external survey specialist may be appropriate), and that managers are assured that the data will not be used to berate them. It may well be apposite, however, to inform managers that the data from this survey will provide a baseline upon which future survey responses will be benchmarked, and that it is the company's intention to demand explanations where poor performance on work-life balance remains poor or deteriorates further.

The data from the survey should be fed back to employees and used as the basis for listening sessions that aim to get underneath the scores. It is particularly helpful to gather specific examples and anecdotes – even if stories have been exaggerated with retelling, they are indicative of the underlying corporate culture. It is tempting to get into solution mode at this point, but that almost always leads to a piecemeal approach to the issues rather than a coherent policy and plan for change. The outcome of the listening campaign should be a deeper understanding of the overt and covert influences that prevent people from establishing an effective work-life balance. In addition, it can be very useful to gain insights into how different demographic segments feel about the issues of most concern to other segments. If young, unmarried people under 25 are likely to resent programmes aimed at parents of young children, then recognising that can make it easier to design initiatives that both groups will perceive as fair.

On the latter point, an Institute for Employment Studies report in 2002[1] generally found that other employees were highly supportive of flexible working for colleagues with family or other caring responsibilities. The study did find a minority of employees, however, who were resentful. One commented:

> *Work-life balance is nearly always interpreted as being about childcare – if you don't have kids, then it is assumed you don't need to work flexibly. We would all like the opportunity to leave early once in a while ... Work-life policies need to be fair and equitable to all.*

In its survey, IES found that 42 per cent of HR professionals believed that policies which help staff balance work and other interests are often unfair to some employees, against 26 per cent of employees. In the same vein, a *Management Today* survey of 500 male managers found that only 7 per cent thought their company did too much to accommodate staff who have families.[2] However, 30 per cent of managers over 45 felt that government policies on work-life balance have gone too far.

Inform and educate – phase 1

The telling part of communication should not begin until the listening campaign is completed. Initially, all that is required is to make it clear what the company intends, and why – ie to state the business case without going into the detail of specific policies. The intention is to raise overall awareness and to stimulate an extensive and constructive debate about how to resolve the issues identified.

Involve and empower

Having raised interest and made people aware of both the company's aspirations with regard to work-life balance and the practical difficulties of achieving those aspirations, HR can begin the process of practical engagement. Through focus groups, team meetings, project groups and other forums, it can pose the key questions:

- What business problems could be alleviated or even solved by more creative approaches to work patterns?
- What changes in policy and practice would contribute to greater work-life balance?
- What ought to change in the organisation culture?
- How can we create a win/win situation for employees, customers and the organisation?

It is permissible and perhaps advisable to place some boundaries around this dialogue. For example:

- Solutions that do not involve extra cost to the company will be given priority – where investment is needed, there should be a demonstrable payback within 12 months.

- Customer service must not be affected adversely.
- Moving problems to someone else's shoulders is not acceptable.

Training a steering group of HR and line employees to act as facilitators for these discussions helps to keep the dialogue solution-focused. It also provides a steady and accurate stream of feedback about implementation issues.

One of several excellent case studies provided by the IES in its survey of how organisations are implementing the Working Time Directive[3] is of Barclays' Technology Services. To raise employee awareness of long hours as an issue, the company used a wide range of one-way media, including e-mail, newsletters, videos and the staff newspaper. It also used lots of opportunities for discussion of the issues, starting with board meetings and working down through team briefings and workshops available to all staff.

Inform and educate – phase 2

There will be a continuing need for information and advice as the initiative progresses. Employees and their managers will want to be kept abreast of the progress of various project groups – it is very easy for them to assume that the topic has gone on the back burner, because they have heard no more about it. Members of the steering group should have the responsibility of reporting back to their areas of the business. Having a website is useful, as long as it is constantly updated; but getting information this way requires people to make the initial effort to access the site. It is usually most effective to have a variety of media with broad messages that signpost to the greater detail that can be found on the website.

Once the company has agreed with top management a detailed work-life balance policy and strategy, the process of information and education enters a new cycle. Now there is real clarity about the direction of the work-life balance initiative, employees will need rapid access to practical guidance such as:

- How do I know what flexible options I am eligible for?
- How do I make the case for a different working arrangement?
- What is expected of me as a manager?
- What tools and techniques are available to help me?
- What other sources of advice, outside the organisation, are available?

Again, a mix of media is likely to be more effective than just one communication channel.

Carry on listening

Because circumstances, both organisational and individual, change constantly, the work-life balance equation is dynamic and must be assessed regularly. We recommend revisiting the initial questionnaire annually and carrying out focus groups across the year with particular segments – for example, junior managers or people over 50. The annual survey provides the benchmark to assess overall progress; the focus groups keep HR in touch with the evolving needs of particular groups of employees.

It also helps to have some form of hotline through which employees can (anonymously, if they wish) raise concerns about how work-life balance policies are being implemented. While it probably will not be used a great deal, it provides a valuable safety valve for issues that are not picked up in the more formal listening processes.

CASE STUDY

Communicating the work-life message to managers and employees

BAA is the owner and operator of seven airports in the UK, including Heathrow and Gatwick. The company employs a total of around 10,000 staff working in a variety of operational and office-based functions. Many staff work shifts.

As a responsible employer committed to sustainable development and providing quality of life, BAA believes it is important that its staff have the ability to balance home and work. The company is in the process of launching enhanced flexible working opportunities and has also been active in promoting to staff the range of support available to help get the work-life balance right.

Its aim is to raise awareness of its staff of the options available to balance work and life, and to ensure that the right processes and services are in place to support the choice.

Flexible working
BAA's flexible working policy extends beyond its statutory obligations and will have been launched to all staff by early summer 2003. The policy has been developed in conjunction with a working group with representation from trade unions and various functions across the business.

A booklet outlining flexible working options is being developed and will be sent to every member of staff at their home address. The literature covers examples of flexible working – for instance, part-time, job-sharing, home-based working – and outlines the process staff and their managers should follow to determine requests for flexible working.

BAA's commitment to provide a working environment that enables staff to give their best as well as ensuring a balance with home life, is highlighted within the booklet. The company makes it clear, however, that requests for flexible working should benefit the business as well as the individual.

Prior to the launch of the booklet – which will be phased across BAA's seven UK airports – BAA's HR department is running a series of focus groups for line managers throughout the company to engage in two-way debate about the implications of work-life balance and flexible working.

The groups are designed to examine BAA's approach and to discuss some of the changes that will need to take place – under such thematic headings as:

- Culture – it's an opportunity, not a problem
- Facilities – office accommodation, IT
- Trust
- Behaviour – managers leading by example.

Outputs from the group are helping to shape the communication of the work-life policies and the supporting internal processes.

A communications plan is being drawn up to promote the policy to staff by using delivery of the booklet to home addresses, the intranet site, staff newsletters and team briefings.

Work-Life Balance Week
Opportunities for flexible working were previewed as part of a week-long Work-Life Balance Week, held at BAA's south-eastern airports during October 2002. Exhibitions highlighted case studies of staff within the company who already use flexible working to help balance home commitments. These included identical twin sisters who job-share at Heathrow.

The Week was designed to be upbeat and interactive. All communication was branded with an established house style used to communicate sustainability issues to staff. Communications included:

- PC desktop messages
- branded e-mails to staff
- intranet features
- posters
- articles in the staff newsletter
- pull-out supplements within staff newsletters.

Highlights of the week were two all-day exhibitions at Heathrow. During the days staff were invited to have free massages, to get their blood pressure and cholesterol checked and to learn more about BAA's approach to work-life balance. Staff canteens supported the event by offering a greater choice of healthy eating menus.

There was also promotion of the services which exist at the airports to help staff be effective at work while meeting the demands of home life. These include:

- an employee assistance programme: independent confidential advice on any topic is available free of charge to all employees, 24 hours a day, initially through a telephone service
- occupational health: confidential advice, including advice on stress management, is available through the occupational health provider for BAA
- Travelcare: this is a charity which, among other things, offers counselling and social work advice to airport staff
- corporate membership of health and leisure clubs.

Branding the change

Any major change initiative requires an identity, if it is to achieve a sustainable prominence in people's minds. Companies which have been particularly successful in raising awareness of work-life balance issues have almost all branded the change in some way. Barclays' Technology

Services branded its development initiative on work-life balance 'the Renaissance Programme'. Lloyd's TSB has branded its overall benefits programme 'FLAVOURS', whereas Nationwide named its flexible working package 'CHOICES'. All such brand names give the impression of progress and choice, in an attempt to make these packages appealing to employees.

TRAINING AND OTHER SUPPORT

Our survey asked companies about how and whether they backed up the policies on work-life balance with processes to help people achieve work-life balance goals. A significant minority of companies (36 per cent) had no process for people to make changes in their working patterns, receive advice on how to make their case, receive advice on how to manage new working patterns, or appeal against refusal. However, 55 per cent had put in place processes to listen to people's concerns about work-life balance issues. Relatively few (43 per cent) offered any training to employees in how to achieve greater work-life balance; or had any process to identify and counsel workaholics.

There seem to be four basic training needs to support a work-life balance programme, as illustrated in Figure 6 below. The *individual employee* will benefit from a programme that offers a mixture of information about how to manage one's own work-life balance and about the opportunities available, and some specific help on the broader issues of personal effectiveness in all parts of one's life. Barclays' Technology Services ran a five-day programme, split into three chunks, covering learning to learn, learning to think, learning to manage your life, learning to lead your life, and learning to live your life.

This is a substantial investment, to say the least, especially as the company has put several hundred people through the programme. Organisations looking to provide a more modest, but nonetheless impactful, training intervention with regard to awareness and general work-life skills may prefer to adopt a course that provides employees with:

- some practical insights into their own current situation (for example, through the *Work-Life Balance Self-Diagnostic*)

- understanding of the pros and cons of various flexible working options

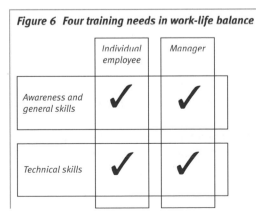

Figure 6 Four training needs in work-life balance

	Individual employee	Manager
Awareness and general skills	✓	✓
Technical skills	✓	✓

- some tools for discussing different options with their partners, colleagues and line manager, and for gaining their support
- tools and techniques for thinking creatively with work colleagues about alternative ways of working.

Participants on these courses might also subsequently be offered individual counselling about work-life issues.

The core work-life programme will be strengthened if it is integrated into a wider programme of development from which people can select as they need and as they agree with their manager. Among relevant topics would be:

- time management
- personal effectiveness
- decision-making
- effectiveness in meetings.

... and perhaps some topics outside the strict work domain, such as parenting skills.

Employees who will be taking on flexible working options may require specific training to prepare them. Home-workers, for example, will need to be taken through:

- the pros and cons of working remotely
- how to organise their time
- how to cope with technical failures (they may need to have to do minor fixes themselves)
- health, safety and legal issues
- how to maintain contact with their manager and work colleagues.

Managers may need separate general training in how to:

- develop a supportive climate for work-life balance
- engage the team in designing smarter work arrangements
- feel comfortable with managing remote employees or virtual teams.

At a technical level, they may need to learn more robust project management and motivational skills appropriate to a different working environment.

REFERENCES AND READING

1 KODZ J., HARPER H. *and* DENCH S. (2002) *Work-Life Balance: Beyond the Rhetoric*. Report 384. Brighton, Institute for Employment Studies.

2 GWYTHER M. (2003) *Working Dads Who Want it All. Management Today*, April; pp44–53.

3 KODZ J., KERSLEY B., STREBLER M. T. *and* O'REGAN, S. (1998) *Breaking the Long Hours Culture*. Brighton, Institute for Employment Studies.

6

The role of the line manager

The third leg of the work-life balance stool is the line manager. He or she holds the key to empowering people to take practical steps to improve their work-life balance.

The line manager is in an invidious position. He or she is faced with demands both from above for greater productivity and from below to try to accommodate demands from direct reports that may conflict with that goal. At the same time, he or she has to ensure that the company adheres to a wide swathe of regulations and laws, including those on working time and flexible working. It is not surprising that many complain of being pulled in several directions. Commented one harassed manager:

The main impacts of our work-life balance initiative on me have been to increase my workload, because of the additional administration, and to make it more difficult to meet my production targets. As a result, my bonus this year is going to be smaller – and I'm the one with increased stress!

He has a point. Without supportive and confident line managers, it will not be possible to make a work-life balance initiative stick. Yet some companies approach the issues in a way that makes line managers feel as if they are the villains of the piece, rather than just another set of victims. A more productive approach views the line manager as potentially the most powerful ally in bringing about a culture change with regard to work-life balance. Placing the priority on resolving the issues for managers ahead of other groups makes sound practical sense, because line managers have the power to either put real momentum behind the culture change or stop it dead.

In Chapter 5 we noted the use of listening to groups to understand the kind of issues various employees faced. Managers, either as a whole or by level in the organisation, are a key group with whom to conduct such research. More than anyone else they are likely to have an overview of some of the causes of excessive hours and family-unfriendly working arrangements.

They may also be the audience most resistant to change, because they have most to lose. The move to a culture supportive of work-life balance can appear highly threatening if it means learning new skills and/or exposing old weaknesses. Managing by line of sight, on inputs, is relatively easy and comfortable. Managing remote employees and employees who may work very different hours from the manager's requires new skills. So does managing performance by focusing primarily on outputs. Steven Poelmans at IESE, the business school in Barcelona, points out that many managers are under intense pressure to provide better work-life balance for others while having very little control over workload and work arrangements themselves.

The stark reality is that many managers live a fiction of being in control of what happens in their departments. This fiction is encouraged from above, by managers who share the fear of being found out! Allowing greater flexibility and being measured on aggregated results of a team who make decisions for themselves and may only rarely be present in person requires moving well beyond these managers' comfort zones.

In supporting the line manager, the HR function needs to recognise that there are at least four levels of response they may have to deal with, each of which is demanding in its own way.

Resistance

Resistance is inevitable in those managers who feel most under threat. The first step is to recognise that their fears are, in their eyes at least, well-founded. Says Pauline Henderson, of the Department for Trade and Industry's Work-Life Balance Team:

It's a big tension for managers – being afraid of implementing work-life balance policy – because decisions might come back and haunt them for inconsistency. They simply aren't sure how to make it work. They are afraid to say no and afraid to say yes, because that might make it more difficult to say no to the next person.

Other factors which managers identify as contributing to their resistance include perceived lack of support from their own managers, lack of support from HR and lack of information.

The solutions to resistance lie in:

- patient explanation of the personal and business benefits
- patient explanation *and demonstration* of the benefits to their department and team
- providing practical and relevant examples of solutions other managers have tried successfully – especially if they are presented by peers they regard as credible.

Patient presentation of the business case will be needed over some time and, perhaps more importantly, presentation of the benefits to the line manager himself or herself. If the managers can be won over, they may become the champions of work-life balance – but they need to be wooed! It will be necessary to demonstrate to them that flexible working is practical in their departments and to convince them of the value of limited experimentation. As long as there is safe ground to which they can retreat, most sceptical managers will be prepared to try a limited amount of new working. When Peter Ambrose, HR manager of P&O Ferries, was faced with reluctance by line managers to accommodate employees' requests for different working schedules, he made it clear that the first thing they had to do was forget the past. Starting with a clean slate, assuming that there was no former practice, stimulated creative and accepting approaches. (See the case study, pages 145–146.)

It will also be necessary, as mentioned in Chapter 5, to provide the information and training they need to feel confident in fulfilling their responsibilities with regard to managing work-life balance issues. The most common reason given by managers for resisting work-life balance issues is lack of confidence in their own ability to make them work.

It may also be appropriate to invite them to work-life briefings with their spouses. This greatly increases the chances that the issues will be discussed at home and brings a little (or perhaps a lot of) extra pressure to bear!

If persuasion doesn't work, there is always coercion. The problem with coercion, of course, is that it can sometimes lead people simply to dig their heels in. However, the organisation must, at a minimum, comply with the law, and managers who obstruct the implementation of policy will need to be dealt with firmly.

Feedback from employee surveys (as discussed in Chapter 5) can be helpful in distinguishing those managers who are making genuine efforts from those who are fighting a rearguard action. The more HR can use feedback to demonstrate to managers that they are affecting the performance of their team, the easier it will be to bring the latter on-side. In one case, a line manager insisted that the work his team did could not possibly be reorganised to make it possible for people to work variable hours. He felt that he was vindicated by the fact that his team was one of the few that consistently exceeded its targets. However, HR was able to point out that he also had the highest staff turnover and that the cost of replacing staff actually put his team at the lower end of profit contribution. Once he took the message on board, this manager began to listen to his team and set himself the triple goals of maintaining performance against production targets, getting into the top quartile of productivity and reducing staff turnover. This inevitably led to some experimentation with flexible working. After a few false starts, the results were more than enough for him to feel justified in taking more steps towards supporting work-life balance policies.

Such feedback is not the norm in most organisations, however. In our survey, only 19 per cent of organisations included work-life balance issues (how the manager established or supported work-life balance in the team) in the appraisal process. If what doesn't get measured doesn't get done, no wonder work-life balance is not a priority issue.

Compliance

In many ways *compliance* is a more difficult barrier to culture change than resistance. With resistance it is possible to have open discussion, to recognise concerns and to attempt to meet them half-way. Compliance blocks discussion – 'I'm doing what you want, so what's to talk about?' – and breeds a rule-book mentality on all sides. Employees recognise quickly when flexibility is granted to them on sufferance only.

Unfortunately, compliance is a frequent outcome of coercion, so HR must take great care not to alienate line managers by the way it introduces work-life balance initiatives. There is a subtle but important distinction between *reluctant compliance* and *exploratory compliance*. Reluctant compliance is simply resistance taken to a less overt level. With exploratory compliance, managers agree to take a neutral stance and to participate in experiments aimed at assessing how different work patterns actually turn out. Engaging managers in the process of experimentation, both design and implementation, provides a safe ground for them to step onto. Many of the companies we encountered in our research reported that this tentative step was enough in most cases to overcome the most serious resistance.

Again, employee feedback can be useful in getting below the surface of what is happening on the ground, but more may be needed. HR needs to continue the dialogue with line managers, attempting to understand their lack of enthusiasm as a first step to winning them over.

Enablement

Enablement is essentially a shift in attitude from caution to wanting to make it work. The manager treats work-life balance like any other project, pushing changes through and responding positively to people's requests by seeking to find ways to meet their needs without negative effects on the customer, the business or their colleagues. The control, however, still rests almost entirely with the manager, who gives permission on a case by case basis. Such managers will often take genuine risks in the cause of determining whether new working patterns are viable. They are relatively patient in waiting for results, and they encourage discussion of work-life balance issues within the team.

Empowerment

Some line managers are prepared to go that step further. Instead of making decisions for the team, they let the team take the authority to make its own decisions about how, when and where the work should be done, within clear boundaries. These managers are typically amongst those who have given most thought to their own work-life balance and who provide good role models.

Understanding where various groups of line managers are on this spectrum enables HR to develop and enact a detailed plan of campaign. If, as is often the case, there are a number of different segments of the management population, each at different levels of engagement with work-life balance, HR needs to address them separately. Wherever possible, it should try to use the enthusiasts to infect the cynics.

Expecting a rapid evolution through these attitudinal stages is not reasonable in most cases. But having a plan that establishes the intended journey gives HR clarity of goals and gives those line managers who want to move faster than their colleagues a degree of freedom to do so. It is these pioneers who will often be the primary drivers of culture change.

Whatever attitudinal stage they are starting at, managers need to feel confident that they understand the business case and the rules about when they should say no or yes to employees' requests for flexible working. Lack of knowledge by line managers appears to be one of the most common problems in meeting employees' needs. It may be appropriate to take many of the decisions out of the line manager's hands altogether. Research by the Institute for Employment Studies[1] found that take-up of flexible working arrangements was higher when managers had no discretion over eligibility.

The new legislation giving employees the right to ask for changes in their working times places the line manager in a difficult position. Firstly, he or she must provide considered, reasonable reasons for turning down a request (and it helps, in terms of consistency and transparency, to give considered reasonable reasons for accepting a request, too). Secondly, he or she must be ready to cope with arguments of the 'If it was OK for her, why isn't it OK for me?' variety.

Other problems relate to having to make judgements that may be outside their skills set. For example, how does a manager seek to prove how accurate his or her opinion is about whether someone has the self-discipline to work from home, or whether an individual is sufficiently trustworthy to set his or her own hours? How does the manager establish equitably how much work should be done in a three-day week compared with a five-day week? (Assessing what makes up a reasonable workload is very difficult, and HR often struggles to get the balance right for its own staff!) And if there is a limited amount of work that can be done flexibly, how should it be divided amongst the team? Is it fair that it should all go to one individual who has young children? Practical support, ranging from data on a website to a hotline to call for specific advice, is essential if managers are not to feel abandoned by HR.

To bring about any kind of meaningful culture change, line managers need to become comfortable with being positive role models for work-life balance and with some substantial changes in leadership style.

THE LINE MANAGER AS ROLE MODEL

The line manager's influence over the work-life choices made by direct reports lies partly in the decisions he or she makes about how and how much people work, and partly in the example he or she sets. An Institute for Employment Studies report[2] found that managers are substantially less likely than other employees to take up work-life balance options and less likely to leave on time for family commitments.

Consider the following negative examples:

- 'If your manager is on vacation and e-mailing people daily, that sets a terrible precedent for other people at the company.'[3]

- 'They play car park "chicken" at this company. The managers race to get here early enough in the morning to be sure they park close to the building entrance. That way everyone sees they were first in. Then they watch the car park at night to see when the managing director leaves. As soon as he goes, so do they.'

- 'Whenever I complain about my workload, my manager points to his own in-tray. I guess I'm lucky he doesn't have the time to think about what more he could delegate to me from that pile!'

- 'My manager sent me 23 e-mails on Boxing Day. I don't know how many he sent to other people. Thank goodness the office was closed.'

- 'What does it say when a manager leaves early but takes a briefcase of work with him?' (A colleague of mine always used a large cardboard box because he couldn't get everything in a briefcase!)

- 'My boss couldn't understand why I didn't want to take my computer on holiday with me.'

To some extent, these managers are victims as much as culprits. They are reacting to the examples set for them by yet more senior managers. Our survey found that only 28 per cent of HR respondents thought their top managers provided a good role model in terms of how they managed work-life balance issues. A US writer on work-life balance issues, Gary Powell, summarises the problem thus:

> *Corporations tend to be run by workaholic top executives who strive for mastery and control in their lives and find they are better able to control what's going on at work than at home. They tend to avoid intimacy in their relationships with others and are more than willing to sacrifice family and outside interests whenever business needs call, however minor these may be. These executives in turn set the standard by which managers who are earlier in their careers are judged . . . lower-level managers are expected to mimic top executives in their unwavering and absolute devotion to work . . . A manager who expresses an interest in a work-family program is doing the equivalent of committing career suicide.*

This may seem a trifle extreme, especially as there are also many examples of top managers who do offer a positive example. One of the common complaints I hear from HR directors is that the people who would make the best leaders are often those who are not prepared to make the personal sacrifices to reach the top. If this is true, then those who select for the top jobs are fishing from a relatively small pool of talent which is likely to be biased towards those who will not make good role models for work-life balance.

A contrary view is expressed by Winston Fletcher in his book *Beating the 24/7*,[4] who found 16 business leaders all of whom claimed to have achieved a good balance between time spent at work and time spent with their families, with friends and pursuing their leisure interests. While none found it easy, and all suffered from the intrusion of work into their weekends, all perceived work-life balance as critically important and preached that message to their line managers and employees. One of the common factors, in most of the organisations we interviewed or found as case studies elsewhere, which have made a significant change in culture with regard to work-life balance, is that top management has taken the issue seriously. The top managers have reiterated the work-life balance message and attempted – even if not always successfully – to put that message into effect in their own lives.

For example, SAP UK and Ireland launched an internal marketing campaign named 'Your SAP' in 2002, in which both managers and employees were filmed talking about how work-life balance initiatives have affected them. The video was then shown to employees, who embraced the success stories of their managers and colleagues alike, and became more aware of how work-life balance could impact on their lives. At BT, the importance of role models for work-life balance is recognised at all levels, and the company intranet site presents profiles of both managers and employees who have a good work-life balance. Similarly, Nationwide has profiled managers and employees in its internal magazine, presented on the company intranet site. During its Work-Life Balance Week, quotes from executive directors appeared on the site to show employees how work-life balance could benefit them.

At Barclays' Technology Management, for example, an important factor in changing the work-life culture was the impact of top management's telling others to go home and taking their own medicine.

It's one thing to say that good leadership is not working 15 hours a day, but another to demonstrate it in practice. Employees often have an illogical but powerful dual image of top management. On the one hand, they may see them as overpaid 'fat cats'; on the other, they expect the demands of a top management job to require very long working hours. It is a sad reflection of the ineffectiveness of communication between the top of an organisation and the employees that such contradictory images persist. Talking about their own struggle to achieve work-life balance lends credibility to both the top managers as individuals and to the work-life balance message. It also brings home the issues to top management in a way no amount of paper-based or electronic reports can. The key, once again, is for HR to encourage and make arrangements for top managers to sit down and talk these issues through with employees.

In spite of good intentions from the top, however, in our survey only one company in four actively encouraged line managers to set a personal example of good work-life balance. Yet there are managers who present themselves as very positive role models for work-life balance. For example:

- 'My manager works late at least two evenings a week, sometimes up to eight o'clock. But he leaves at lunchtime on Friday. If we have worked late with him, he encourages us to do the same.'

- 'My manager employs the goodnight story test. He insists on being home to read to his children at least three nights each working week. When he's travelling, he makes a point, wherever he is, of ringing them just before bed-time. He once walked out of a very important meeting in New York saying he had an urgent family matter to attend to.'

- 'My manager admits he hasn't got his own work-life balance right yet. But he says that's no reason for preventing other people from doing so. It's clear he's trying to find sensible answers both for us and for himself.'

- 'Rather than prove to my manager that I'm working after hours, my problem is to prove I'm *not* working.'

- 'My manager took me aside and said we needed a plan. I was puzzled at first, because I thought she meant the project I've been working on these past few months, which has meant I'm working much longer hours than I like. She explained the plan was how to ensure that I didn't work more than one weekend in three, and how to make sure I took my holiday, which I'd already postponed once.'

Being a good role model is not something that can easily be taught. People evolve into the role gradually. HR can help by ensuring that those people who are positive role models are given support and recognition, and are used to influence peers and more junior managers.

LEADERSHIP STYLE

If the line manager is to become champion and guardian of work-life balance in the team, he or she may need to make both attitudinal and behavioural changes. Among the elements of this new style of leadership are:

- seeing the employee as a whole person
- recognising what prevents work-life balance
- recognising the symptoms of overwork and stress
- being generally supportive with regard to work-life balance issues
- relaxing control
- allocating work
- creating a climate that encourages experimentation and learning
- managing up
- making work satisfying and fun.

Seeing the employee as a whole person

Three authors writing in *Harvard Business Review*[5] describe a vision of a new breed of manager, who sees work and personal life not 'as competing priorities in a zero-sum game, in which a gain in one means a loss in the other' but as collaborative, mutually beneficial arenas. Instead of knowing only casual facts about people, these managers recognise and support the full range of their people's life roles. They find that being sincerely interested in an employee's personal life creates a bond, and with it, trust. Identifying people's various roles helps these managers tap into the full range of their employees' talents.

These managers spend time helping direct reports understand how their work and non-work roles relate to each other – where they mesh and where they need to be kept separate – to establish effective boundaries. This helps remove distraction, allowing people to be more focused on the task at hand. It takes skill to do this without being intrusive, but their genuine interest in other people is usually a passport to such discussions.

Some of the simple but effective behaviours we have observed by such managers include:

- turning up with their own families to cheer on an employee participating in a charity row-a-thon
- encouraging employees to consider what lessons could be transferred from their non-work roles into the workplace
- allowing a group of employees to use the corridors of the office as an exhibition space for their paintings and sculptures – other employees and visitors showed their appreciation by purchasing some of these works of art, which boosted the employee-artists' confidence even more
- including non-work learning as part of the employees' regular development review.

Once they open up about their own non-work interests, line managers are frequently surprised at how easy it is to persuade other people to do the same. Says one:

I had no idea of the richness of interests some of my people had. One of them was a superb classical guitarist. We've done an exchange. I'm teaching him conversational French, which could be useful in the role he hopes to move into, and he's teaching me to play. It's something I've wanted to learn since I was a kid!

Recognising what prevents work-life balance

The new leader is sensitive to work-life conflicts and actively looks out for them, rather than hoping no one will bring them up. Predicting potential workload surges well ahead of time allows him or her to plan with direct reports how to mitigate the impact. It helps to monitor hours worked, to identify when individual employees are under pressure and to balance workload planning with input from employees about their non-work commitments. For example, can the manager help the employee avoid the typical pre- and post-holiday work overload by reassigning some tasks for those weeks?

Such managers are sufficiently self-aware to recognise and moderate their own negative behaviours, such as putting pressure on direct reports to take on additional workloads, and making them feel they are letting the side down if they refuse. They listen to what they are saying, and gather feedback from direct reports about the impact of what they say. They recognise the difference between positive and negative stretching. (Positive stretching gives the employees new challenges that develop their intellect and skills; it is usually accompanied by a degree of nurture – support in acquiring the knowledge and skills necessary to do the new task. Negative stretching simply gives employees more and more of the same work to do; it often makes any remaining interesting and intellectually challenging work less beneficial, because there is no time to do it properly or to think about learning from the experience.)

The sensitive manager also develops an awareness of the subtle discriminations that disadvantage people who work flexibly. For example, author Lotte Bailyn says:

> *A manager can be very understanding of the needs of an employee (particularly a woman with children) to be unable to stay after 5 pm. But if he nonetheless continues to hold the meeting, he contributes to the view that those with family constraints on time are less important employees and, probably, also less competent.[6]*

He or she is also careful to relate flexible working solutions to the bigger picture of the team's goals. Says Bailyn: 'Individual accommodations lead to gratitude, which make it harder to ask for more work changes.' Maintaining a constant dialogue with direct reports about how an arrangement is delivering ensures that they do not feel inhibited from asking for further changes.

Recognising the symptoms of overwork and stress

Many of the symptoms of overwork and stress are obvious, as long as the manager is on the lookout for them: tetchiness, unnecessary mistakes and rework, people taking bundles of work home with them in the evenings and at weekends, and so on. The difference between the traditional manager and the new manager is that the latter *wants* to recognise these symptoms, because they represent a threat to the efficient working of the function. They try to protect direct reports from pressure from above, while making sure that they do not take on such a workload themselves that they are too busy to notice other people's problems.

Being generally supportive with regard to work-life balance issues

A US study[7] found that the behaviour of managers, especially in terms of how supportive they were perceived to be, was the most significant factor in managing work-life balance. Another, carried out in 2000,[8] found that 61 per cent of 1,862 employees of US companies said that the active support of their boss was key to determining their attitude at work. It's one thing to have policies and programmes; another to listen to people, show them respect, try to take their needs into account, and demonstrate empathy. It is as important for a manager to show that he or she cares as to permit an employee to adjust the way he or she works; and when an accommodation cannot be made, or when needs can only partly be met, the fact that the manager tried is worth a lot of brownie points.

An important element of support is visible fairness. The manager has, for example, to ensure that he or she is equally supportive of the non-work requirements of those who do not have children as he or she is of those who do. Similarly, he or she should seek to avoid casting some jobs as critical and therefore not appropriate for flexible working, and some as non-critical and therefore available for flexible working. (If jobs are categorised in this way, the flexible jobs tend to assume lower status, and so do the people occupying them.)

Relaxing control

Giving people more control over their work is directly associated with greater enjoyment of their work, with higher motivation, reduced stress and a reduced sense of being under pressure.[9] Control is not just about *when* to work, it is also about *how*.

A study of IBM employees[10] found that the length of the working week was of far less importance in the perception of conflict between home and work than the degree of control people felt they had over the hours they worked. Among people who were able to work from home when convenient, work a compressed week, and/or shift hours to fit around the family, a little over a quarter experienced difficulties balancing the two halves of their lives, compared with nearly half of those who did not have such flexibility.

Virtually every leadership course examines the process of the gradual empowerment of direct reports by giving them greater control over what they do, so the idea should not be alien to managers. Gradual relaxation of the reins gives both the employee and the manager time to adjust.

Allocating work

Line managers' reluctance to make major changes in how work is done in their department often stems from very reasonable concerns about the potential for disruption and a reduction in overall team performance. Studies of change management often place initiative fatigue near or at the top of the list of contributory causes.

Attempts to restructure and re-engineer are often undermined because the stresses and strains on employees caused by the changes and the pressure for cost containment exert such pressure on employees' concentration and peace of mind that they actually decrease productivity and the work quality. Says author Lotte Bailyn:[11] 'The only solution ... is to bring the family needs above the line and include them up front in the reconsideration of how work is organised.'

The *Harvard Business Review* authors mentioned earlier point out that open discussions of work-life issues are often the 'catalysts for identifying inefficiencies in the workplace'. Depending on whether the manager is comfortable in an enabling or empowering style, he or she can engage the team in designing practical ground-rules for managing work allocation.

One of the simplest and most powerful ways in which HR can help the line manager is to provide greater clarity about what exactly is meant by 'management by results'. It's one thing to tell managers that they should stop managing by line of sight and manage on results, but how do they interpret that in practical, measurable day-to-day procedures?

We can define management by results *as a process to agree and monitor the outputs expected of an employee, and how these contribute to the overall team task.* Some tasks are relatively easy to define in output terms – for example, produce a report, mark so many examination papers, or make a set number of sales calls. Even here, however, quality of work may be an issue – in particular, service quality. It is a lot harder to assess how an employee deals with customers if the employee is not observed either by peers or by a supervisor. And some tasks can be much more difficult to supervise – for example, a piece of research in which the outcomes are expected to emerge as the work progresses.

None of these problems is new, however. The nature of knowledge working means that very few tasks can be measured wholly or even primarily with hard data, even if they are performed in line of sight. What generally emerges in discussing these issues with line managers is that they have difficulties *measuring performance in general*. It is not surprising, therefore, that they feel nervous about letting out the rope even further.

Line managers require education and example to help them establish with each employee a mixture of soft and hard measures which reflect accurately what is expected from each task assigned. They need to feel confident that these measures are reasonable, non-discriminatory and equivalent to measures that would be applied if the individual was working in the office under supervision. Many of the skills required here are similar to those required to manage virtual project teams. Ensuring that managers have the chance to experience working in a virtual team themselves exposes them to some of these practices and gives them a taste of what it is like to be on the receiving end of distant management.

A good first step is to make clear, within the team, just what the ground rules are, and to involve the team in thinking through the implications of different forms of working. Key questions include:

- What cover must we provide at all times/at core times?
- How much should we take into account personal circumstances in allocating opportunities for flexible working?
- How do we make sure that people, who work 'normal' hours do not end up with all the most boring, unwanted jobs?

With these questions in mind, the manager can focus any rearrangement of work around *how long does the job really require to do?* This question can be answered in several chunks – for example, core tasks, peripheral tasks and liaison tasks. If the core tasks of a job amount to 35 hours a week or more, and the remaining tasks another 15, it is almost certainly too large for one person, but not large enough for two. The most efficient mechanism may be to turn the job into a job-share with, say, two people working 25 hours each. In this way, responsibility for the task remains focused. You will, however, need to allow between two and four hours for increased liaison time between the job-sharers.

Creating a climate that encourages experimentation and learning

Our seminal study of team learning,[12] carried out for the European Community, found that most teams are so focused on task achievement that they fail to build in sufficient reflective space to review learning and plan for future learning. This narrow focus inevitably leads to reduced performance as the team becomes busier but less effective.

Leaders of high-performance teams create a balance of focus between task and learning while encouraging supportive behaviours between team members. In the context of work-life balance, the manager can ensure that occasions when work demands become burdensome are analysed within the team to establish what has happened and how to prevent or diminish the impact of any recurrence. He or she can also encourage the inclusion of achieving work-life goals in personal and team development plans.

Managing up

My manager often has the best of intentions. He knows we are hard-pressed and can't really take on more. But the moment he is with his boss, he says yes to everything. Then he brings back a whole load more work and blames it all on his boss. He feels guilty about it, but at the end of the day he is more concerned with not upsetting his career prospects than in protecting us from unreasonable demands from above.

This employee speaks with feeling – he had had less than six hours' sleep the previous night, having worked till nearly midnight and returned for seven the next morning.

Being a leader demands courage – it can be very hard to say to more senior managers, 'This job can't be done with the resources available.' If the manager is not prepared to renegotiate the team's workload, or to refuse to take on work that will seriously disrupt their work-life balance, who will? The failure to do so is only partly to do with lack of courage, however; equally important is the need to present a reasoned and verifiable case to the management layers above.

The reality in most organisations is that much of the work that gets passed down is of little real value to the organisation. Requiring senior managers to think before they ask for work to be done is by and large good for the organisation, as well as for the employees on the receiving ends of such requests.

Harold Leavitt, the leadership guru, provides several examples of unnecessary workload resulting from careless requests from the top. One of these tells of the experience of a former domestic-policy staffer in President Jimmy Carter's administration. On a Friday afternoon, instruction came from above to produce an urgent report for the President on a particular subject, to be on the President's desk by the following Monday. The staff worked the whole weekend on the report – one worker even cancelled his young son's birthday party in order to get the job done properly. The report was ready and on the President's desk on Monday morning, but by Wednesday the staff who had slaved the whole weekend to complete it still had not received any recognition or thanks for their patience and hard work. It eventually came to light that the President had not needed the report – he merely commented to a few senior staff that he would like to see how the problem was progressing. This remark had subsequently turned into a suggestion of the need for a report, which in turn became more and more suggestive and urgent as it moved through the chain of command, eventually becoming a crisis that had to be dealt with immediately.[13]

In the regular CIPD workshop I run on Marketing the HR Function, one of the tools we use is a simple matrix. Along the horizontal axis are the key business goals; in the vertical axis the various activity areas or key competencies of HR. In the boxes created by this matrix we write in all the specific projects or activities that could usefully be delivered, with a time and cost budget attached to each. Almost invariably, the sum of all these projects exceeds the total budget allocated to the department. HR can then engage the rest of the executive team in deciding which projects or activities they want to drop. The same principle applies to the workload of any department: the clearer the manager makes the choices, the more difficult it is for top management to demand more. If they insist on trying to squeeze more projects into the plan, the manager's response must be: 'Which of these do you accept can be only partly done or will not be done as well as it should?'

Of course, the manager may still be told, 'How you do it is your problem – you are paid to solve these issues.' Now comes the key question for HR: *how and to what extent are you prepared to support the line manager in resisting this kind of pressure?* It is a question many HR directors are unhappy to address publicly, and in private they sometimes admit that they do not carry the clout to intervene. At the very least, however, the HR director can raise the broad question at board level and attempt to discuss specific instances with senior management colleagues in private.

Other practical measures HR can take are:

- providing line managers with confidential advice when they feel that pressure from above is undermining the work-life balance policy
- using the employee survey to identify pockets of poor practice
- offering assertiveness training and negotiation skills training to line managers
- persuading the chief executive to give public recognition to managers who stand up against this kind of abuse
- providing an internal arbitration service to help resolve disputes over what is an appropriate workload (for teams or individuals).

Making work satisfying and fun

One of the outcomes of our work on learning teams is a distinction between *fizz* (the enjoyment people gain from the work they do) and *buzz* (the enjoyment that comes from socialising with colleagues). A manager who can instil both of these attributes into the team culture can reduce the impact of long hours that do have to be worked by making them fulfilling. There is a big difference between going home tired but content and simply going home tired!

It often doesn't take much to create buzz, even when people are flat out doing jobs with negative stretch. Simply saying 'Right – everyone stop for a pizza break!' can make all the difference. For the manager who is stuck on how to inject more fun into the workplace, there are several excellent books full of ideas.[14]

CASE STUDY

P&O Ferries

P&O Ferries' decision to invest in work-life balance was part of a much larger culture-change initiative. The company was born out of a merger in the late 1990s, and one of the first actions by the new board was to undertake an extensive staff survey. The results showed that employees and the local community did not regard it as a good employer. It was, says HR manager Peter Ambrose, 'seen as very hard'. In part this was due to memories of a major strike in 1987, during which the company fired all the striking staff and re-engaged on new contract terms those who eventually came back. In part, too, it was related to tradition – the ships were run with a strict hierarchy of uniformed managers, from the captain to pursers.

The new board determined to change the culture, making it more open, more friendly and more participative. Top management spent a great deal of time consulting with staff about how to change the culture.

When the issue of flexible working arose, therefore, Ambrose found he was pushing at an open door. Although flexible working legislation was some time away, the board readily agreed that the company should welcome the idea, rather than resist it. It would be an effective way to demonstrate the company's commitment to family-friendly policies, they reasoned.

Implementing flexible working on-shore was not difficult. It was relatively easy to convince managers and employees of the benefits and to establish practical systems. On board, however, it was a different story. Most of the managers had very long service (often 20 to 30 years) with the company and were instinctively resistant to change. 'A common attitude was to resist anything "soft" and any privilege they had not had when they were on their way up the organisation,' says Ambrose, 'and there were relatively few women in senior positions, not least because the way work was organised made it difficult for them to take on those jobs.'

Ambrose decided to tackle the issue head-on. For three months,

I went into the lion's den. I travelled on every ship and had sessions with senior, middle and junior managers to allow them to talk about their concerns with regard to introducing flexible working. They were concerned it wouldn't work, but they couldn't explain why. I told them 'If you can justify to me why it can't be done, with good reason, then I'll accept that.' They never could.

This gradual persuasion was far more effective, he believes, than trying to impose behaviour changes from head office. Wherever possible, he worked with specific cases, such as a stewardess who wanted to halve her hours. When the manager said it would cause havoc with the roster system, Ambrose made him work through the process until the manager convinced himself it was fully feasible.

To emphasise the importance of thinking creatively, P&O promoted the concept of *Taking the T out of Can't*. On-shore workshops were held to open managers' eyes to wider issues of managing people within the new business values and to encourage them to be proactive in finding ways to accommodate employees' individual needs. Ambrose and his team also emphasised that flexibility was not just a matter for employees with young children; the company should support any employee who wanted a different pattern of work, wherever it was feasible to do so. If an employee wanted time to pursue a particular hobby, or wanted to take a year's sabbatical, the company would try to comply. 'I'm sure we'd have lost a lot of staff', says Ambrose, 'if we hadn't changed to working in this way.'

SOME PRACTICAL STEPS TO PROMOTE WORK-LIFE BALANCE

In educating and supporting managers to become local champions of work-life balance, HR will need to provide simple, relatively undemanding templates to get them started. A typical template might include the following headings:

- Make work-life balance a regular item on team meetings
- Educate the team in how to deal with remote colleagues
- Encourage feedback on how you are supporting/hindering work-life balance
- Be clear in setting expectations about work output, teamwork, and what the team should expect of the leader
- Promote multi-skilling and interchangeability of roles.

Make work-life balance a regular item on team meetings

It all becomes a lot easier if roles, responsibilities and working patterns are frequently discussed at team meetings. Although the manager cannot hand over fully to the team the responsibility for sorting out individual working arrangements without risk of falling foul of the legislation, he or she can resolve a lot of problems simply by airing them within the team as a whole. One company I encountered years ago hit upon the idea of 'auctioning' work. A project-based IT company, it conducted a weekly auction at which employees could bid for specific tasks against an estimate of hours to complete. For large tasks, several employees could make a consortium bid. In this way people were able to manage their hours week by week.

Educate the team in how to deal with remote colleagues

My own company's experience with remote employees is that it is vital to make them feel involved. The manager should make sure they and the rest of the office-based employees allow adequate time for them to talk to remote colleagues, and not just about work issues. Interestingly, time spent chattering to someone by telephone often appears to be much longer than that spent face to face. The actual amount of social conversation time spent with teleworkers is almost always less than that spent with colleagues at the next desk or around the coffee machine.

Encourage feedback on how you are supporting/hindering work-life balance

Although the feedback from formal employee surveys may be useful, it is neither sufficiently immediate nor frequent enough to enable the manager to reflect on day-by-day behaviour and decisions. The manager needs in addition to gather informal feedback whenever the opportunity presents itself.

Be clear in setting expectations about work output, teamwork and what the team should expect of the leader

Given the legislative framework, it will not be surprising if line managers are concerned about discussing individual requests for flexible working. How the manager lays the foundation for the discussion is critical. He or she should start by stating the ground rules. For example:

1   Any alternative working pattern must ensure that the job continues to be done as well as under the current arrangements.

2   Neither manager nor individual must place an undue burden on other employees without their consent.

3   Both the individual and the company are expected to suggest options wherever possible.

4   If a role cannot be adapted to allow a more flexible or different pattern of hours, the manager and the employee should explore alternative roles (for example, shifting from customer service to project management), bearing in mind, however, that they may have different views on the employee's ability to do an alternative role.

5   A probationary period will often be reasonable, on both sides, to assess whether a different routine works. The criteria for assessment include ground rules 1 and 2 above. If the employee is trying out a new role, the basis of assessment should be reasonable, agreed and clearly understood on both sides.

6   Not everyone is able to work effectively using flexible schedules and/or flexible location. Both the manager and the employee must be realistic about what will be practical in any particular case.

With the ground rules set, the manager can begin to explore with the employee his or her personal priorities. The end result should be a high level of clarity about what the employee wants to achieve in both the work and non-work sides of his or her life, and a similar level of clarity about the business objectives, which should be defined as far as possible in terms of measurable outputs.

Promote multi-skilling and interchangeability of roles

The more people can substitute for each other, the wider the range of alternative working options available. One small engineering firm of 36 people invested in training them so they were multi-skilled and worked out individual working patterns. It ended up with 32 different patterns, but gained 32 extra hours of machine time.

Although it takes time and a lot of energy on the part of both the manager and the team members in terms of explaining and coaching, plus, in some cases the expense of putting some people on training courses, the net result is a much more flexible team, better able to manage its workload and better able to respond to changes in requirements from internal or external customers. Managers also typically find that they can delegate more in a multi-skilled team, relieving some of their own work pressures. HR can help by advising on how to develop a training needs analysis, providing access to appropriate training courses and facilitating the coaching skills of team members.

HOW HR CAN SUPPORT THE LINE MANAGER

In general, our survey suggests that the HR function has tended to leave line managers to sink or swim on their own with regard to work-life balance issues. Only 19 per cent provide training in how to organise work to accommodate work-life balance; only slightly more provide training in how to manage people who work remotely or at non-standard times. However, nearly half (47 per cent) say they do provide a support system to help line managers deal with work-life balance issues in their team.

Some of the supportive practical steps HR can take are:

- choosing easy wins, and using them to spread the message
- training
- making full use of feedback from employee surveys
- ensuring that there is clarity at all levels about work-life balance rules and expectations
- sharing good practice.

Choosing easy wins, and using them to spread the message

When Pauline Henderson – now with the Department of Trade and Industry but formerly with Nationwide Building Society – wanted to break through to top managers in Nationwide's technical division, she chose to do so through a successful programme of home-working. The main reason this team was so successful, she explains, is that it was formed specifically to accommodate teleworking, so both the team members and the manager were enthusiastic. In teams where teleworking had been grafted on, the managers had much more difficulty accepting the new ways of working. The board was sceptical, so she took some of the home-workers to the board meeting to explain how it worked. Faced with positive reports from both the home-workers and their manager, the board had to accept that this was a practical alternative way of working.

Training

Support line managers and team members with a wide enough portfolio of training opportunities to meet both the technical and the behavioural requirements, as discussed in Chapter 5.

Making full use of feedback from employee surveys

Make sure that survey feedback is conducted in a way that builds managers' confidence, rather than undermining it. Provide sufficient counselling to support managers in dealing with this feedback, and encourage them to seek more immediate, more frequent feedback directly.

Ensuring that there is clarity at all levels about work-life balance rules and expectations

Research by the Institute for Employment Studies[15] found that take-up of flexible working arrangements was higher when managers had no discretion over eligibility. That may be an argument for taking the decisions as much out of managers' hands as possible – or for making sure they are sufficiently educated about work-life balance issues to make good judgements most of the time. The problems with relying on centralised rules include inflexibility (it is impossible to foresee all the circumstances that might occur in the field) and the danger that managers will abdicate the issues to HR.

Nationwide engaged managers in discussion on how to apply policy consistently in the workplace and take the risk out of it. Based on these discussions, it was able to issue very clear guidelines that were in managers' own language. These guidelines are used to objectively evaluate an employee's request for flexible working, at which time the employee is required to present a business case. Such a procedure is in place in order to avoid making value judgements on the employee's reason for wanting to work flexibly, and focuses on feasibility in a purely business context.

Some of the programme managers we interviewed emphasised the importance of checking the understanding of work-life policies and of reviewing process with line managers frequently, at least for the first year. Simply issuing information is not enough. Managers need to talk it through and share experience in handling real cases before they feel comfortable with incorporating the policies in their day-to-day routines.

Sharing good practice

HR can boost confidence by creating forums for exchanging experience – newsletters, chat rooms and, most importantly, face-to-face gatherings where they can share concerns and ways of dealing with them. Overcoming line managers' sense of isolation on work-life issues should be a key objective in the plan of campaign.

The ultimate aim is to make line managers feel valued – that they are a key part of the solution, not the core of the problem.

REFERENCES AND READING

1 KODZ J., HARPER, H. *and* DENCH, S. (2002) *Work-life Balance: Beyond the Rhetoric*. IES Report 384. Brighton, Institute for Employment Studies.

2 See reference no. 1 above

3 CONFERENCE BOARD. (1998) *Work–Family Roundtable: Technology's Effect on Work-life Balance*. New York, Conference Board.

4 FLETCHER , W. (2002) *Beating the 24/7: How Business Leaders Achieve a Successful Work-life Balance*. Chichester, Wiley

5 FRIEDMAN S.D., CHRISTENSEN P. *and* DEGROOT J. (1998) 'Work and life: the end of the zero-sum game.' *Harvard Business Review*. Vol. 76, 6. pp119–129.

6 BAILYN L. (1997) 'The impact of corporate culture on work-family integration' in S. Parasuraman and J. Greenhaus (eds.) *Integrating Work and Family: Challenges and Choices for a Changing World*. Westport, CT, Quorum Books.

7 DUXBURY L., HIGGINS C. and COGHILL D. (2003) *Voices of Canadians: Seeking Work-life Balance*. Ottawa, Health Canada. Available at http://labour-travail.hrdc-drhc.gc.ca/work-life/welcome-en.cfm [Accessed 16 July 2003]

8 Survey by Careerbuilder Inc.

9 Study by London School of Economics and the Policy Studies Institute (2001).

10 HILL J.E., HAWKINS A.J., FERRIS M. *and* WEITZMAN, M. (2001) 'Finding an extra day a week: the positive influence of job flexibility on work and family life'. *Family Relations*. Vol. 50, 1. pp209–219.

11 See reference no. 6 above.

12 CLUTTERBUCK D. (2003) 'Teams and learning: the agenda has changed'. *Development and Learning in Organizations*. Vol. 17, 2. pp10–16.

13 LEAVITT H. (2003) 'Why hierarchies survive'. *Harvard Business Review*. Vol. 81, 3. pp96–102.

14 MACERLEAN N. (1998) *Get More from Work – and More Fun*. London, Institute of Personnel and Development.
HEMSATH D., YERKES L. *and* MCQUILLEN D. (1997) *301 Ways to Have Fun at Work*. San Francisco, Berrett-Koehler Pub.

15 See reference no. 1 above

7

Work-life balance and the team

Work-life balance isn't just about coming to arrangements with individuals. It's also about enlisting the creativity and goodwill of the team in designing and implementing on-the-ground solutions.

Almost all the texts we have read about creating change to support work-life balance focuses either on the organisation (through policy and process) or on the individual as manager granting flexibility or as employee seeking it. Yet the role of the team is equally important. The willingness of team members to accommodate each other's needs, to see work-life balance as a shared concern rather than as an issue between each individual and the organisation, is influential in determining the pace of change.

Just why the team's role has been assigned so little importance it is difficult to establish. But in this chapter we attempt to rectify the omission. First, though, let's define what we mean by a 'team'. The simplest definition is *a group of people who work together to achieve a common purpose*.

An *effective* team is characterised in addition by:

- relative adaptability in the roles people play
- sharing information, understanding and expertise
- supporting each other
- accepting personal discomfort or disadvantage for the good of the team as a whole.

Effective teams, therefore, provide a fertile environment for establishing work-life balance. The six critical steps in doing so are:

1 Understand the nature of the team and how the team type will influence the potential to achieve work-life balance.

2 Understand what each team member wants, in terms of work-life balance in both the short and long term.

3 Assess the climate for work-life balance within the team.

4 Commit to supporting each other in achieving work-life balance and other goals.

5   Develop a plan to make these goals happen.

6   As the plan is being implemented, continuously review each of the previous five steps.

UNDERSTANDING THE NATURE OF THE TEAM

Teams are not all the same. They may have major differences in composition, type of task, duration, and so on. These differences mean that each team may have very different issues to address in terms of how it approaches work organisation, learning and other aspects of co-operation and collaboration. It is clear, for example, that a team that has to provide 24-hour cover for customers (for example, telephone operators) has different issues to address from a team whose job is only to provide cover from 9 am till 5 pm. Understanding the type of team and its essential dynamics is critical in designing workable solutions to work-life balance.

We can look at team typologies in two ways:

- by the degree of stability of the task and of the membership
- by the nature of the task (and in particular by the degree of *interdependence* of the tasks each member performs).

Six different types of team

In our study of learning in teams,[1] we identified six common team types:

- stable teams (where the membership and the task remain broadly the same over long periods)
- project teams, which may be drawn from various parts of the organisation, or partly from outside the organisation, but which concentrate on a specific, new task – generally the membership stays the same for the duration of the task or series of tasks
- evolutionary teams, characterised by having waves of new members joining at different points as a project progresses
- cabin crew, where the team members change frequently but the task is constant and consistent
- learning alliances, such as mentoring relationships or action learning sets, where there is stable membership but a constant evolution of topics
- virtual teams, either geographically distributed or not part of the official hierarchy (or both); these can be either stable or unstable in both task and membership.

Teams with high stability of membership have greater opportunity to influence those aspects of work assignment that affect work-life balance and to support each other than those with low stability of membership. Teams with high stability of task will normally have greater opportunity to plan workload and to find ways to systematise what they do. Teams with low stability of task need to focus on ways to increase overall flexibility and range of possible responses to variations in workload.

Team interdependence

The issue of interdependence is explored by Robert Keidel,[2] who proposes three layers:

- pooled, where team performance is the sum of individual performances (eg Ryder Cup golf or sales)

- sequential, where team performance relies on a mixture of individual and orchestrated performance (eg American football or assembly-line manufacture)

- reciprocal, where team performance is more than the sum of the individuals' performance (eg basketball or a cross-functional task-force).

Clearly, in a pooled performance team what counts is not when or how each member carries out a task but whether he or she delivers what he or she has been tasked with. Each team member performs a similar task, independently. One person's work only affects that of the others if he or she fails to deliver or if he or she behaves in a way that either damages the reputation of the team as a whole or provides encouragement and support for each other. (Included in support, in this instance, is learning from each other.)

In this environment there is often an issue of making sure that everyone pulls his or her weight and is felt to do so by colleagues. The pressure not to let the others down can be a source of stress and lead people to overcommit.

In a sequential team, overload, absenteeism or poor performance by one member can have a rapid and expanding impact on the work of the others, as the classic Charlie Chaplin film *Modern Times* illustrates. For example, a high proportion of the quality costs of hospitals, in terms of patient care, relates to sequential breakdown between teams from different disciplines.

In a reciprocal team, roles are shared out broadly, with considerable overlap. Critical tasks are carried out by the team member who happens to be in the right place at the right time. When this happens, the other team members adapt their roles to provide the appropriate support. This adaptability can be a trap, however, because it is not always clear when the team is reaching (or has exceeded) the limits of its capacity to respond effectively to demand.

Reciprocal teams can be very adaptable in terms of work-life balance, different members taking the stress of being in the front line at different times. They are characterised by periods of routine activity punctuated from time to time by a demand for concentrated effort by several or all members of the team. Where they fail to function well, it is often for one or other of two reasons:

- one or more members is unable to perform at the required level

- the periods of routine activity are too short or non-existent, so the team never gets a chance to regroup and draw breath. (There may also be problems arsing from having too long periods of routine activity, which result in people going stale.) In essence, what has happened here is that the team is in permanent overload.

How does team type affect the potential to achieve work-life balance?

A good starting point for developing awareness within the team of the broader issues relating to work organisation is to establish some clarity about the team type and the implications that it has for work-life balance. Questions to discuss in this context include:

- Could you achieve greater productivity and work-life balance by changing the team type?
- What model would best fit your team task?
- Could the team learn from other teams?
- Could you change the boundaries of the team to include people who have other skills that would complement the existing team's?

One of the most powerful illustrations I have seen of this kind of thinking was a crumbling factory in the depths of Tennessee.[3] The product was car mirrors. As an experiment, one production line was given the freedom to redesign its work practices, with work-life balance (that was not the term they used – this was 30 years ago! – but the intent was the same) and improved production quality as the dual objectives. The team were all smallholders as well as factory workers. Where they really wanted to be most of the day was back on their farms. The new working patterns and processes they implemented cut at least two hours off their working day. Other teams, suspicious that they were cutting corners, kept checking their output for any sign of reduced quality, but found precisely the opposite.

PREPARING THE GROUND: UNDERSTANDING WHAT EACH TEAM MEMBER WANTS, IN TERMS OF WORK-LIFE BALANCE

Having clarified the work-related factors that may help or hinder a particular team in terms of maintaining work-life balance, it is time to examine the people issues. The team needs to build a strong awareness of what the ideal balance between work and non-work looks like for each member, and the extent to which each is prepared to work outside that ideal. Simply talking about expectations, personal obligations and life circumstances builds an understanding about what each person is looking for and a greater degree of empathy with each other's situations.

A useful basis for discussion is the matrix in Figure 7, which looks at each team member's requirements from four different perspectives. One of the benefits of this is that it presents the individual in a more holistic manner. Another is that it distinguishes between what he or she wants/needs now and what he or she will want/need in the future. Given that it is not always possible to accommodate people's work-life balance requirements immediately, this gives the team scope for planning solutions over the medium to long term.

The matrix also typically brings out people's life-career objectives. For example, a colleague wanted to reduce working time to four days a week now, and after two more years to split her time between her current role and a new area of career development, for which she is presently studying. After that, she is less clear about what she wants; she will examine the options nearer the time. Having shared these objectives with her colleagues and listened to theirs, finding solutions that met the needs of all the team relatively closely proved remarkably easy.

Figure 7 My work-life goals

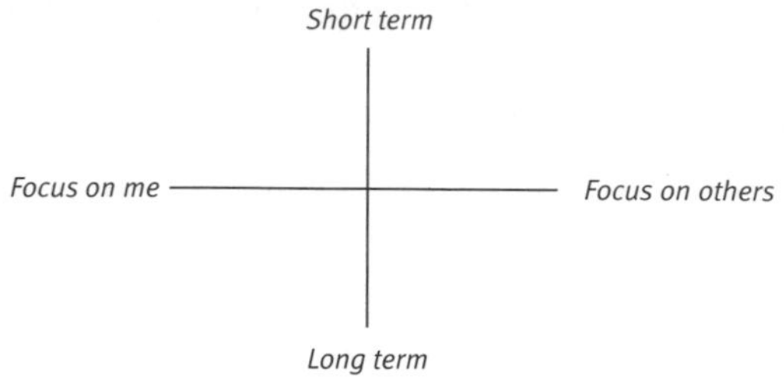

```
                    Short term
                        |
                        |
                        |
 Focus on me  ——————————+—————————  Focus on others
                        |
                        |
                        |
                    Long term
```

ASSESSING THE CLIMATE FOR WORK-LIFE BALANCE WITHIN THE TEAM

Like the larger organisation, each team has its own culture. The team leader plays a major role in creating this culture – he or she can either foster a climate of openness and mutual support-iveness or, at the other extreme, create a climate of 'divide and rule'.

The manager should explore with the team their perceptions of what factors encourage people to/prevent people from:

- taking actions and decisions that permit a better work-life balance
- discussing work-life balance concerns openly
- considering different ways of doing things
- taking advantage of work-life opportunities offered to them
- admitting when they are under pressure
- saying no to unacceptable additional work burdens.

COMMITING TO SUPPORTING EACH OTHER

Difficulties team members experience in any of these areas can be discussed by the team as a whole, with a view to changing the climate, so that it is more supportive. One of the most power-ful outcomes can be a simple commitment, by all team members, to supporting each other's goals in work-life balance, learning and task achievement. Discussing the goals regularly pro-vides a frequent reminder and gives people an opportunity to speak up where they might in other circumstances suffer in silence.

DESIGNING AND IMPLEMENTING THE WORK-LIFE TEAM PLAN

Figure 8 outlines the four key areas the manager and the team must address in planning how they will optimise work-life balance and team performance. (It could be argued that work-life balance is a measure of team performance, and some organisations are already using the scores from employee surveys as part of managers' bonus calculations. It is only a small step to awarding team bonuses in part from how well the team achieves work-life balance.)

As our study of team learning established, just as it is important to link the business plan with a team performance plan and individual performance plans, so it is equally important over the medium term to link individual, team and learning through a planned approach. The same

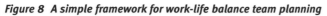

Figure 8 A simple framework for work-life balance team planning

principle applies to work-life balance – the organisational aspirations can only be delivered by linking planning processes at the three levels. Without a clear chain of planning, supervision and monitoring, in which the team plan plays a pivotal role, implementation will either be very patchy or require coercion from above.

Goal clarity

Goal clarity is an essential first step in the planning process. Whatever the team type, the team will have to define precisely what is expected of it, in terms of performance against both quality and quantity targets. But goal clarity, as we saw in Chapter 3, is equally important for the individual. Team goals for work-life balance may be generic (eg everyone here feels they have a reasonable work-life balance, or at least has the opportunity to do so) or specific (no one works more than five hours a week over those contracted more than once a quarter). They may seek to apply one broad approach to all, or establish the flexibility to accommodate very different needs.

In deciding what kind of work-life balance goals the team should set, it is important that each individual has some degree of personal clarity about what an appropriate work-life balance would mean for him or her. These personal goals should always be accepted as valid, unless the individuals themselves question them. Whether they can be accommodated within the constraints imposed by the needs of the organisation and the aggregate needs of the team will emerge from the second and third stages of the planning process.

Resources

The key resources a team needs include time, emotional energy, creative energy, equipment/technology, space and money. The plan should detail how much of each is required, when and how it can be accessed, and how flexible each is. In terms of time, the team may agree to make available a certain number of hours each week as a routine 'top-up' that recognises the difficulty of delivering the work goals in the time contractually available, in return for some elements of job security, opportunities to develop new skills and/or establish a track record, and so on.

However, unlike what happens in the vast majority of teams, in these teams it will be very clear how well the team is resourced to deliver the tasks assigned to it. Likely problems with work-life balance can then be identified and dealt with in a number of ways, from accepting that work-life balance may have to take a back seat temporarily, to renegotiating what is expected of the team. The latter may require courage on the part of the team leader – it can be very hard to say to more senior managers, 'This job can't be done with the resources available' – but some advice on approaches has been given in Chapter 6.

Competencies

Competencies define the skills the team needs in both individuals and across all the members. For example, a local branch sales office may need everyone to have customer service skills, but only one or two people to be competent at book-keeping. How competencies are defined and distributed can have a major impact on resourcing – for example, if the whole team grinds to a halt because the one person who understands the intranet system is on holiday. The cost of building greater flexibility, by equipping more people with more competencies, can almost always be justified in terms of greater work efficiency, as well as in terms of work-life balance. Aggregating the benefits and the costs of increased skills flexibility should make the choice clearer. However, it should be noted that the costs of increasing team competence are often not borne by the organisation alone; the individual will often have to make an investment of time and energy – perhaps studying at home or working longer hours to catch up with work that did not get done while he or she was on a course.

Determination

Determination underlies all the other three elements of the planning process. Integrating work and non-work goals at the team level will not happen if the team members are not sufficiently motivated to achieve change. Flexibility in resourcing will not happen if people are not willing to make trade-offs with other team members in a mutually supportive atmosphere. And people will not learn new skills if they are not convinced of the payoffs, both personally and for the team as a whole. The team has to commit at the very least to making a strong effort to implement the work-life balance plan. If the members do so, experience in most reported cases is that their attachment to the new ways of working will increase with exposure to them, even if some adjustments have to be made along the way.

SOME KEY QUESTIONS FOR WORK ALLOCATION IN THE CONTEXT OF WORK-LIFE BALANCE

- What are the critical task goals for this team? (What needs to be done? What is really important?)
- How do we integrate these with individual and team development goals? (What needs to be learned?)

- How do we identify the resources available in terms of time, intellectual effort, creativity, emotional effort, supporting others? (What is each person able to contribute in terms of each?)

- What is the anticipated demand for each?

- How do we cope with peaks and troughs in demand for each? (How can we reduce crisis working?)

- What support structures do we have to help colleagues overloaded in one or more areas?

- How can we build in more thinking/ planning time? (How do we create reflective space?)

- How do we distribute the burden in each area more fairly?

SOME TECHNIQUES FOR BUILDING FLEXIBILITY IN THE TEAM

The urgent/important matrix

One of the simplest tools for answering the first of the questions in the box (What needs to be done? What's really important?) is the urgent/important matrix, as shown in Figure 9. Essentially, this requires the team to list all the tasks they have to perform, whether regular or one-offs, and score them in terms of how urgent they are and how important. Items that are urgent and important will normally be given a high priority, but as Stephen Covey[4] would argue, tasks that are important but not urgent should also receive a high, or equal, priority. Tasks that are urgent, but not important, come well down the list and those that are neither urgent nor important are relegated to a status where they only receive attention if there is nothing else to do.

The four categories of task give rise to four levels of response, with regard to whether employees put work ahead of home-life. In category A (both urgent and important) employees are expected do their best to accommodate the work need and accept that some sacrifices of their non-work life may be needed. They will also have the responsibility to drop non-important tasks both to help each other get the task done and to prevent too great an incursion of work into non-work life for other members of the team.

For tasks in category B (not urgent, but important), employees contract with each other and the team leader to ensure that they get done within a given timeframe. If this means working some extra hours, so be it. Unlike category A, where the urgency may cause a clash with specific per-

Figure 9 The urgent/important matrix

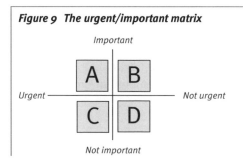

sonal commitments outside work, there is much more capacity to plan when and where to carry out category B tasks, so minimising the work-life conflict. Category C tasks (urgent but not important) should never be allowed to take up more than, say, 20 per cent of the team's resources. In a conflict between work and non-work priorities, these tasks will usually lose out. Category D tasks (not urgent and not important) will *always* lose out in the competition for time and attention.

Our experience is that teams, like individuals, spend far too much time on urgent but not important tasks. The team therefore needs to ask itself:

- How do we distinguish between tasks to allocate them to the four boxes?
- How much agreement is there?
- How do we ensure that we do have the same expectations?
- What processes allow us to focus on the important?
- What compromises are appropriate for members of the team in dealing with each of these four situations?
- How much effort could we save by not doing unimportant tasks?
- How will we monitor what we do to maintain a focus on the important?

Task interchangeability

The more easily the team can move work between members, the better equipped it is to achieve its priority tasks and the easier it is to accommodate individual needs. As part of the planning process, the team should discuss such questions as:

- What tasks can we substitute for each other on now?
- Do we experience problems in performance or work-life balance in those tasks where we have low interchangeability?
- How could we develop a higher level of interchangeability?
- What would the benefits be, and how could we measure them?

Obligations banks

'Obligations banks' borrow from the annualised hour concept and also from the practice outside work of babysitting circles. Team members build 'credits' or 'debits' in taking on tasks out of assigned hours, or in covering for colleagues.

Key questions for the team to ask here are:

- What activities would be included in this?
- What value would we assign to contributions? (For example, is an extra couple of hours early one week-day morning worth as much as the same amount of time on a Saturday afternoon?)
- How can we ensure fair play?
- Who will keep the bank records?
- How can we make this concept work with our team?

Keep on reviewing

It is an obvious point to make, but like any other business process the work-life balance plan needs constant monitoring and review. For a start, people's circumstances change, tasks change and new members join the team. Says a line manager in a pharmaceutical company:

You don't just solve the work-life balance issue and expect it to go away. You've got to revisit it time and again. We've found that it's essential to include it on our team meeting agenda as part of a broader discussion about how we manage the work. That way, work-life issues get incorporated into all the major decisions we make.

CASE STUDY

BT

BT has engaged its teams in work-life balance in a number of ways. Workshops are run on how team members can work flexibly while recognising the impact their working practices have on their colleagues. Virtual workers can use a 'virtual café' to liaise with other team members, and workers can attend 'smart lunches' with their colleagues to catch up with team activities and learn of any new work developments.

HR'S ROLE

HR's responsibility is to help teams and team leaders develop the capability and commitment to drive work-life balance proactively rather than simply respond to individual circumstances. Unless the team takes on the task of managing the work-life issues, any culture change will be at best superficial. Basic ways in which HR can help include:

- endorsing and emphasising the role of the team in managing work-life balance
- facilitating team discussions at the beginning; or training some line managers to be roving facilitators of the process
- raising awareness of the processes for managing learning within teams
- creating forums for sharing good practice within teams.

From the interviews we have conducted, the team appears to be an area of least investment by HR with regard to making work-life policies deliver change. Nonetheless, the potential to make change happen faster and in a more sustainable manner is considerable.

REFERENCES AND READING

1 HERTS TEC (2001) *Learning Teams,* project reports. Herts, Herts Tec.
2 KATZ N. (2001) 'Sports teams as a model for workplace teams: lessons and liabilities'. *Academy of Management Executive.* Vol. 15, 3. pp56–69.
3 CLUTTERBUCK D. (1975) 'Semi-autonomous working at Harmon Industries'. International Management.
4 COVEY S. R. (2001) *The Seven Habits of Highly Effective People : Powerful Lessons in Personal Change.* London Simon & Schuster.

8

Pulling it all together

Because changing the culture so that it is truly supportive of work-life balance requires changes in perception and in practice from the organisation, line managers, individuals and the team, HR needs to play a co-ordinating role. Simply appointing an HR professional to manage initiatives is not enough; for sustainable change to occur, work-life balance has to be integrated within the key management processes of the organisation.

Let's be realistic. Work-life balance is not a solvable problem any more than teenage rebellion or growing old. The more complex our lives become, the more conflict we will experience between different aspects of our lives. But the real problem is one of choice. Most people could choose to live on a much smaller income and spend more time with their children, but doing so usually means accepting a more limited scope of life interests – we may not be able to afford holidays, meals out, membership of the gym, and so on. Employees submit to long hours and other demands of work either because they enjoy what they do, or because they feel the sacrifices they make will result in other rewards they value, or for both reasons. Only by accepting less complex lives, with less richness of stimulation, can most people 'solve' the issue of conflict between their work and non-work lives. And few of us are prepared to choose that option.

It follows, then, that it is not reasonable to expect an employer to sort out an individual's work-life problems. It *is* reasonable, however, to expect an employer to ensure that it does not make things worse by making unreasonable demands on employees, and to seek ways to organise work which help people better manage work-life balance issues for themselves. As we saw in Chapter 1, there are strong business reasons why such an approach can benefit the business as much as the individual.

HR is increasingly becoming the arbiter and stimulator of culture change around work-life issues. It is arguably one of the most difficult challenges the function has faced, because the necessary involvement extends beyond the boundaries of the organisation and into people's non-work lives, where HR professionals are (rightly) wary of treading. It also requires a re-examination of attitudes and practices across virtually every business process, from production processes to financial reporting, all of which have an impact on what the organisation demands of its people.[1]

If the reference to financial systems is puzzling, consider the following examples – the general panic and long hours necessary in many companies when the budget process is added to normal, regular duties; and the similar 'all hands to the pumps' requirements of annual stock-taking in retail. Neither of these panics is really necessary – there are practical methods of spreading out the load – but they have become ingrained in the culture.

In short, it requires HR to oversee an integrative process which recognises and supports:

- dual goals for the organisation of commercial success and assisting employees to achieve self-fulfilment and well-being in both work and non-work

- dual goals for individuals of reaching achievements in both their career/work and in other lifestreams

- a recognition and accommodation by both the organisation and the employee that they have complementary obligations to the community

- a commitment by the company to make work itself a positive and enhancing experience

- the flexibility to respond to changing needs and crises in both work and non-work

- the ability by both the organisation and individuals to develop and implement processes to 'manage out' frequent, conflict-causing crises

- active and open processes to raise awareness and stimulate constructive dialogue around alternative solutions to conflict between work and non-work demands

- a close alignment between the *perception* of work-life balance and the *reality* (for example, ensuring that a long-hours culture does not become so institutionalised that people do not realise they are missing out on important family experiences).

This is precisely the opposite of what three *Harvard Business Review*[2] authors describe as viewing 'work and personal priorities as competing priorities in a zero-sum game, in which a gain in one area means a loss in the other'. An Institute for Employment Studies[3] report expresses a much more integrative view:

> *Work-life balance is about culture, values and managing people to create a climate where they feel empowered to state their own demands ... and the ability to enter into a conversation to work out a solution ... Separating work-family issues from the strategic business concerns helps neither the individual nor the organisation. At the heart of the work-family perspective is a notion of reciprocity that speaks to the need for a more ecological view of workers and the workplace.*[4]

So what precisely should HR do to provide this integrative role? The critical elements appear to be:

- Gain a clear understanding of where the organisation is now.

- Develop the structures which will support a sustainable culture change.

- Adopt a quality management approach to the planning and management of work-life balance.

WHERE IS THE ORGANISATION NOW?

One of the problems raised by HR professionals and by leaders in general is how to assess where the organisation is in terms of tackling the work-life balance issue. Has it achieved 10 per cent of what it needs to do, or 50 per cent, or 90 per cent? How does it compare with other organisations which have different market and employment circumstances? It is like setting out on a journey without knowing quite where you are going, how far it is, how long it will take, or what it will cost.

There is a Work-Life Balance Standard[5] in existence which provides a checklist of activities and indicators, but these do not seem to be integrated into a coherent framework. Indeed, the lack of such a framework has, we believe, been one of the factors holding back the development of work-life culture change within organisations. As we conclude the writing of this book, Investors In People has announced a rival standard. Its 'Work-Life Balance Model'[6] covers four principles, with indicators and subsequent evidence attached to each one:

- culture (one in which WLB is recognised and valued)
- strategy (WLB strategy is central to the organisation's aims and objectives)
- action (successful WLB solutions)
- effectiveness (evidence that the WLB strategy is delivering positive results).

In essence, they provide a basis for assessing whether the organisation is investing appropriate effort in work-life balance. However, what they do not do is provide a route map for achieving these results. Our research indicates that there is a need for a clear underpinning theory of work-life balance and a framework for designing a practical and effective implementation plan.

Later in this chapter we provide a suggested framework in which tools such as the Standard can play a role. The key for HR, however, is to start with a clear assessment of the big picture. Focusing too much on the detail at the start is unlikely to have much impact on culture change.

One way of looking at the big picture is to be very clear about the culture change required. For example, Table 6 contrasts a typical starting culture with an alternative vision.

Table 6 What would a WLB-friendly culture ideally be like?

It would entail a change from:	*To:*
Work-life balance issues are seen • *as a problem* • *as a source of cost*	*Work-life balance issues are seen* • *as an opportunity* • *as a source of profit/competitive advantage*
The customer comes first	*The employee is equal (or first)*
Long hours are the norm	*Long hours are the exception*
Senior managers provide poor role models	*Senior managers provide good role models*
Discussion of work-life balance issues is discouraged	*Discussion of work-life balance issues is encouraged and open*
Work-life balance is the employee's responsibility	*Work-life balance is a joint responsibility for employer and employee*
There are rigid rules on how, when and where people work	*Any working arrangement that benefits the organisation, the employee and the customer is fine*
Discussion of WLB is discouraged	*There is open dialogue on WLB issues*
Few or no senior manager role models	*Many senior manager role models*
Low clarity of business case	*High clarity of business case*
Low clarity of individual WLB goals	*High clarity of individual WLB goals*
Very narrow definition of WLB stakeholders	*Definition includes non-employees such as family members, dependants and the community*
WLB is at the periphery of corporate values	*WLB is a core corporate value*

Your organisation may produce a different – perhaps much longer – list of cultural variables. Having such a list, however, gives people clarity about the journey to make, and where they and the organisation are now.

CASE STUDY

The National Health Service

The NHS, which has embarked upon a major culture change initiative built around work-life values, began to take the issue particularly seriously in 1999. Improving the working lives of existing NHS staff and those intending to join is now a well-established Department of Health campaign. One of the key driving factors is recruitment, retention and return of staff. It has identified three levels of organisational achievement:

Pledge – making a public commitment to putting in place the people, policies and plans to deliver against a set of Improving Working Lives Standards

Practice – putting many policies in place and implementing them, but allowing for areas where further progress is required

Practice Plus – meeting in full a set of consistent standards for all staff.

One of the key criteria for achieving the Standard is the requirement for employers to provide evidence that they 'understand that staff work best for patients when they can strike a healthy balance between work and other aspects of their life outside work'. The six elements of the Standard were developed through consultation with the service, unions and staff, and Regional Taskforces, led by 'champions' were set up, with the role of selling in to senior management teams the benefits of a constructive and forceful approach to work-life balance.

Each organisation was expected to appoint an internal group representative of the organisation reporting to the chairperson or chief executive, to support the implementation of the Standard throughout the organisation. Financial assistance has been available and continues to be available to support NHS employers in working towards meeting the Standard.

To achieve Practice status, Trusts have carried out an internal assessment against 29 indicators that make up the six elements of the Standard. This self-assessment, or benchmarking exercise, has been validated by an on-site inspection by nationally trained assessors from the Service, hearing from front-line staff how the implementation of the Standard has made a difference to their working lives and the service they deliver.

The whole exercise is reinforced by inclusion of the standard in the 'star' system of performance rating for NHS organisations, so there is a small but significant financial penalty for not addressing work-life balance issues.

Improving Working Lives has been very successful to date, and is increasingly a feature of everyday management in the NHS, making tangible improvements to the working lives of most staff. It is and continues to be a crucial measure of NHS HR. There is now clear evidence that modern employment practices and flexible working policies are delivering results. For example, of the respondents to the recent Return to Practice Survey, 86 per cent of those who completed the course in the previous three years still remained in practice; 94 per cent of respondents stated they had been able to negotiate flexible working arrangements.

There has also been a significant increase in the exchange of good practice across the NHS, and in some areas they have already set up benchmarking systems to compare data against the 29 indicators.

Stage 3, Practice Plus, is now being developed. The main problem, says organiser Mary Best, is 'how do you turn pockets of good practice into an organisation-wide culture change?' Some Trusts have provided strong leadership on work-life balance issues and now need to work more to engage and involve staff; others have not and will not. Both within Trusts and across the NHS as a whole there is an issue of consistency of performance that cannot be met by the Standard alone. What the Department of Health is aiming for is the spread of achievement in a wide range of good HR policies right across the NHS, built into decision-making and business planning at all levels and applied equally to all staff groups.

Our own examination of the stages of progress in creating a culture supportive of work-life balance suggests the model shown in Table 7.

Our survey revealed an intriguing (but not unexpected) dichotomy between HR's overall perception of the culture with regard to work-life balance and the reality underneath. As is so often the case, the devil lies in the detail.

When asked how supportive the culture is in general towards work-life balance, most respondents were relatively upbeat. On a scale of 1 (very high) to 5 (very low), 27 per cent scored their organisation as 1 or 2, and 38 per cent as 3. However, when we asked about specific cultural indicators, a different pattern emerged. Relatively few respondents believed their organisation gives people much control over where and how they work; nor did they believe the organisation

Table 7 Levels of work-life balance evolution

Compliance	*Doing the legal basics*
Policy proliferation	*Ad-hoc policies, not coherently linked and may be undermined by organisational processes*
Coherence	*An overall, cohesive approach to WLB policies, HR policies and work organisation. People take the opportunity to use WLB policies and can change options from time to time*
Integration	*WLB is incorporated into the culture and thinking of the organisation. It has genuinely become a source of competitive advantage. The impact of WLB policies is clear on employees, the organisation and other stakeholders*

promoted people primarily on results rather than being seen to work hard. Moreover, when it came to a choice between customer first and employee first, it was clear that employees ran a very poor second. To the question *In general, do people in this organisation genuinely believe that their careers will not be adversely affected, if they have greater work-life balance?* the noes (60 per cent) were strongly in the majority.

Equally telling was the question *Is changing the culture to become more supportive of work-life balance a high priority for this organisation?* – only 38 per cent were able to say yes.

The identification of four levels of progress provides a more accurate benchmark with which organisations can assess where they are, how far they want to go, and how far along the journey they are. Organisations at the compliance level must accept that they are unlikely to have a very positive employer brand. They may have trouble attracting the talent they require and retaining the talent they have. For a small number of organisations where the need for skills or commitment among employees is low, this may still be a rational approach.

Policy proliferation is the level at which most organisations currently seem to be. Even if there is a single overall statement of intentions with regard to work-life balance, there seems to be little attempt to link these together with each other and with the mainstream of business process. As a result, the level of overall take-up of opportunities to work flexibly may be lower than might be expected.

Coherence implies a significantly higher level of co-ordination from HR and of involvement by senior managers. The organisation recognises that achieving widespread work-life balance requires a substantial shift in culture and is determined to identify and manage the myriad factors that influence work-life balance.

Integration is the nirvana of work-life balance, when the organisation and the individual employees are able to achieve win/win solutions most of the time. The benefits of flexibility are clear for both, and new circumstances for either side are accommodated relatively easily. Both sides feel sufficient confidence in their ability to manage work-life issues to be able to shift focus to include community involvement as an important element in how they measure the success of their approach to work-life balance.

Do organisations have to move through these various stages one by one to reach integration? There is not enough experience to be sure. Moreover, where companies are in the progression is not necessarily as clean-cut as the table suggests. It is possible, for example, to have elements of both compliance and policy proliferation at the same time. However, the four levels provide a practical baseline for planning and measurement.

STRUCTURES TO SUPPORT CULTURE CHANGE THAT SUPPORTS WORK-LIFE BALANCE

Those organisations which have been successful in shifting from one level of work-life balance management to the next tend to have in common:

- strong support from top management
- a strong, well-connected and patient programme co-ordinator

- a steering group representing a diverse set of interests and circumstances
- budgets that allow them to gather and analyse the data they need to understand and react to work-life conflict as it arises.

Without the endorsement and encouragement of top management, it is difficult to move much beyond the compliance stage. Even if a basket of more advanced policies exists, implementing them and making them part of the culture will be an uphill task. Employees will constantly be looking over their shoulder for signs of approval of flexible working, and failing to find them, will prefer not to ask. Signs of a top team that has got the message include:

- Work-life balance issues appear regularly on the board's agenda.
- Most of the top team recognise and are attempting to manage their own work-life conflicts.
- There is a buy-in to the business case for investment in supporting work-life balance.
- They spend time discussing these issues with employees at a variety of levels.
- Their requests for measurement data indicate a real grasp of the implementation issues.
- They are prepared to commit to a timetable for progressing to the next level of work-life balance evolution.

The role of the work-life balance co-ordinator is fundamental. He or she not only liaises between the various stakeholders (including top management, employees and HR itself) but:

- makes sure the planning process is robust
- develops a wide portfolio of education and training options in support of work-life balance
- ensures that the debate about work-life issues is open, frequent and continuing
- oversees the measurement process
- identifies barriers to a work-life-balance-friendly culture and suggests policies and practices to overcome them
- is available to provide counselling and guidance to employees and their managers alike.

At SAP in the UK, it is the HR consultant and recruitment manager who takes on the work-life balance co-ordinator role, having ultimate responsibility for work-life balance issues in the company. The major responsibility in the role is helping SAP to achieve an 'employer of choice' status, for which work-life balance plays a major role. In addition to rolling out policies and practices, and the responsibilities mentioned above, the co-ordinator in this case attends conferences, studies the latest work-life balance research, ensures entry into the *Times* newspaper work-life balance award, and is highly involved in developing the Voluntary Service Overseas (VSO) scheme in which the company also participates.

The steering committee has to have enough clout to get things done and to ensure access to top management, along with a sufficiently broad spectrum of membership to ensure that it hears and responds to the views of both the most obvious target audiences for flexible working and those who are less obvious. It should be a broad church, including stakeholders such as line managers, those with young children and those with elderly parents, those who travel frequently on company business, and so on.

At Nationwide, the work-life balance steering committee role is taken by the board that controls all diversity issues within the company. Headed by the deputy chief executive, the board consists of managers from across the whole business who have a variety of backgrounds and work-life balance needs.

The budget for work-life balance management does not have to be large. It simply needs to be enough for HR to assess what is happening and to invest in appropriate programmes of education and training. Most of the training should be justified as an investment with other, often more direct benefits for the business – for example, better project management or negotiation skills.

The cost of specific initiatives can usually be contained by integrating them within a flexible compensation policy or by making them available but expecting employees to contribute to them (for example, crèche or gym facilities). Making bulk deals with external suppliers often allows companies to offer substantial savings to employees on such facilities.

Whatever the cost, a strong co-ordinator and well-informed top management and steering group can ensure that the budget is affordable and built around clear, achievable and measured returns to the business and to the employees. Once this process is established and proven, it provides credibility for the whole work-life balance management approach.

A QUALITY MODEL FOR WLB

The deeper we delved into the organisational issues relating to work-life balance, the more obvious it became that this was an issue of quality – quality of life and quality of working life. HR's role in improving the quality of people's non-work life must be at best marginal; it can, however, help by ensuring that work does not become the destroyer of an enjoyable and fulfilling home life and intrudes on non-work space only within limits that are reasonable and appropriate. It can also do its best to ensure that work itself is an enjoyable and fulfilling experience – that it has *fizz* (opportunities to enjoy the company of others) and *buzz* (opportunities to gain satisfaction and positive challenge from the work itself).

The quality model – inspired in structure initially by that of the European Foundation for Quality Management – emerged gradually. It incorporates all of the critical elements required to design and implement an effective approach to institutionalising good practice in managing work-life balance. The key line is the top row (in the lightest shade) and represents the steps in a quality model – policies, processes to implement them, the human dimension, and measurable outcomes.

The planning dimension we have already encountered in Chapter 5. Both individuals and the organisation need clarity about the goals they want to achieve and why these goals are important to them. They need to marshal appropriate resources and ensure that the resources (time, energy, money, etc) are adequate to the task. They need knowledge and skills to leverage those resources into practical activities and appropriate behaviours. And they need the reinforcement that comes from experiencing progress towards the goals.

Policies

As indicated in Chapter 3, work-life balance policies fall into three obvious categories:

- those that relate specifically to working times, both in terms of duration of work and when the work is done, and in terms of when it is permissible to take time off work for non-work responsibilities and activities
- those that relate to the location of work (office, home, client site, neighbourhood centre, or a combination of these)
- those that relate to making choices easier (eg assistance with childcare or dependant care).

The aim, in quality terms, is to provide a portfolio of policies that are 'fit for the purpose'. This means in essence that they must:

- conform to both the spirit and the letter of the relevant legislation
- be appropriate to the circumstances of the business and the employees, at both the macro level and the micro (ie there has to be sufficient flexibility to adapt to the specific needs of each business unit and to most, if not all, employees)
- be reviewed and amended regularly to ensure that they remain appropriate.

Processes

Policies are of little value without pragmatic, workable processes to put them into practice. Teams at all levels must have the ability, authority and resources to design and implement

Table 8 The quality model for work-life balance

POLICIES	PROCESSES	PEOPLE	OUTCOMES
Time flexibility	Work organisation	Role models	For individuals
Location flexibility	Technology	Inform/educate/ consult/empower	For the organisation
Benefits and support	HR systems	Training	For society/ the community
Measurement BENCHMARKING	AUDIT	FEEDBACK	REVIEW
Implementation PLANS	RESOURCES	BEHAVIOUR	SUSTAINABILITY

© Clutterbuck Associates 2003

different work arrangements. There must be effective processes for identifying both needs and opportunities for alternative working practices, for making both the personal and the business case, and for resolving conflict.

Technology is often part of the solution. Equipping people with broadband telephone connections encourages home-working, for example. Opening intranet data to access from employees' homes helps too. Even simple technologies, such as baby monitors, can be a boon to a new mum who is able to bring her baby to work.

HR systems relate to what actually happens in key areas, such as promotion and reward. If the people who get promoted or who receive the biggest bonuses are the manifest workaholics, that sends a clear message. If, on the other hand, managers receive public recognition for their achievements in helping others achieve work-life balance, and/or for retaining and motivating their direct reports, then a very different message is broadcast. HR systems also include having well-publicised resources, such as an employee assistance programmes or concierge services, to support people.

People

People within the organisation need to know what they want, in terms of work-life balance, and to know what is on offer. Their managers must have the confidence and competence to accommodate a wide variety of business and individual needs, or at least to establish workable and acceptable compromises. The key people elements in the quality model appear to be:

- It is essential to have appropriate role models, both at top management and down the line. Exactly what proportion of managers should demonstrate effective work-life balance behaviours to change the culture is not clear. What can be said with reasonable confidence Is that 10 per cent is too small in most cases to make a difference, whereas 80 per cent or more would suggest that a positive work-life balance climate is well established.

- Communication operates at a number of levels. Simply informing people about work-life balance and their legal rights is a base-level of activity. Educating them requires some dialogue, with information from employees playing as great a role (or more) than information to them, as they develop an understanding of what is possible for them and for their colleagues. Consulting employees with a view to engaging them in the design of work-life balance policies and processes requires a great deal more dialogue. A step beyond is empowerment, where the responsibility for organising work is left entirely to the employees themselves. Although there are one or two well-publicised and very successful examples of this (for example, Semco in Brazil), there are few organisations that aspire to this level of letting go of the controls.

- Training is important for all the key internal participants. Top management needs a deep understanding of the issues in order to agree policies, provide the resources to implement them and ask the right questions to establish where and how the investment is being returned. Line managers need help in acquiring the skills and courage to manage in new ways. And individuals often benefit from help in working out what they want to achieve and why. They may also value training in life skills such as parenting, or in other skills such as time management, which have applicability both within and outside work.

Outcomes

There are three primary stakeholders in the work-life balance model, plus a number of subsidiary stakeholders. Individual employees may be looking for a variety of results – less stress, more enjoyment of work, a reduction in guilt, the achievement of goals in other lifestreams, and so on. Through them, benefits accrue to their families in terms of quality of family life.

The organisation is looking for the benefits promised in Chapter 1, where we examined the business case. The emphasis each company places on retention, creativity, productivity and other outcomes will differ, of course. Subsidiary beneficiaries may include subcontractors and other suppliers who are less likely to face unreasonable demands from a culture that respects people's non-work lives.

The community benefits of an effective approach to work-life balance were also examined briefly in Chapter 1. The impact of having employees with the time and commitment to serve as school governors or community mentors, for example, is considerable, although difficult to measure in quantitative terms.

The concept of an integrated model of work, family and community is explored by Googins,[7] who says:

> *The community is the forgotten stakeholder . . . The future of the family is tied to an active community role . . . Communities remain not only a silent partner in the work and family arena, but one that has neither been appreciated nor exploited in a broader conception of work and family.*

Googins points out that schools and government institutions often increase work-life conflict by being inflexible in their own schedules. He advocates dialogue between employees, employers and the community to find ways to make it easier for people to integrate the various time-bound demands upon them.

Measuring the impact the organisation has upon the local community can be done in many ways, but key elements from a work-life perspective would include:

- What proportion of employees have voluntary roles outside of work?
- Does the company have a reputation as a concerned and responsible employer?
- How does the community rate the company in terms of response to requests for non-monetary help on community projects?
- Do employees feel they have time, energy and encouragement to engage in community activities?

Measurement

At the policy level, organisations need to measure themselves against other organisations through practical benchmarking. At the process level, it is important to audit – to establish, for example, what people need and want, the levels of stress they feel, and how supported they feel by the organisation, their managers and their peers. At the people level, feeding back the results of surveys becomes a major driver of change, and the response of people to that information creates a positive cycle of feedback and discussion. Finally, at the outcomes level, regular review of what has and has not been achieved enables the organisation to measure progress and revisit the model at the plan/policy/benchmark stage.

HOW TO USE THE QUALITY MODEL

The quality model is being developed into a systematic process for analysing an organisation's state of progress through the four levels of evolution of a culture supportive of work-life balance. In principle, each of the 12 core elements will be scored at up to 60 points, making a possible maximum of 720. In addition, there are 60 points each for the quality of the planning/implementation process, the measurement process, and for the level of innovation demonstrated by the organisation and its employees in creating practical solutions to work-life balance issues. This makes a grand total of 900 points. It is hoped that a Work-Life Balance Quality Management Award will be created, in respect of which organisations can benchmark their own efforts against those of their peers.

CONCLUSION

Since I first became interested and started writing about this subject, a great deal has changed. There is a much wider spread of good practice and much, much more legislation. However, I was surprised, on delving into the copious literature on the subject, to find a lack of *practical theory*. Of course there are academic studies that pick at the psychology of work life balance, or at some detail of implementation, but very little that was of much use to the HR professional aiming to create fundamental change in the way his or her company approached these issues.

I hope this book redresses some of the balance. It has been a useful learning journey for me and the colleagues who have worked on it with me. The difficulties individuals and organisations face in fitting in all the activities and achievements they aspire to will not diminish in the near future – quite the reverse. It may be that in a few decades we will be able to clone ourselves electronically, letting each separate self live a part of our ever more complex lives, integrating into one persona periodically. Whether that would solve more problems than it would create, I doubt. Till then, however, organisations and the people in them are going to have to be ever more flexible, more innovative and more tolerant.

REFERENCES AND READING

1 FRIEDMAN S. D., CHRISTIANSEN, P. *and* DEGROOT, J. (1998) 'Work and life: the end of the zero-sum game'. *Harvard Business Review*. November–December. pp119–129.

2 KODZ, J., HARPER, H. *and* DENCH, S. (2002) *Work-life Balance: Beyond the Rhetoric*. IES Report, No. 384. Brighton, Institute for Employment Studies.

3 FRIEDMAN D. E. *and* JOHNSON A. A. (1997) 'Moving from programs to culture change: the next stage for the corporate work-family agenda', in S. Parasuraman and J. H. Greenhaus (eds.),

Integrating Work and Family : Challenges and Choices for a Changing World. Westport, CT, Quorum Books.

4 *The Work-Life Balance Standard,* available from WLBC Ltd, 17 Packers Way, Misterton, Crewkerne, Somerset TA18 8NY/ www.wlbc.ltd.uk.

5 INVESTORS IN PEOPLE. (2003) *Work-life Balance Model.* London, Investors in People.

6 GOOGINS, B. K. (1997) 'Shared responsibility for managing work and family relationships: a community perspective', in S. Parasuraman and J. H. Greenhaus (eds.), *Integrating Work and Family : Challenges and Choices for a Changing World.* Westport, CT, Quorum Books.

Appendix 1:

Examples of work-life balance policies

1. THE EQUILIBRIUM COMPANY

MODEL WORK-LIFE BALANCE POLICY

OUR COMMITMENT TO WORK-LIFE BALANCE

The Equilibrium Company is committed to supporting all employees in the achievement of work-life balance.

The long-term success of this organisation depends, to a large extent, on the commitment, expertise, creativity; and dedication to quality and customer care of our employees. To remain competitive and successful in a changing world we must be flexible and prepared to adapt to circumstances.

We believe that our employees, regardless of age or personal circumstances, will work best when they are able to maintain a satisfactory personal balance between their paid work and other aspects of their lives. We understand that individual needs are likely to change as people progress through the life-cycle and we will make available a range of flexible working arrangements and leave provision to accommodate these circumstances.

We will continue to foster a culture within this organisation which makes it acceptable for individuals to discuss openly their concerns about work-life balance.

Responsibility for the success of our work-life balance strategy lies jointly with *the Equilibrium Company* as an employer and with every employee. The decision to alter working arrangements or allow a period of leave must be based on a sound business case. Along with their legal rights, it is important that both parties recognise their responsibilities to work together to create a win/win situation.

Our efforts to achieve work-life balance are supported by the following policies:

- Annual leave
- Appraisal
- Carer's leave
- Disability

- Employee Assistance Programme
- Flexible benefits
- Flexible working
- Health and safety (in respect of home-working and mental health at work)
- Parental leave (adoption, maternity, parental, paternity)
- Right to request flexible working patterns

2. THE AUDIT COMMISSION

AUDIT COMMISSION WORK-LIFE BALANCE POLICY

[gratefully reproduced with permission]

We believe in the importance of a balanced lifestyle where staff can achieve their best at work and manage other areas of their life effectively.

Andrew Foster

Juggling work and personal responsibilities can be a challenge for all of us. Sometimes the strain of keeping on top of things can lead to feelings of pressure. Life events such as the arrival of a baby, bereavement, divorce or a house move can intensify the problem and occasionally bring you to a crisis point.

Keeping healthy and maintaining a good balance between work and the rest of your life is something the [Audit] Commission fully supports. We know that everyone is different and will have individual needs. Our work options and support schemes recognise this so that you can select what will work best for you.

We hope that by taking full advantage of the help available when you need it, you will be able to enjoy and give your best at work, and develop your potential in a supportive environment.

FLEXIBLE WORK OPTIONS

We offer a number of flexible work options to suit different needs. These are open to men and women of all grades. There are many reasons why people might wish to work a different pattern from the 'norm'.

Reasons for flexible working may include:

- a wish to undertake further education or training
- working fewer hours due to health problems or a disability
- transport problems or distance from work
- wanting to be involved in voluntary work or other interests
- improving general quality of life
- wanting to 'phase down' when approaching retirement, or
- caring for and supporting children or other dependants.

WHAT FLEXIBLE OPTIONS ARE AVAILABLE?

The following options are available to staff. Line managers will consider applications positively, discussing the practicalities of how the arrangement could work with the individual and affected team members.

In a few cases, the nature of the job or other practical constraints may make it impossible to agree to a request. This will be rare and, in most cases, a workable solution that meets both business and individual needs can be found.

Flexible start and finish times

Subject to the needs of our customers and clients, the organisation is flexible about agreed start and finish times. Flexibility must fit with the demands of the job, and managers must agree in advance. This might enable you to avoid the rush hour or take children to school.

Career breaks

When you have worked for the organisation for two years you can apply for a career break. Breaks are available for up to five years with a guarantee of a return to work on the same grade as before. It is important that contact is retained throughout the break so that the return to work can be as smooth as possible for both parties. We therefore ask those on breaks to attend for training or work experience for two weeks a year. They will also remain on the mailing list for any regular information circulars as well as being encouraged to keep in touch on an informal basis.

Part-time working

Part-time working is open to new and existing employees at all grades. Benefits will be reduced on a pro rata basis. Different working patterns are possible. Some people may choose to work three or four full days a week, while others may prefer shorter hours on some [days] or every day.

Term-time working

Staff with children in school or term-time care may ask to work during school terms only, to enable them to care for their children during the holidays. Benefits will be reduced on a pro rata basis.

Job-share

It is possible for two individuals (with the right skills and experience) to apply to share a job between them. Appropriate handover arrangements need to be agreed between the sharers to ensure that the work is properly covered.

Homeworking

In certain circumstances (for example, where your office base is a long way from home), home-working on a partial or full-time basis may be possible with IT and other support. Suitable contact and management arangements are needed, and health and safety procedures must be followed.

HOW DO I APPLY?

Firstly, look in the Staff Handbook (Section C – Terms and Conditions) for fuller details of the schemes including eligibility criteria and effects on benefits.

If you feel that working flexibly would help you in your current circumstances you should approach your line manager having done some initial thinking about the impact of your request on your work role. Prepare a 'business case' setting out the advantages of the proposal, implications and possible solutions. The types of questions you and your manager should consider include:

- Is the role suitable for the type of option requested?
- How can my role be effectively covered for the hours/period I will not be working?
- What will be the effect of the arrangement on colleagues, and what support will they need?
- Will the arrangement involve any additional costs, and if so, can they be met or offset in some way?
- How long is the arrangement envisaged to last, and what are the future plans for the individual and [his or her] role?

If, on closer examination, the preferred option is not feasible, consider whether there are any alternative, compromise options.

Remember that flexibility works both ways. As a flexible worker you should be prepared to attend key meetings/training events that may fall outside your normal working times where possible. Of course, adequate notice should be given to allow you to change your arrangements.

FURTHER DETAILS

For further details please see Staff Handbook Section C – Terms and Conditions, Section 13 on Flexible Working Arrangements or contact Employee Services.

WHAT IS FLEXIBLE WORKING?

Flexible working, put simply is any working arrangement which is different from the traditional 'nine to five' working day. For many of us this is already a reality through shift work, part-time working, job-share, etc. BAA wishes to extend the options available to staff which will both benefit them, the business and our customers. These may include a range of flexible hours options or homeworking on a regular or ad-hoc basis. Each request for flexible working must demonstrate the benefits to the individual and the business. If you need help with developing the business case, then you can get advice from your manager, TU rep or HR adviser.

WHY ARE WE PROMOTING WORK-LIFE BALANCE IN THIS WAY?

All of us have changing responsibilities outside work, which may include family commitments, community or other non-work-related activities. We value the contribution made by our staff and through approaching the way we work in a positive and creative way we believe that the quality of the work we do will be enhanced.

Some of the benefits can be defined as:

- improving the quality of working life
- avoiding rush hour travel
- offering customer service over a longer period in the day
- making fewer car journeys
- causing less demand for BAA office space and car parks
- helping to meet the demands of home life

JOB-SHARING

As the name suggests, this is where two people share one job. Identical twins Sonia and Adrienne double up as special facilities officers at Heathrow, looking after VIPs who travel through the airport. Their job is shift working seven days a week. Splitting the shifts between them helps with childcare.

SOME EXAMPLES OF FLEXIBLE WORKING

Part-time

This is familiar to most people and simply means working less than the normal full-time contract of 40 hours per week. The actual number of hours will vary from individual to individual and from job to job. It can be a permanent arrangement or can be used as an option on a temporary basis to help with a particular issue for the individual.

Job-sharing

This involves two people sharing the responsibility for a full-time job. Each person has a full-time contract with pro rata terms and conditions and usually shares a job description. How the job-share works depends on the individuals and the business need. It could be morning or afternoon working, $2\frac{1}{2}$ days per week, working alternate weeks, etc. Some jobs can be split into component parts and these can be shared.

Flexible working hours

These allow teams or individuals to work in a way which brings benefits to the business and at the same time helps to meet their home commitments. This could mean agreeing different start and finish times each day, to work longer hours on some days or shorter hours on others which could be in line with term-time for parents. It could also mean working contractual hours over a shorter working week (eg the nine-day fortnight). Such arrangements are beneficial where there are peaks and troughs in workload over the year.

FLEXIBLE WORKING

Mike Millard is BAA Gatwick's external business relations manager. One of his areas of responsibility is car parks, and in order to be around at the busiest time, he sometimes comes in at weekends. He then takes time off during the week, allowing him to manage work effectively with the added benefit of time off with his wife who is a shift worker.

Nomadic and home-based working

Nomadic workers move between locations – which enables them to meet customers and team members that are based in other locations – and on occasion work from home. They have a permanent base but probably spend 60 per cent of their time elsewhere. Permanent home-based working is unusual in BAA, but some staff, especially those who have easily defined and measurable work, are able to work from home on one or two days per week, [which] can prove very beneficial for individuals and the business, allowing them uninterrupted time to prepare reports etc as well as saving them the cost and time of travelling to work. Home-workers will need computer and telecommunication links in order to work effectively and to enable them to keep in contact with their manager and colleagues.

Other policies and services

In addition to the examples above, there are a number of other policies and services which can help with balancing work and home life. The full details of these can be found on the RDMP intranet site – if you do not have access to a PC, then ask your manager for details.

Carer leave policy

Parental leave, adoption and paternity leave as well as emergency and extended carer leave are covered in this policy.

Special leave

Leave for jury service, medical appointments, reservists, community support activities and special leave (unpaid) are covered here.

Maternity leave

BAA provides benefits over and above the statutory provisions for mothers before and after the birth.

EMPLOYEE ASSISTANCE PROGRAMME

A free 24-hour confidential telephone service [is] available 365 days per year to all staff and their families. Help with everyday and more serious problems, including stress management, debt counselling, bereavement and housing problems. The Employee Assistance Programme can be contacted on 0800 XX XXXX.

The process

- The initiative for changing working arrangements may come from managers, teams or individuals. BAA allows every individual to have a discussion with their line manager about the best way of working for them and the business. It is important to note that these discussions focus on the dual benefit, and that all proposed arrangements are in line with company policy.

- All requests should be dealt with promptly, and this process is helped if a business case is prepared in advance. This should include details of any casts or changes in service levels.

- If a request cannot be met, then full reasons will be given. If you feel that your request has not been given adequate consideration, then you can refer it to a more senior manager.

- If you are working in a flexible way, then you are responsible for making sure that your manager is always aware of how/where/when you are working. You must make sure that HR and the Business Support Centre (where appropriate) are aware of your patterns of work.

- Arrangements should be reviewed regularly in [the] light of any changes to the individual or business need. It is important also that the trust placed in the individual is not abused.

We are committed to providing a working environment that helps you to give your best as well as ensuring that you can balance this with your home life.

If you have any questions, please speak to your line manager or HR adviser.

THE FLEXIBLE WORKING REGULATIONS

Any employee who has been in employment for 26 weeks and is the parent of a child up to the age of 6 or of a child with disabilities up to the age of 18 has the right to request flexible working arrangements.

The employee must make the request in writing to [his or her] line manager.

The request should outline the proposed new working arrangements.

The manager and member of staff must meet to discuss the proposal within 28 days.

If the proposed date of the meeting is inconvenient, then another date must be agreed and the meeting take place within 7 days of the original meeting date.

The meeting should discuss the proposal and the request [be] considered using the following points:

- possible additional costs, if any

- detrimental effect on ability to meet customer demand

- the need to reorganise work among existing staff, if appropriate

- the need to recruit additional staff, if appropriate
- any impact on the quality of work or service provided
- any impact on the performance of the individual.

Following the meeting the manager must write to the individual with a decision within 7 days.

If the request has been refused, then the manager must justify this refusal based on the above points.

If a member of staff believes that [his or her] request has not been considered fully, then [he or she has] the right to appeal.

[He or she] must make the appeal in writing within 14 days of receiving the decision, and state [his or her] reasons for the appeal, again based on the points above.

An appeal meeting must be held within 14 days of receipt of the appeal letter, and a decision must be communicated to the member of staff within 14 days of that meeting.

A member of staff may be accompanied by a colleague or staff representative at any of the meetings.

If you need any help understanding the flexible working regulations, then please contact your local HR adviser.

JOBSHARE POLICY

Below is an example of a job-share policy, taken from the *Family Friendly Policies* document available to staff at Boots The Chemist in the UK.

1 JOBSHARE CONTRACTS

1.1 Information

Job-sharing involves two people voluntarily sharing one full-time post and dividing the responsibilities, tasks, hours of work and pay and benefits between them. A job-shared post remains essentially a full-time function undertaken by two people.

Job-sharing requires attention to the working relationship between two partners in terms of communications and compatibility. (In contrast, part-time posts tend to be separate jobs with self-contained duties.)

Reasons for considering job-share may include women returning from maternity leave wanting to spend more time with their children; members of staff who care for relatives; to allow for part-time study.

Advantages of job-share to the Company include:

- retention of staff
- high commitment (individuals want it to work)
- high-calibre applicants may apply because the hours suit them
- there is a wider range of skills and experience in the one post
- greater potential for innovation and creativity

- [it] allows a reduction in hours without changing the job
- the job-share partners can cover holidays, sickness and each other's absence
- both parties can work together to cover peak times
- job-share is often very attractive to external candidates who are highly skilled and looking for a flexible option.

Key areas to the success of job-share:

- choosing partners that match
- managing when one job-share partner leaves
- planning training to maintain cover and invest in both individuals
- managing handover
- allocating duties and responsibilities.

Although the job-share needs to be managed well (eg careful thought given to handovers, etc), and occasionally more training required, generally, any extra cost is more than compensated for by higher productivity, lower absenteeism and reduced staff turnover.

1.2 Procedure

Members of staff may speak to their personnel representative to register their interest in job-share in confidence. A job-share register has been set up in Nottingham to assist members of staff in finding suitable job-share partners. Names of staff on the register should not be released to anyone without [the] permission of the employees concerned. Anyone may join the register by completing the standard form and forwarding to [his or her] personnel representative. Applications for positions will take place in the usual way regardless of whether the member of staff has registered.

1.2.1 Setting up a job-share

There are a number of situations when the need for a job-share may arise:

- an individual may request that [his or her] current role be considered for job-share
- a vacancy may be advertised as suitable for job-share
- one individual may apply to job-share.

1.2.2 Eligibility criteria for job-share

Male and female staff may apply for a job-share, depending upon the nature of the job. There is no service qualification for job-share applications.

1.2.3 Other points to consider

As well as using the criteria in section 1.2, the following points also require consideration:

- Will the needs of the business be met?
- How will customer and client needs be met?

- How will handovers be managed to ensure consistency?
- How will overtime be dealt with?
- How will sickness absence be dealt with?
- Could partners cover for each other?
- How is training organised?
- Is the job-share to be equally/unequally shared?
- Will the sharers cover for each other's holidays?
- Will salaries be equal?
- Does the job-share split allow sufficient cover through the week?
- Is the split to be by:
  - specialist knowledge?
  - location?
  - alternate weeks?
  - alternate days?
  - $\frac{1}{2}$ week split (Mon–Wed; Wed–Fri)?
  - morning/afternoon split?
  - other split?
- What important external contacts are there, and how will they be managed?
- Can contact be made at home during non-working periods?
- How might any selection for redundancy be made?

There may be other criteria specific to a certain function/role. These criteria should also be assessed as appropriate.

- Are there any members of staff who will report into the job-share partners, and [if so,] how will they be managed?

1.2.4 Is the member of staff suited to job-share?

- Does the member of staff have a job-share partner in mind, or can a job-share partner be found by advertising?
- What is the timescale for finding a job-share partner?
- Are the methods/systems used by the partners the same? Do they need to be? Do they work well together?
- Are the partners at the same level in terms of their competencies? What differences are there?

- Are the hours worked acceptable to both partners?

- How conscientious are the partners likely to be in relation to handovers?

- Do the individuals have good planning and organisational skills, and time management skills?

- Is there evidence of the partners being involved in any teamworking situations in a previous role?

- What have partners' previous performance contracts been like?

- Are both partners committed to and enthusiastic about job-share?

1.2.5 Forming the job-share partnership

A good working relationship is fundamental to the success of the job-share. These guidelines are intended to help management to encourage such a working relationship.

a) recruitment

The position should be advertised in the usual way but any advertisement should include the phrase 'This position is available as job-share'.

There should be no discrimination shown towards any full-time staff who wish to become a job-sharer.

Where there is only one suitable job-sharer available for a full-time job, obviously the position cannot be offered to [him or her]. [His or her name] should be noted in all registers of job-sharers for future reference.

When a job-share position is offered, the letter must emphasise the need for positive teamwork. (See sample letter at end of job-share section.) It may be appropriate to send out the Statement of Particulars with the offer letter (see POM Recruitment and Selection).

b) induction

Where a job-share partnership is set up, the new partners should be encouraged wherever practical to go through the induction programme together. This saves time and also allows a relationship to be established.

When a job-share position becomes vacant within an existing arrangement, the remaining partner should be involved in the induction of the new partner.

There should be some overlap time built into working hours, especially during the first three months. This helps to avoid situations in which one job-holder is 'played off' against the other.

Job-share needs to be communicated to other members of the team in a positive manner, emphasising the difference between job-share and other forms of part-time work.

c) training

Job-sharers must be eligible for training in exactly the same way as other staff.

Before the start of employment it should be made clear that some degree of flexibility will be required of job-sharers in attending off-the-job training.

d) performance contracts

Each job-sharer must have [an] individual Performance Contract. It must be made clear to the job-sharer at commencement of the arrangement that [he or she] will also be assessed on the level to which the job-share is effective and this should, therefore, be covered in the Contract. The usual guidelines relating to Performance Management should apply.

e) promotions/opportunities/prospects

Job-share partners can apply for promotion or other opportunities individually or as a partner-ship.

1.2.6 Terms and conditions of employment

A statement of particulars has been drawn up for job-share (item code 99-05-979). NB This is not the same as the part-time Statement of Particulars.

1.2.7 Completion of statement of particulars

Please refer to Contracts Section for guidance.

1.2.8 Calculation of holidays

All job-share contract holidays are calculated on a pro rata basis, dependent on contractual working hours. It is unlikely that both partners would be allowed holiday at the same time. Please refer to the Holidays Section for guidance on the calculation of holidays.

1.2.9 Company-nominated days

Members of staff on job-share contracts have four Company-nominated days between them included in their holiday entitlement. Discussion as to allocation of these days needs to take place prior to agreement of the contract.

1.2.10 Customary holidays

Members of staff on job-share should have customary holidays allocated on a pro rata basis. This needs to be agreed prior to agreement of the contract.

1.2.11 Bonus and share schemes

Members of staff on job-share contracts are eligible for any applicable bonus and share schemes based on their working hours. The usual rules apply. (See BTC Staff Bonus Scheme Section.)

1.2.12 *One partner leaves*

Every effort should be made to replace a partner who leaves. If a job-share partner leaves, the position is advertised as a job-share.

If, eight weeks after the first advert, a partner has not been appointed, the remaining partner is offered the role on a full-time basis.

If full-time work is not acceptable, the Company will endeavour to make acceptable, alternative arrangements. This may include employment at lower status, salary and different working hours.

If the arrangements above are not accepted, the Company reserves the right to terminate the job-share partner's employment.

1.2.13 *Maternity leave*

If a job-share partner goes on maternity leave, the Company has a responsibility to keep the position open for her to return to following her maternity leave. The remaining partner should be offered the opportunity of the full-time role. If this is not acceptable, the maternity vacancy should be advertised as a job-share position.

Appendix 2:

The state of work-life balance survey

QUESTIONNAIRE

PART 1 POLICIES FOR WORK-LIFE BALANCE

1   Does this company have an overall policy on WLB?   Yes/No

2   Do you measure the impact of that policy?   Yes/No

3   How effective has the overall policy been, on the spectrum below?

5	4	3	2	1

Substantial changes   No impact at all
to many people's lives

4   Which of the following are important *as work-life balance issues* for your company?

Do you have a *WLB-related* policy for each of them?

Do you measure them?

	Important Yes/No	Have policy Yes/No	Measured Yes/No
Long hours			
Conflict with home demands			
People unwilling to be promoted/ take on major assignments			
Recruitment calibre			
Retention of talent			
Non-return from maternity leave			
Sickness absenteeism			
Productivity			
Employee motivation			
Equal opportunities			
Legal claims (eg constructive dismissal, industrial injury)			
Corporate reputation (employer brand)			

5 Which of the following opportunities for greater work-life balance do you offer employees?

Are they open to all, or just some, employees?

	Offer made? Yes/No	To all? Yes/No
Flexible working hours		
Job-sharing		
Part-time work		
Nine-day fortnight		
Childcare facilities		
Term-time working		
Sabbaticals		
Working from home		
Working from a neighbourhood centre		
Other (please specify)		

6 How do you communicate these policies to employees? (Please tick all that apply)

  ❐ Employee handbooks

  ❐ WLB-specific website

  ❐ Team briefings

  ❐ Employee periodicals

  ❐ As part of appraisals

  ❐ Individual counselling

7 How aware do you think people are of these policies?

5	4	3	2	1

Very aware   Not at all aware

PART 2 SUPPORT FOR THE INDIVIDUAL

1 Is there a process for people to:

  • request changes in their working patterns?   Yes/No

  • receive advice on how to make their case?   Yes/No

  • receive advice on how to manage new working patterns?   Yes/No

  • appeal against refusal?   Yes/No

2 Do you offer training/briefings on how to achieve greater work-life balance?   Yes/No

3 Do you have processes to listen to people's concerns about work-life balance? Yes/No

4 Do you have processes to identify and counsel workaholics?   Yes/No

PART 3 CULTURAL FACTORS

1   In general, is the culture in your organisation supportive of work-life balance?

5	4	3	2	1

Very supportive   Very unsupportive

2   Do top managers provide good role models for work-life balance?   Yes/No

3   How much control do people in your organisation generally have over when and how they do their work?

5	4	3	2	1

Substantial control   Very little control

4   Are people promoted primarily on results, rather than on being seen to work hard?

5	4	3	2	1

On results   On being seen
                                                           to work hard

5   Where is your organisation on the *customer comes first* to *employee comes first* spectrum?

5	4	3	2	1

Customer   Employee
comes first   comes first

6   In general, do people in this organisation genuinely believe their careers will not be adversely affected, if they have greater work-life balance?   Yes/No

7   Is changing the culture to become more supportive of work-life balance a high priority for your organisation?   Yes/No

PART 4 SUPPORT FOR THE LINE MANAGER

1   Are line managers encouraged to set a personal example of good work-life balance practice?   Yes/No

2   Does work-life balance within the team feature in their appraisal?   Yes/No

3   Do managers receive training in how to organise work to accommodate work-life balance?   Yes/No

4   Do they receive training in how to manage people who work remotely or at non-standard times?   Yes/No

5   Is there a support system to help managers deal with work-life balance issues in their team?   Yes/No

And finally, more discursively, please feel free to add your thoughts on any of the following topics:

> Do you believe work-life balance adds significantly to competitive advantage? If so, how?
>
> What do you perceive the role of HR is in changing the culture to become more supportive of work-life balance?
>
> What is the biggest challenge in enabling people to achieve greater work-life balance?
>
> What is the biggest step forward your organisation has made?

Appendix 3:

Sources of further information

in alphabetical order

Alliance of Work Life Professionals (AWLP)
AWLP Headquarters, 515 King Street, Suite 420, Alexandria, Virginia 22314 USA
Tel: 00 1 (800) 874-9383 www.awlp.org

Carers UK
20–25 Glasshouse Yard, London EC1A 4JS
Tel: 020 7490 8818 Fax: 020 7490 8824
www.carersonline.org.uk

Chartered Institute of Personnel and Development
35 Camp Road, London SW19 4UX
Tel: 020 8971 9000 Fax: 020 8263 3333
www.cipd.co.uk

Chwarae Teg (Fair Play)
Companies House, Maindy, Cardiff CF14 3YZ
Tel: 02920 381331 Fax: 02920 381336
www.chwaraeteg.co.uk

Daycare Trust
21 St George's Road, London SE1 6ES
Tel: 020 7840 3350 Fax: 020 7840 3355
www.daycaretrust.co.uk

Equal Opportunities Commission
Overseas House, Quay St, Manchester M3 3HN
Tel: 08456 015901 Fax: 0161 838 1733
www.eoc.org.uk

Federation of Small Businesses
2 Catherine Place, London SW1E 6HF
Tel: 020 7592 8100 Fax: 020 7233 7899
www.fsb.org.uk

Home Office Partnership
55 West Street, Comberton, Cambridge CB3 7DS
Tel: 01223 264485 email: info@hop.co.uk
www.hop.co.uk

Homeworking.com
c/o Knowledge Computing, 9 Ashdown Drive, Borehamwood, Herts WD6 4LZ
email: info@homeworking.com
www.homeworking.com

International Telework Association
401 Edgewater Place, Suite 600, Wakefield, NA 01180, USA
Tel: 00 1 202 547 6157
www.telecommute.org

Kids' Club Network
Bellerive House, 3 Muirfield Crescent, London E14 9SZ
Tel: 020 7512 2112 Fax: 020 7512 2010
www.kidsclubs.com

National Group on Homeworking
Office 26, 30–38 Dock Street, Leeds LS10 1JF
Tel: 0113 245 4273
www.gn.apc.org/homeworking

New Academy of Business
17 Clare Street, Bristol BS1 1XA
Tel: 0117 925 2006 Fax: 0117 925 2007
www.new-academy.ac.uk

New Ways to Work
26 Shacklewell Lane, London E8 2EZ
Tel: 020 7503 3282 Fax: 020 7503 2386
www.new-ways.co.uk

Parents at Work
45 Beech Street, London EC2Y 8AD
Tel: 020 7628 3565 Fax: 020 7628 3591
www.parentsatwork.org.uk

Parents.com
www.parents.com

Public Service Partnership Ltd (Working Lives
In Public Service)
Houldsworth Mill, Reddish, Stockport,
Cheshire SK5 6DA
www.workingbalance.co.uk

Telework/Telecottage Association
Tel: 0800 616008 www.tca.org.uk

The Women and Equality Unit
10 Great St George Street, London SW1P
3AE
Tel: 020 7273 8880 Fax: 020 7273 8813

TUC
Congress House, Great Russell Street,
London WC1B 3LS
Tel: 020 7636 4030 www.tuc.org.uk

UK National Work-Stress Network
9 George Drive, Drayton, Norwich, Norfolk
NR8 6ED
Tel/fax: 01603 868249 www.workstress.net

UK online for business (formerly the
Information Society Initiative)
Tel: 0845 715 2000 email:
info@ukonlineforbusiness.gov.uk
www.ukonlineforbusiness.gov.uk

Unison
1 Mabledon Place, London WC1H 9AJ
Tel: 020 8545 4187 www.unison.org.uk

WLBC Ltd
17 Packers Way, Misterton, Crewkerne,
Somerset TA18 8NY
Tel: 01460 77713 email:info@wlbc.ltd.uk
www.wlbc.ltd.uk

Women Returners' Network
Chelmsford College, Moulshan Street,
Chelmsford, Essex CM2 0JQ
Tel: 01245 263796 Fax:

Work Foundation
Peter Runge House, 3 Carlton House Terrace,
London SW1Y 5PG
Tel: 020 7479 2107 Fax: 020 7479 2222
www.theworkfoundation.com

Working Options
14–16 Hamilton Road, London W5 2EH
Tel: 020 8932 1462
www.working-options.co.uk

Work-Life Balance Trust
10 Duncan Terrace, London N1 8BZ
Tel: 020 7837 4509 www.w-lb.org

Work-Life Research Centre
Manchester Metropolitan University,
Hathersage Road, Manchester M13 0JA
Tel: 0161 247 2569 www.workliferesearch.org

Work-Life Research Group
University of Kent at Canterbury, Tyler Hill,
Canterbury CT2 7NZ
Tel: 01227 827272
www.kent.ac.uk/psychology/worklife/

Worklifebalance.com Inc
7742 Spalding Drive, Suite 356, Atlanta,
Georgia 30092, USA
Tel: 00 1 (770) 997-7881, 00 1 (877) 644-
0064 Fax: (770) 668-9719
www.worklifebalance.com

Index